The Discourse of Financial Crisis and Austerity

T0347521

This book demonstrates the importance of understanding how political rhetoric, financial reporting and media coverage of austerity in transnational contexts is significant to the communicative, social and economic environments in which we live. It considers how aspects of moral storytelling, language, representation and ideology operate through societies in financial crisis and through governments that impose austerity programmes on public spending. Whilst many of the debates covered here are concerned with UK economic policy and British social contexts, the contributions also consider examples from other countries that reflect similar concerns on the ideological operations of austerity and financial discourse. The multiple discursive contexts of austerity demonstrate the breadth of social concerns and conflicts that have developed in societies and institutions following the global economic crisis of 2008. Through its interdisciplinary focus on this topic, this book provides an important contribution across multiple subject areas, with shared interests in critical and analytical approaches to discourse, power and language in social contexts reflecting the healthy collaborative scope of critical discourse studies as a field of research.

This book was originally published as a special issue of *Critical Discourse Studies*.

Darren Kelsey is Head of Media, Culture, Heritage at Newcastle University, UK. Darren's publications have focused on media mythologies and ideology, war and terrorism, moral storytelling, the banking crisis, right wing populism, journalism ethics, social media, surveillance and affect theory. Darren is a co-convenor of the Newcastle Critical Discourse Group.

Frank Mueller is Professor of Strategy and Organisation at Newcastle University Business School, UK. His overall research focus is on understanding organisational change as a discursive, political and strategic project under conditions of neo-liberalism and managerialism.

Andrea Whittle is Professor of Management and Organization Studies at Newcastle University Business School, UK. Her research is driven by a passion for understanding the role of language in business and management settings, and is informed by theories and methodologies from the fields of discourse analysis, narrative, discursive psychology, ethnography, ethnomethodology and conversation analysis.

Majid KhosraviNik is a Lecturer in Media and Discourse Studies at Newcastle University, UK. His research interests lie in theory, methodology and application of critical discourse analysis in a range of topics including the intersection of discourse and (national/ethnic/group) identity. He is a co-convenor of the Newcastle Critical Discourse Group.

The Discourse of Financial Crisis and Austerity

Critical Analyses of Business and Economics Across Disciplines

Edited by
**Darren Kelsey, Frank Mueller,
Andrea Whittle and
Majid KhosraviNik**

Routledge
Taylor & Francis Group

LONDON AND NEW YORK

First published 2017 by Routledge

2 Park Square, Milton Park, Abingdon, Oxfordshire OX14 4RN
52 Vanderbilt Avenue, New York, NY 10017

Routledge is an imprint of the Taylor & Francis Group, an informa business

First issued in paperback 2018

British Library Cataloguing in Publication Data
A catalogue record for this book is available from the British Library

ISBN 13: 978-1-138-28097-7 (hbk)
ISBN 13: 978-0-367-22049-5 (pbk)

Typeset in Myriad Pro
by RefineCatch Limited, Bungay, Suffolk

Publisher's Note
The publisher accepts responsibility for any inconsistencies that may have arisen during the conversion of this book from journal articles to book chapters, namely the possible inclusion of journal terminology.

Disclaimer
Every effort has been made to contact copyright holders for their permission to reprint material in this book. The publishers would be grateful to hear from any copyright holder who is not here acknowledged and will undertake to rectify any errors or omissions in future editions of this book.

Contents

Citation Information

The chapters in this book were originally published in *Critical Discourse Studies*, volume 13, issue 1 (January 2016). When citing this material, please use the original page numbering for each article, as follows:

Chapter 1
Financial crisis and austerity: interdisciplinary concerns in critical discourse studies
Darren Kelsey, Frank Mueller, Andrea Whittle and Majid KhosraviNik
Critical Discourse Studies, volume 13, issue 1 (January 2016), pp. 1–19

Chapter 2
Accounting for the banking crisis: repertoires of agency and structure
Andrea Whittle and Frank Mueller
Critical Discourse Studies, volume 13, issue 1 (January 2016), pp. 20–40

Chapter 3
Protesting Too Much: Alastair Darling's constructions after the Financial Crash
Catherine Walsh
Critical Discourse Studies, volume 13, issue 1 (January 2016), pp. 41–56

Chapter 4
Evaluating policy as argument: the public debate over the first UK austerity budget
Isabela Fairclough
Critical Discourse Studies, volume 13, issue 1 (January 2016), pp. 57–77

Chapter 5
How Malthusian ideology crept into the newsroom: British tabloids and the coverage of the 'underclass'
Steven Harkins and Jairo Lugo-Ocando
Critical Discourse Studies, volume 13, issue 1 (January 2016), pp. 78–93

Chapter 6
'I think it's absolutely exorbitant!': how UK television news reported the shareholder vote on executive remuneration at Barclays in 2012
Richard Thomas
Critical Discourse Studies, volume 13, issue 1 (January 2016), pp. 94–117

Chapter 7
Organizing the (Sociomaterial) Economy: Ritual, agency, and economic models
Amanda Szabo
Critical Discourse Studies, volume 13, issue 1 (January 2016), pp. 118–136

For any permission-related enquiries please visit:
http://www.tandfonline.com/page/help/permissions

Notes on Contributors

Isabela Fairclough is Senior Lecturer at the University of Central Lancashire, UK. Her publications focus on the critical analysis of political discourse from the perspective of argumentation theory and include the monograph *Political Discourse Analysis* (with Norman Fairclough, 2012), as well as research on transition to liberalism and a market economy in Eastern Europe.

Steven Harkins is an ESRC funded PhD student in the Department of Journalism Studies at the University of Sheffield, UK. His research examines representations of poverty and inequality in the British media. The research looks at the agency of journalists and their sources in creating narratives of poverty and inequality.

Darren Kelsey is Head of Media, Culture, Heritage at Newcastle University, UK. Darren's publications have focused on media mythologies and ideology, war and terrorism, moral storytelling, the banking crisis, right wing populism, journalism ethics, social media, surveillance and affect theory. Darren is a co-convenor of the Newcastle Critical Discourse Group.

Majid KhosraviNik is a Lecturer in Media and Discourse Studies at Newcastle University, UK. His research interests lie in theory, methodology and application of critical discourse analysis in a range of topics including the intersection of discourse and (national/ethnic/group) identity. He is a co-convenor of the Newcastle Critical Discourse Group.

Jairo Lugo-Ocando is Associate Professor of Journalism Studies in the School of Media and Communication at the University of Leeds, UK. He has worked as a journalist, correspondent and news editor for several news media outlets. His books *Blaming the victim: How global journalism fails those in poverty* (2015) and *Developing News: Global journalism and the coverage of "Third World" development* (2017) deal with how the international media reports poverty.

Frank Mueller is Professor of Strategy and Organisation at Newcastle University Business School, UK. His overall research focus is on understanding organisational change as a discursive, political and strategic project under conditions of neo-liberalism and managerialism.

Amanda Szabo is currently a PhD student in the Department of Communication at the University of Colorado Boulder, USA. She is studying the role of communication in the production of economies.

Richard Thomas is a Lecturer in Journalism at Leeds Trinity University, UK. His research examines how through conventions, protocols, language, imagery and graphics, television news presents a range of key political and economic issues including elections, remuneration, wealth, poverty and income distribution.

Catherine Walsh is a Lecturer in Public Communications at Cardiff University, UK. Her research concerns the rhetorics of political and financial elites, studying the exchanges that they have, their agency, how they teach one another what the economy is and should be, and how they disseminate their preferred meanings into wider discourses with us all.

Andrea Whittle is Professor of Management and Organization Studies at Newcastle University Business School, UK. Her research is driven by a passion for understanding the role of language in business and management settings, and is informed by theories and methodologies from the fields of discourse analysis, narrative, discursive psychology, ethnography, ethnomethodology and conversation analysis.

Financial crisis and austerity: interdisciplinary concerns in critical discourse studies

Darren Kelsey[a], Frank Mueller[b], Andrea Whittle[b] and Majid KhosraviNik[a]

[a]School of Arts & Cultures, Newcastle University, Newcastle upon Tyne, UK; [b]Newcastle University Business School, Newcastle University, Newcastle upon Tyne, UK

ABSTRACT
We begin our introduction to this special issue by considering the interdisciplinary collaborations behind this project before reviewing previous research on political rhetoric, financial reporting and media coverage of austerity in transnational contexts. We consider aspects of moral storytelling that have arisen through the contextual complexities of societies in financial crisis and other moral tales of austerity in political rhetoric. Whilst much of the literature and debates covered here are concerned with UK economic policy and related British social contexts, we will expand to include examples from other countries that reflect similar concerns on the ideological operations of austerity and financial discourse. Finally, some critical theoretical approaches to ideology and political economy are discussed in relation to the socio-economic areas covered in this special issue. The multiple discursive contexts of austerity that are covered here demonstrate the breadth of social concerns and conflicts that have developed in societies and institutions following the recent global economic crisis.

Introduction

In early September 2013, Newcastle University hosted an international conference entitled: *The discourse of austerity: Critical analyses of business and economics across disciplines*. Our aim was to bring together scholars across a range of disciplines to analyse discursive constructions of financial crisis and austerity. The aim of the conference was not simply to debate the rights and wrongs of austerity policies or discuss the causes and consequences of the financial crisis. Rather, we were concerned with a more critical approach to this topic: we wanted to explore how financial crisis and austerity measures have been *represented* through ideological mechanisms of language and discourse. In doing so, the conference provided an opportunity to understand how political decisions, assertions and agendas in support of particular financial structures and strategies had become accepted as possible, desirable or inevitable in various socio-political arenas and institutions. It is this position that has informed our event and this special issue: regardless of one's opinion on the legitimacy of austerity policy, it is crucial to understand how such a sensitive and highly politicised form of legislation – that has a major impact on peoples' lives and contextualises the ideological preferences of governments transnationally – is communicated through the language and representations of media, financial and political institutions.

By demonstrating our interdisciplinary focus on this topic, this special issue provides an important contribution across multiple subject areas. The editorial team has collaborated from different academic backgrounds with shared interdisciplinary interests. Within Newcastle University, co-convenors of the *Newcastle Critical Discourse Group* found significant common ground with colleagues in the *Strategy, Organisations & Society* group. Shared interests in critical and analytical approaches to discourse, power and language in social contexts forged interdisciplinary partnerships that continue to reflect the healthy collaborative scope of critical discourse studies (CDS) as a field of research. CDS has consistently proved to provide an academic forum and intellectual space for innovative collaboration amongst academic disciplines, which makes projects like this possible. Therefore, we would like to thank the journal of *CDS* for providing us with the opportunity to compile this special issue.

This introduction will take the opportunity to recap previous literature on financial discourse and austerity whilst introducing the papers in this special issue. We will consider aspects of moral storytelling that have arisen through the contextual complexities of societies in financial crisis and other 'moral tales' of austerity that have occurred in political rhetoric. Whilst much of the literature and debates covered here are concerned with UK economic policy and relevant social contexts, we will expand to include examples from other countries that reflect similar concerns on the ideological operations of austerity and financial discourse. Finally, some critical theoretical approaches to ideology and political economy are discussed in relation to the socio-economic areas covered by this special issue. The multiple discursive contexts of austerity that are covered here demonstrate the breadth of social concerns and conflicts that have developed in societies and institutions following a global economic crisis.

Financial reporting, moral storytelling and the banking crisis

A number of scholars have critically analysed financial reporting and the banking crisis in transnational contexts (Berry, 2013; Kelsey, 2014; Manning, 2013; Olson & Nord, 2015; Philo, 2012; Vaara, 2014). Manning has examined the 'failure of financial journalism, together with the global news agencies, to alert us to the signs of imminent catastrophe' (2013, p. 173). Manning argues that other than a 'handful of honourable exceptions, most financial journalists and most international news agencies simply failed to report much of the emerging evidence of the growing possibility of collapse' (2013, p. 173). Within the UK specifically, Barber (2015, p. xxvi), the editor of the Financial Times, acknowledges that 'the British press might be accused of not questioning more closely the foundation of prosperity in the City'. In a piece critical of financial journalists, Starkman (2015) attributes this failure to their 'capture' by Wall Street institutions, driven by journalists' reliance on Wall Street for their stories: 'Burning a bridge is hard. It is far easier for news bureaucracies to accept ever-narrowing frames of discourse, frames forcefully pushed by industry, even if those frames marginalize and eventually exclude the business press's own great investigative traditions' (p. 15).

Olson and Nord (2015) scrutinise the Swedish press for its role in legitimising the government's response to the financial crisis in 2008. They argue that the typical styles and conventions of descriptive journalism were responsible for representations that portrayed 'political actors as credible crisis managers rather than tactical politicians, with the result being that they appear more trustworthy and competent'. Furthermore, they claim that 'due to unbalanced coverage, actors who are framed as competent crisis managers succeed in further strengthening their positions'. Similarly, Berry's analysis of the UK press suggests that because City sources dominated BBC Radio 4 coverage of the banking crisis, 'listeners were offered a prescribed range of debate on the UK government's bank rescue plan and possible reforms to the financial sector' (2013, p. 253). Studies like these are important since they address the construction and ideological implications of media coverage concerning the financial crisis. They demonstrate how journalists and the sources that appear in media coverage are engaged in a highly political process that impacts upon financial discourse – and the type of economic policies deemed legitimate as a result. However, concerns regarding media responses to the financial crisis stretch beyond the specific reporting of financial journalism. (See also Thomas's contribution in this issue.)

The financial crisis became a widely reported issue that was often played out as a moral spectacle in mainstream news sources beyond the generic parameters of financial reporting (Kelsey, 2014). Since the financial crisis, we have seen a significant shift in UK press discourses about the City over a relatively short period of time. Kelsey's (2012) analysis of (pre-crisis) media coverage in 2005 considered how British bankers featured as heroic figures: symbolising British national identity after the July 7th bombings when the economy recovered after an initial crash. Kelsey shows how wartime mythology prompted invocations of resilience and defiance against terrorism in discourses about the City (2012). However, just a few years later following the banking crisis, bankers were vilified and their greed was held responsible for causing mayhem (Hargie, Stapleton, & Tourish, 2010; Kelsey, 2015a; Whittle & Mueller, 2012). The press, public and politicians questioned their lack of moral values and lack of empathy for working people. But within these criticisms of the banking sector, Kelsey (2014) has shown how the mythological characteristics of these discourses actually functioned in more complex and paradoxical contexts than those of archetypical vilification: the spectacle of the City banker reflected archetypal conventions of trickster mythology.

In a case study of the *Mail Online*, Kelsey showed that whilst some stories featuring the *banker as trickster* suppressed discussions of systemic economic failings, other cases actually raised concerns about the global free market. But the latter did not reflect an ideological compromise or opposition to hegemonic systems of global capitalism. Rather, paradoxical mechanisms occurred in representations of bankers as immoral individuals, tricksters, who exploit the system:

> … [W]hilst these criticisms call for some form of punishment or legislation to control the problem, there is reluctance to compromise free market values or legitimise state regulation of the banking sector. The complex characteristics of trickster figures in the stories analysed demonstrate current dilemmas and anxieties about the power and practices of financial institutions. Whether bankers are the genius providers of wealth or the reckless destroyers of economies, their ridicule highlights a sensitive balance of values and interests in journalistic storytelling. (Kelsey, 2014, p. 307)

Contradictions occur when bankers were held responsible for the financial crisis; yet, at the same time, the public were told it is bankers whom we need for our economic recovery. In other words, we are told that financial systems and models of banking do not need to be fundamentally redesigned, but some immoral individuals working within them need to behave more responsibly (see also Walsh's contribution in this issue). In line with the paradoxical traits of destructive trickster mythology, Radin sums up this archetype: 'If we laugh at [the trickster], he grins at us. What happens to him happens to us' (1956, p. 169). Hence, Kelsey (2014) concludes: 'If it is true that we need the expertise of bankers to recover in the global market then this provides [a] dilemma for publics, politicians and storytellers to consider', as we continue to try and make sense of the challenges society faces following a global financial crisis.

But these mechanisms of moral storytelling have functioned beyond the discourse of journalism and the City. Whittle and Mueller (2012) analysed the moral stories told during a public hearing involving senior banking executives in the UK. Their analytical framework draws together insights from a range of discourse fields, including discursive psychology, ethnomethodology, dramatism, rhetoric, ante-narrative analysis and conversation analysis, to cast light on 'discursive devices' (micro-linguistic tools) employed in the stories about the recent financial crisis during a public hearing with senior UK banking executives. They identify two competing storylines that 'were used by the bankers and their questioners to emplot the events preceding the financial crisis' (Whittle & Mueller, 2012, p. 111). In doing so, they enhance previous understandings of storytelling by 'highlighting the power of micro-linguistic tools in laying out the moral landscape of the story' (Whittle & Mueller, 2012, p. 111).[1] As they point out, 'stories surrounding the financial crisis are important because they shaped how the crisis was made sense of and acted upon' (Whittle & Mueller, 2012, p. 111). In the stories, they show how 'bankers, for instance, casting themselves as 'victims' enabled responsibility and blame to be (potentially) avoided. This is not simply about 'saving face', it is also about maintaining the legitimacy of the system that, to date, has also benefited them' (Whittle & Mueller, 2012, p. 111). Metaphors such as 'tsunami' play an important role in framing the causes of the crisis, presenting it as akin to a natural disaster, as research into the metaphors of failure used by bankers to explain the banking crisis has shown (Tourish & Hargie, 2012).

On the other hand, Whittle and Mueller (2012) also uncovered an alternative story narrated by the politicians, who cast the bankers as 'villains', thereby enabling a convenient 'scapegoat' to be found which individualised responsibility. In the hearing, they analysed it was also possible for the MPs undertaking the questioning to project themselves as 'public servants' who were trying to locate and punish any perpetrators, 'while also avoiding any questions about the role of government in the crisis' (Whittle & Mueller, 2012, p. 111). Therefore, as Whittle and Mueller argue, discursive devices in these social environments are more than just rhetorical tools; they serve crucial political and ideological purposes in the stories that they construct (see also papers by Mueller & Whittle, Fairclough, and Walsh, in this special issue).

Whilst it is true that moral storytelling can enhance or enlighten our understanding of an issue, it can also be used as a tool for manipulating an audience or suppressing other knowledge. For these reasons, Gabriel argues, 'this makes stories particularly dangerous devices in the hands of image-makers, hoaxers, spin doctors, and fantasists'

(2004, p. 19). Storytelling and moral positions in political rhetoric remain central components of economic discourse in arguments that support or oppose particular ideological agendas in responses to the financial crisis. Austerity policies, for instance, were only one of many potential responses to the global financial collapse, the subsequent bank bailouts and budget deficit that followed, but were presenting in the media as a *fait accompli* (Berry, 2013; Philo, 2010). The moral positions of governments are constructed according to those political agents and institutions who seek to legitimise or delegitimise particular economic strategies. The following section continues to account for the moral components and mechanisms of political rhetoric that feature in discourses of austerity in particular.

'Moral tales' of austerity in political rhetoric

This is not the place for us to *evaluate* the effectiveness or effects of austerity policies: other authors have done plenty of this in the last few years (Blyth, 2013; Krugman, 2013; Stiglitz, 2012a, 2012b). Our argument here is that austerity is, crucially, a 'morality tale' that exists partially detached from the pure economics – which are of course themselves open to discursive contestation. Our aim is to outline the discourses and discursive contexts of the austerity and anti-austerity morality tales.

The core element of the austerity morality tale is that 'it is an undisputable fact that excessive state spending has led to unsustainable levels of debt and deficits' (Schäuble, 2011). In this respect only, there was agreement between Merkel-Schäuble and the Conservative euro-sceptic right-wing British Member of European Parliament, Daniel Hannan, who pronounced on his popular blog that 'you cannot spend your way out of recession or borrow your way out of debt' (*Daily Mail*, 2009). Whilst Hannan's discourse was directed at Brown's left-wing Labour government in power at the time, the Merkel-Schäuble discourse was meant for the EU's Southern periphery: Greek and Italian parliaments, and governments, who are accused of having for many years failed to put their house in order, or according to Merkel, 'do their homework' (*The Daily Telegraph*, 2013). Doing one's homework, for the PIIGS[2] basically means to reduce government spending and enacting deep structural 'much-needed reforms' (Schäuble, 2011).[3] Such reforms would include the removal of labour market rigidities, increasing their tax-collecting capacity, and making significant changes to retirement ages, in particular for public-sector workers. Cutting state pension benefits and public-sector wages was also often part of this package.[4]

In the UK, a significant policy reversal took place between 2008 and 2010, from a £20 billion stimulus programme in late 2008, to a £40 billion austerity budget in (Osborne's, 2010) emergency budget consisting of cuts and tax increases (Coates & Dickstein, 2010, p. 67). In 2010, George Osborne, the Chancellor of the Exchequer, pledged: 'It is a hard road, but it leads to a better future' (Osborne, 2010). Four years later, Osborne confirmed that spending cuts were only half done. When asked in an interview if this meant that some departments would face cuts of 37% in real terms, he did not confirm the figure, but responded as follows:

> Well we do have a lot more difficult decisions to come because the truth is this country got itself heavily into debt. It racked up a very big budget deficit. I think the question by the way for Ed Balls [Shadow Chancellor of Exchequer] is, 'Why would he give the keys back to the person who crashed the car?' ... But you know we've got to make these decisions. You

saw us in the last week … take difficult decisions on public sector pay, difficult decisions to make sure that we can afford public sector pensions. So we have to go on making these decisions and that will include decisions in the next Parliament. (Osborne, 2014, p. 5)

The 'hard road' and 'difficult decisions' are characteristics of government rhetoric that have projected austerity as an inevitability in a situation where they have no choice since spending cuts are their only option. As Philo (2010) amongst others has proposed, there were other options available to the government even if they were radical alternatives that might have cost some wealthier members of society more money. Philo's research showed that 74% of the British public were in favour of a one off tax on the rich – to free up wealth tied in areas such as property and other investments from the boom years – which would clear the national debt. But as Philo points out, a discourse of inevitable austerity has functioned at the forefront of government and media rhetoric – to the point where the *BBC* hosted a 'choose your cut' webpage (ibid). This discourse of inevitability in Government rhetoric has often denied austerity is an ideological agenda and presents spending cuts as the only option. As Osborne's quote (above) shows, the ideological design of a hegemonic financial system that crashed and failed on a global scale is often reduced to simplistic blame targeted at one previous government. On this point, it is also interesting that we have seen recurring accusations that the previous Labour administration was responsible for insufficient regulation of the banks in the build-up to the crisis. Discourse analysts might like to speculate on the reaction that a pre-crisis pledge to regulate the banking sector in order to avoid a major financial crisis would have caused: presumably, it would have been dismissed as government scaremongering, red tape and left-wing state regulation of the market, among other things. Nonetheless, since the new Conservative–Liberal coalition government was installed in Downing Street in 2010, a discourse of austerity has become dominant in the UK and the blame game of 'irresponsible spending' and 'the mess left behind' by a Labour government has prevailed.

The idea of 'growth-friendly fiscal consolidation', or 'expansionary contraction', is predicated on rational expectations held by consumers and investors, who approve of *present* consolidation and who expect *future* tax cuts: hence, there is a *positive* confidence effect (Kinsella, 2012, p. 232). Included here is the widespread notion – among German commentators in particular – that worries about public-sector deficits, especially if they are perceived to be widening, will have negative effects on consumer confidence. According to this logic, addressing public-sector deficits will put both investors and business owners at ease and increase their confidence with regard to the economic outlook. Schui (2014, p. 2) examines the pro-austerity argument, which proposes that the renewal of 'economic dynamism is also expected to result from the reduction of government expenditure and debt: a smaller state is believed to leave more space for private initiative and inspire confidence among private investors and consumers'. Examples of this were explicated both by then European Central Bank (ECB) chief, J-C Trichet and German Finance Minister Wolfgang Schäuble in the run-up to the G20 meeting in Toronto in June 2010 (*The Economist*, 2010; Blyth, 2013, p. 61). Both Canada and the UK's Cameron government sided with Germany and the ECB, which left the Obama administration isolated (Blyth, 2013, p. 61).

By 2012, Ireland managed to separate itself from the Portugal, Italy, Ireland, Greece, Spain (PIGSS). Merkel praised Ireland for their 'stoicism and determination' (The

New York Times, 2012b) in working their way successfully through austerity. Others on the 'it can be done' side of the austerity debate would include the Baltic states[5]– even though, in light of their post-Soviet union history and being outside the Eurozone, in the case of Latvia and Lithuania, during the recovery,[6] the story is more complicated (Blyth, 2013, p. 216; Sommers & Woolfson, 2014; Sommers, Woolfson, & Juska, 2014). As part of the pro-austerity tale and in light of their post austerity growth rates since 2011, the Baltic States have sought to show that through determination and sacrifice, 'putting one's house in order' *can* work and deserves to be rewarded. For example, in 2011, Estonia's economy grew 7.6 per cent, Lithuania's 5.8 per cent and Latvia's 5.5, which were the fastest growth rates of the EU economies (*Financial Times*, 2012). Given Estonia and Lithuania's continued growth figures in 2012 and 2013,[7] they have become part of the 'austerity can work' narrative.[8] Blyth (2013, p. 216) puts it well, 'how policy elites in Europe and elsewhere saw the morality tale playing out between the Baltic countries and Southern Europe in the summer of 2012: guts versus surrender, work versus sloth, real austerity versus fake austerity'. The potential role of the Baltic countries as role models for, say, Greece, Portugal or Spain, is part of an ongoing discussion, partly conducted in the blogosphere between Nobel-prize winning economist Paul Krugman and Estonian president Toomas Ilves, where even the *Financial Times* (2012) refused to take clear sides.[9]

In order to demonstrate the meaning of 'real austerity', Chancellor Angela Merkel and the Federal Minister of Finance Wolfgang Schäuble managed to get a 'balanced budget amendment to Germany's constitution' approved by the German parliament in 2009. This law will go into full effect in 2016, after which date the federal government is permitted maximum annual borrowing of 0.35% of gross domestic product – currently equating to about €10 billion (*Spiegel Online*, 2014). Again, a strong moralising element is present: we not only preach frugality, but we also practise what we preach. In a December 2008 speech to the Christian Democratic Union party congress, Merkel lauded the image of the 'Swabian housewife', who is known for her frugality, her strong work ethic and her clear understanding that you should not spend more than you have coming in (*The Guardian*, 2012). In Swabia, loans and overdrafts are for emergencies only, not for regular consumption. In addition, for both her and Schäuble, and other political leaders, there is a strong sense of a morality tale being enacted, serious sins having been committed, and the sinners first having to suffer pain in purgatory before absolution can arrive (*The New York Times*, 2012a).[10]

Both sides in the austerity debate have their morality tales and both sides hold opposing theories of how confidence is created. On the anti-austerity side, at the G20 summit in London, April 2009, Prime Minister Gordon Brown had fairly successfully propagated and 'appeared to have convinced other governments to embrace global Keynesianism, expanding global spending to boost their economies rather than cutting spending to narrow Budget deficits' (Schifferes & Knowles, 2014, p. 49). The morality tale here is that everyone needs to do his or her share for global confidence building. Being frugal is presented as a *sin* rather than a *virtue*: it is free riding at others' expense (Blyth, 2013; Krugman, 2013; Stiglitz, 2012a, 2012b). This ethos states that strengthening consumer confidence is crucial during a downturn and the nourishment of such confidence requires counter-cyclical spending.

Furthermore, the anti-austerity camp turns the 'good frugal North versus bad slothful South' cliché on its head: indeed, a tale can be told that brings out the flip side and emphasises the responsibility of especially German banks in creating the crisis at European level: 'German banks' recklessly bad lending of its excess savings to southern Europe financed property bubbles in Spain and Ireland, funded a consumption boom in Portugal and lent the Greek government the rope with which to hang itself ... ' (Legrain, 2014). In this tale, boom and bust in the PIIGS are no longer explicable with reference to cultural defects, but are the outcome of the dynamics of capitalism, whereby firms in the 'North' have played a culpable role. In the run-up to the euro crisis, 2010, the combined exposure of German and French banks to the PIIGS was estimated at $1 trillion (Blyth, 2013, p. 86) with roughly equal shares for each country, revealing where the money that funded the 'boom' years had actually come from.

We know that discursive positions are always situated within a particular position in an argument (Billig, 1996; Gilbert & Mulkay, 1984). They should not be thought of as permanently held viewpoints. Most ideologies are flexible enough to allow a fair amount a shifting and situational adaptation, or even paradox and contradiction (Wetherell, Stiven, & Potter, 1987). The austerity debate provides some great examples for this argument positing the situated nature of discourse, including amongst leading publications like *The Economist,* which moved from a solidly pro-austerity standpoint in the run-up to the UK May 2010 election, to a mildly anti-austerity standpoint (*The Economist*), and then moved onto a direct critique of German austerity policies (*The Economist*, 2012).

A critical reading of *The Economist*'s discursive practice might see its intervention before the 2010 election as an attempt to lend credibility to the Cameron–Osborne spending plans. But once they were elected, there was less point in taking a blatant pro-austerity stance; a morally more acceptable position could be assumed by criticising the extreme pro-austerity camp in the German government. Whilst we, of course, do not know *The Economist*'s intentions, the contextual production and consumption of texts and their discursive substance are crucial to the different interpretative responses they receive. Hence, the next two sections continue to discuss these concerns by addressing some of the broader implications of austerity on society at large.

Social context, the welfare state and conflicts of austerity

A discourse of inevitability was a significant finding in previous research on *BBC* coverage of austerity. Kay and Salter (2014) analysed the BBC's discursive framing of the government's austerity plan, focusing specifically on BBC coverage of the Comprehensive Spending Review in 2010, in which Osborne's 'austerity' plan was released (see also Fairclough in this issue). By carrying out a framing analysis that applied critical theory, the authors analysed 'three online *BBC* features and compare their framing of the economic crisis – and the range of possible policy responses to it – with that of the government's', as well as 'editorial blogs and training materials associated with the *BBC*'s special "Spending Review season"' (Kay & Salter, 2014, p. 754). Their analysis considered 'the historical context of the *BBC*'s relationship with previous governments at moments of political and economic crisis' (Kay & Salter, 2014, p. 754). Despite recurring criticisms that the *BBC* often expresses a left-wing bias, their findings suggest that the *BBC*'s 'economic journalism discursively normalises neoliberal economics, not necessarily as desirable, but certainly as inevitable' (Kay & Salter, 2014, p. 754). (See also Thomas in this issue.)

Nonetheless, the UK austerity programme is set to continue if the Conservatives remain in power after the 2015 general election. One significant area of controversy that has caused controversy is cuts to the welfare state. In the same interview previously quoted, Osborne said:

> I've set out the kind of spending cuts, the size of the spending cuts that are required. I've also said that if you want to try and reduce the impact on some of these government departments, you should also be looking for savings in welfare. (2014)

This contextualises a recurring dilemma that is projected for the British public to weigh up: if certain departments are to face fewer cuts, then one particular area of spending must be compromised (i.e. the welfare state).

The challenges of financial crisis and austerity have become intertextually and interdiscursively entwined in multiple areas of public discourse and political debate. It is important to understand that when we discuss the discourse of austerity this is more than a purely economic topic. The focus of articles in this special issue considers austerity from the perspective of the financial crisis, business and economics (see Szabo in this issue). But these concerns have also been central to debates in areas stretching beyond this. For example, the UK riots of 2011 saw austerity feature as a prominent point of debate. Some argued that the government's austerity programme was to blame for causing discontent among disillusioned communities. Meanwhile, other sources defended the government against these accusations by saying that austerity was being used as a poor excuse for other social issues and a lack of moral values (Kelsey, 2015b). Whilst not blaming any single factor for the riots himself, Kelsey considered those responses from right-wing sources that depoliticised the agency of rioters, stating that they had no political cause or motivation, but recontextualised the rioters as a political problem who were symbolic of a sick society that could only be cured by 'tough' conservative social policies on crime and social disorder. Their solutions often linked back to support for reductions in welfare spending. Bridges (2012) also argues that after riots, the government were in denial of the impact that the financial crisis had on some communities:

> Even when the [*Riots Communities and Victims Panel*] touches on more structural issues, it does so in ways that seem oblivious to the depth of the economic crisis and government austerity cuts, especially as they impact on the inner cities. (p. 9)

Criticisms of austerity have frequently centred on the impact austerity has had on representations of families and social conditions since the crisis. De Benedictis (2012) argued that after the riots, 'feral' parents were 'created as inevitable failures marked with negative value in the current austerity climate'. In recent years, we have also witnessed the growing popularity of 'reality' television programmes focusing on social welfare. Jensen (2014) argues that programmes such as *Benefits Street* – a Channel 4 documentary aired in 2014 about life on benefits in the UK – reflect a culture of 'poverty porn' in broadcasting and audience fascinations with the welfare state. Jensen (2014) argues that the 'genre of poverty porn television functions to embed new forms of commonsense about welfare and worklessness'. In doing so, she explores how these discursive constructions suppress and deny critical perspectives by projecting what Bourdieu (1984) described as 'doxa' – society's unquestioned and taken-for-granted truths which delineate the sphere of what is open for debate. This doxosophy, Jensen argues, makes 'the social world appear self-evident and requiring no interpretation', thereby reinforcing the 'neolib-eral commonsense around welfare and social security'. Jensen's analysis shows how an acceptance of this commonsense is projected in 'poverty porn' programmes such as *Benefits Street*. These programmes appear 'spontaneous' but, as Jensen points out, are in fact highly editorialised and generate significant media debate, 'particularly via "the skiver", a figure of social disgust who has re-animated ideas of welfare dependency and deception' (Bourdieu, 1984). This point about common sense and acceptance was central to our broader interests behind this project. It is important to provide some context to readers, as we have in this section, in order to show how austerity has become intertextually embedded in different discursive corners and niches of society. Through nuanced constructions and attempts to legitimise or delegitimise austerity, an ideological battleground takes place within the hegemonic structures of finance and econ-omic policy.

Another significant example of this ideological battleground lies in the case of Greece. Greece provides a particularly significant case of austerity discourse due to the range and severity of social and economic issues it has faced during the crisis. As Angouri and Wodak point out, following six years of financial crisis in Greece, 'living standards have dropped considerably for the majority of the population, strict austerity measures have been implemented and unemployment has reached a record figure of 27.8% (with a Eurozone average of 12%)' (2014, p. 540). The 'turnaround' anticipated by austerity economics has certainly not arrived. Yiannis Mylonasa argues that neoliberal discourses in Greek media reproduced 'the hegemonic explanations of the crisis that view the crisis as a national and moral problem rather than a global and systemic one' (2014, p. 305).

Following the right of right-wing discourse in Europe (Wodak, KhosraviNik, & Mral, 2013), polarisation of Greek society and the re-emergence of the extreme right-wing party, Golden Dawn, Angouri and Wodak (2014) analyse postings from the *Guardian Online* to consider how discursive strategies function to attribute or resist blame for Greek's financial hardship. Through a micro-analytical and discourse-historical approach, they show how macro and micro dynamics of discourse construct blame and make sense of the crisis: 'Analysis of the data shows that a range of actors is held responsible for the current situation, while the rise of Golden Dawn is constructed both as a 'product of' and 'movement against' the crisis' (Angouri and Wodak, 2014, p. 540). Lampro-poulou (2014, p. 467) also considers the polarisation of crisis discourse in British press cov-erage of the Greek crisis. She argues that Greece was framed as 'either dependent on or independent of Europe' and subsequently recontextualised its national elections as a vote that would decide the future of Europe. She argues that this 'double-voicing' in discourses about Greece's future 'contributes to the maintenance of domination and social control and helps sustain dominant discourses circulating in the broader socio-cultural context' (Lampropoulou, 2014, p. 467). The recent election of anti-austerity party Syriza in Greece in 2015 could well change the terms of the debate and present a challenge to the dominant pro-austerity discourse prevailing in the Eurozone.

Due to the significance of Greece within the Eurozone, coverage of its financial affairs has frequently been analysed in the discourse of other national press. Vaara's analysis of media discourse in Finland examined the 'discursive and ideological underpinnings of the social, political and financial crisis in Greece and other European countries and contributes to research on discursive legitimation more generally' (2014, p. 500). Vaara's work shows how 'discourses of financial capitalism, humanism, nationalism and Europeanism played a central role in legitimation, delegitimation and relegitimation' through discussions about the current and future challenges of the Eurozone (Vaara, 2014, p. 500). Bickes, Otten, and Weymann (2014, p. 424) also analyse discussions about Greece and blame attribution in the German press:

> The German media presentation of the so-called Greek financial crisis caused an unexpected uproar in Germany. An anti-Greek sentiment evolved and spread among German citizens and solidarity for crisis-hit Greece was mostly rejected. Public surveys revealed that many Germans even wanted Greece to exit the Eurozone immediately. This article highlights the crucial role of the media in shaping the negative public opinion.

Interestingly, some of the recurring factors that featured in British discourses of poverty (such as *Benefit Street* discussed above) are echoed in transnational contexts. In 2010, Europe's largest daily newspaper, *BILD*, published numerous reports that 'implicitly and explicitly constituted the myth of the corrupt and lazy Greeks in comparison to the hard-working Germans' (Bickes et al., 2014, p. 424). Nevertheless, we see again these same discursive characteristics that construct the binary mechanisms of poverty myths by blaming those in hardship for their own situation (see also Harkins & Lugo-Ocando in this issue). This attaches responsibility to those with less prevalent or powerful voices than the institutional elites who have greater opportunities to shape financial discourse. This brings us to our final section concerning ideology and political economy. Given the issues we have discussed so far, these are significant critical concepts in our concerns regarding the language of media and political sources in discourses of austerity and economic policy more generally.

Ideology, political economy and discursive practice

Downey, Titley, and Toynbee (2014, p. 878) propose that media studies needed to once again rediscover the critique of ideology. Following on from Hall's (1982) pledge for media studies to rediscover and adopt the tools for analysing ideology, they argue that due to the current problem of growing social inequality that is covered by blaming the poor or migrants, we need more analysis of ideology (Downey et al. 2014, 878). They make this case in their critique of post-2008 responses to the economic crisis before examining 'advocacy of "social mobility" in the public sphere' as an ideological project. Similarly, Baines and Kelsey (2013) have also called for educators, scholars and practitioners to embrace, adopt and apply critical frameworks of ideology and political economy:

> Rediscovering ideology … increases the potential for a more critical, structural awareness and reflective engagement among media practitioners. This is where ideology, in a working and ethical context, becomes intrinsically linked to political economy: when workers – be it journalism graduates or their counterparts from business schools – are increasingly aware (and potentially critical) of the structural systems they work within and the economic, political and social (ideological) interests that they influence, and represent. (Baines & Kelsey, 2013, p. 34)

This brings us back to our earlier concerns regarding the ideological mechanisms of austerity discourse and the naturalised 'common sense' constructions of media, political and financial institutions (see Szabo's contribution in this issue) that project austerity as an inevitable economic policy. An absence of critical reflection and analysis from within

– and beyond – these institutions restricts the substance of financial discourse to the parameters of hegemonic structures and frameworks of economic policy.

As Baines and Kelsey point out, since the rhetoric of New Labour in UK politics, we have often seen discursive constructions of 'post-ideology' financial policy and an economic system based on 'reality' rather than ideology (2013, p. 32). For example:

> … the 'third way' of New Labour supposedly overcame the pulls and persuasions of left and ring wing ideology. As recently as 2011 Blair spoke of post-ideological societies in the 21st century: 'We live today in a post-ideological era of government. The fundamental political divide between left and right is a phenomenon of the 20th century' (Blair, 2011). Of course, Blair's vision of a Third Way always remained ideologically constructed, and maintained, but its perception of socio-economic 'compromise' suppressed the salience of ideology at work. (Baines & Kelsey, 2013, p. 32)

This reiterates the importance of Norman Fairclough's work, which has critiqued New Labour's rhetorical strategies: ' … the pamphlets, speeches and newspaper articles of New Labour politicians are full of descriptions of how the "Third Way" of New Labour differs from the "old left" and "new right" … ' (2000, p. 9). New Labour's Annual Report of 1998 stated Blair's support for Third Way politics: 'The Third Way is a new politics that helps people cope with a more insecure world because it rejects the destructive excesses of the market and the intrusive hand of state intervention' (Fairclough, 2000, p. 10). As Baines and Kelsey point out, 'we have since learnt, market forces in both business and journalistic contexts, are far from the bliss of post-ideological harmony evoked by Blair' (2013, p. 32). Despite the failings of free market capitalism, the literature covered in this introduction shows how the familiar economic structures and practices of past and current governments across periods of boom and bust have remained securely ingrained in the discursive practices of political and financial institutions.

Ghilarducci and McGahey's (2013) special issue of *Social Research* considered the 'persistence of austerity' as a failed but dominant policy in the developed world. Their work considers how the logic of austerity economics 'has become the dominant policy prescription in the developed world, even though a good deal of economic theory and analysis says that austerity will make things worse' (Ghilarducci & McGahey, 2013). In so doing, they consider 'the political economy of austerity in the USA and Europe and why progressive alternatives have a hard time being part of the policy discourse' (2013). Schiffrin and Fagan's (2013) analysis of the US press considered the accusation that business journalists are ideologically influenced and tend to present a pro-business/market perspective. American business journalists 'are often accused of being not only biased, but too ill-informed to write in an analytical or critical way about economics' (Schiffrin & Fagan, 2013, p. 151). To assess these claims, Schiffrin and Fagan analysed US press coverage of the government's 2009 stimulus package:

> We found that although there was robust discussion of the stimulus, it was mostly focused on the political process rather than the economic issues, there was little agenda setting and government and business sources – including many with a 'vested interest' – were overwhelmingly cited the most. (2013, p. 151)

Whilst we should not draw broad or simplistic generalisations about journalism in any given cultural context, it seems that there are challenges and concerns to address in constructions of financial discourse that inform public opinion on economic affairs. There are certainly structural, economic, professional, practical and environmental processes to consider in relation to media coverage and journalistic practice. These contextual nuances are important to bear in mind when we critically analyse the work of journalists. As Richardson (2007) notes, journalists are workers whose professional practice is impacted upon by the pressures, constraints and values of those environments in which they work. Stuart Hall previously described the media's 'professional codes and technological practices as making a decisive 'cut' or 'overcut' into the semiosis of language in culture at large' (see Rojek, 2003, p. 95).

Fowler (1991) also argues that the ideological role of language is central to constructions of reality: 'Anything that is said or written about the world is articulated from a particular ideological position: language is not a clear window but a refracting, structuring medium' (Fowler, 1991, p. 10). Therefore, whilst scholars such as Manning (2013), Schiffrin and Fagan (2013) and Berry (2013) and others all express sound concerns over the input and influence of media sources, it is important to note that journalists are not conspiratorially committed to elite sources or determined to reproduce dominant ideologies. Rather, journalists often need to use authoritative sources in order to protect themselves from criticism and appear to be objective. As Manning (2013) also points out, many explanations have been suggested for the failures of financial journalism, ranging from issues concerning the complexities of alternative perspectives, the power and persuasive role of financial public relations, or the difficulties of conducting investigative journalism when the staff numbers in newsrooms are cut back (2013, p. 173). Hence, we often see those elite sources with the privilege of institutional access and authority appearing more prominently than other marginal or alternative voices. So, it is important to consider how ideology impacts upon language in news media and constructions of financial discourses, as well as being part of the media through which these discourses are promulgated. Furthermore, financial discourse also occurs through institutions beyond the media. Therefore, with critical notions of language, power and ideology in mind, the papers in this Special Issue cover a range of analytical perspectives on social, political and institutional discourses of financial crisis and austerity.

Overview of the special issue

This special issue attends to various aspects of economic and austerity discourses and a range of discursive analytic approaches.

Mueller and Whittle start the issue with an analyses of how the causes – and blame – for the financial crisis were discursively negotiated during a public inquiry in the UK in early 2009. Drawing theoretical inspiration from a variety of fields ranging from ethnomethodology and conversation analysis, discursive psychology, to linguistic anthropology, they analyse how politicians and banking leaders accounted for the events that led to the collapse and subsequent state bailout of several major British banks. The focus of the analysis is on how actors involved in the banking crisis attribute events to internal 'agentic' or external 'structural' causes. The study found that the politicians employed an agentic repertoire that emphasised the choice, will and intent of the bankers, de-emphasising structural issues such as deregulation and globalisation. The banking leaders, on the other hand, employed a structural repertoire which downplayed agency and instead invoked structural or cultural processes and forces that prevailed at the time. The authors conclude by discussing the wider ideological implications of these two repertoires, as they fed into wider public discourse and shaped the desirability of various policy responses, such as increased state intervention in financial markets, increased regulation of banks, and caps on bankers' bonuses – many of which were in fact subsequently implemented in the UK and elsewhere.

Catherine Walsh examines how Alistair Darling, the British Chancellor of the Exchequer from 2007 to 2010, constructs the Financial Crash rhetorically and how his rhetoric on mortgage and finance stands in comparison to other preceding Chancellors. Walsh's analysis maps the discursive tensions in Darlings' rhetoric in marrying the Labour party's socio-economic perspectives while at the same time presenting a defence of the banking and financial sector. Through careful combination of qualitative and quantitative analysis, Walsh shows the subtle discursive manoeuvres and statistical patterns found in Darling's discourse of finance and financialisation. The study reveals that the provision of limited critique has worked as a discursive strategy in managing the electorate's expectations while legitimising fundamental neoliberal principles.

Isabella Fairclough analyses a corpus of newspaper articles covering the first austerity policy in the UK announced by in the 2010 Emergency Budget in order to develop further the analytic framework for evaluating political discourse in Critical Discourse Analysis specifically (see Fairclough & Fairclough, 2012), and advance the 'argumentative turn' in policy studies more generally. Fairclough puts forward a 'deliberation scheme' – a set of critical questions that can be asked in order to evaluate the premises, validity and consequences of a particular argument – in this case, the arguments put forward in newspapers to defend, question or criticise the British government's austerity policy. Fairclough concludes by discussing the profound consequences of this discourse for social inequality. By successfully 'framing' the financial crisis as a case of government overspending, austerity measures directed primarily at those most vulnerable in society are presented as not only inevitable but also morally right.

Steven Harkins and Jairo Lugo-Ocando take up this final point by analysing how those most vulnerable in society who have been hit hardest by austerity policies are represented in the British tabloid press. Using Critical Discourse Analysis, the authors demonstrate the operation of 'Malthusian' ideology in the press coverage of austerity policies, following the arguments of Thomas Robert Malthus. Malthus was an English cleric and scholar known for his influential writings in the early nineteenth century which conceptualised poverty as a problem of overpopulation and scarce resources, arguing against poor relief for the able bodied. The influence in the Victorian era continued through the distinction between the 'deserving' and 'undeserving' poor, and remains one of the principal features of how poverty is framed by the media today (Lugo-Ocando & Harkins, 2014). Indeed, the authors found that Malthusian ideology was the prevailing frame within which austerity policies were presented in the British press, particularly through the notion of an 'underclass'. This discourse feeds into a more general neoliberal ideology which serves to displace responsibility for the financial crisis and maintain the supremacy of 'market forces' as the only logic for wealth distribution.

Richard Thomas examines the other end of the wealth 'spectrum' by analysing media framing of executive remuneration in the banking sector. As a case study, Thomas concentrates on how three major UK broadcast television channels, that is, BBC, ITV and SKY have covered the 2012 dispute over Barclay's bank remuneration package. By adopting a multi-modal critical discourse analytical approach, he positions his study within a substantial body of research on relations of economy and media and attends to general macro-structural issues of political economy in media organisations and news production in particular. The study reveals that, despite differences in Public Service Broadcasting mandates (e.g. BBC vs. SKY), the content and overall framing of the news in three outlets were largely homogenous. The paper argues that while economic, business and finance journalism still has the capacity to hold the corporate world to account, it fails to do so through oversimplification of financialised concepts and an overall reluctance to appear overtly critical of banks.

Amanda Szabo makes a theoretical contribution by showing how critical discourse analysis can be used to study economic policy by integrating it with notions of communicative constitution of organisation, socio-materiality, performativity and rituals. Her research involves a textual analysis of policy-making setting in the USA, focusing in particular on a City Council meeting about the feasibility of municipalising energy utilities. She shows how wider discourses of envisaging economy interact and impact on the discursive processes at play. She argues that, on the one hand, the rubrics of the texts are both emerging from the economic models while at the same time contributing to them and, on the other hand, the texts have an organising effect on the practices of participants, audiences and stakeholders of the session. The study speaks to the two-way impact of text and practice in organisational settings and the implications of this for economic decision-making, in particular the role of the State in the economy – a central issue in economic policy debates since the financial crisis.

Conclusion

The political economy of hegemonic structures impacts upon the ideological dynamics of social and financial discourse, which is interlinked and influenced according to its national or global context. As we have sought to argue in this Introduction, austerity programmes have impacted upon a range of social issues, concerns and contexts. The arguments for and against reform to the banking sector and austerity programmes are often contextualised through the moral mechanisms of storytelling and rhetoric that we have discussed. National austerity programmes are mainly responses to a *global* financial crisis. Therefore, it is important to understand that financial discourse reflects similar traits and raises parallel concerns across the multiple transnational contexts that we have discussed. By adding to the range of interdisciplinary approaches available, the following papers in this special issue will, we hope, enhance our understanding of austerity discourse and financial crisis from original and critical perspectives.

Notes

1. Wodak, Kwon, and Clarke (2011) have similarly shown the function of language in construction and scaffolding of perception of leadership and consent making in business meetings. See also Kwon, Clarke, and Wodak (2014) and Clarke, Kwon, and Wodak (2011).
2. Portugal, Italy, Ireland, Greece and Spain.
3. This is, of course, not a new morality tale. In 1944, Polanyi described the 1871–1914 period thus: 'Finance … acted as a powerful moderator in the councils and policies of a number of smaller sovereign states. Loans, and the renewal of loans, hinged upon credit, and credit upon good behavior' (p. 14).

4. In the case of Cyprus, its status as offshore centre for Russian funds is a major element in the morality tale.
5. Part of the REBLL group: Rumania, Estonia, Bulgaria, Latvia and Lithuania.
6. Estonia joined the euro on 1 January 2011. Latvia joined the euro on 1 January 2014. Lithuania joined the euro on 1 January 2015.
7. http://www.tradingeconomics.com/lithuania/indicators. http://www.tradingeconomics.com/estonia/indicators. http://www.tradingeconomics.com/latvia/indicators.
8. We should not overlook the presuppositions of 'growth discourse' either, since unquestioned notions of 'growth is good' have been critiqued in other research considering growth in other economic contexts (Lewis, 2013; Lewis & Thomas, 2015).
9. The FT (2012) was reluctant to overcommit either way: 'So are the Baltics really a model for, say, Greece or Spain? The answer is probably not – though they may provide lessons.'
10. In Schäuble's home town of Freiburg, the saying goes, 'everyone sweeps their own door step to keep the city clean' and you only help out your neighbour if he is ill in bed. If he retired early, say in his mid-fifties, and then finds he cannot afford to live on his pension, this would not be a scenario where, under a Freiburg ethic, you would help him out.

Disclosure statement

No potential conflict of interest was reported by the authors.

References

Angela Merkel: 'Austerity makes it sound evil, I call it balancing the budget'. (2013, April 23). *Daily Telegraph*.

Angouri, J., & Wodak, R. (2014). 'They became big in the shadow of the crisis': The Greek success story and the rise of the far right. *Discourse & Society, 25*(4), 540–565.

Austerity alarm: Both sides in the row over stimulus v austerity exaggerate, but the austerity lobby is the more dangerous. (2010, July 1). *The Economist*.

Baines, D., & Kelsey, D. (2013). Journalism education after Leveson: Ethics start where regulation ends. *Ethical Space: The International Journal of Communication Ethics, 9*(4), 29–37.

Barber, L. (2015). Overview: Soothsayers of doom? In S. Schifferes & R. Roberts, (Eds.). (2014). *The media and financial crises: Comparative and historical perspectives* (pp. xxiii–xxviii). London: Routledge.

Berry, M. (2013). The 'today' programme and the banking crisis. *Journalism, 14*(2), 253–270.

Bickes, H. Otten, T., & Weymann, L. (2014). The financial crisis in the German and English press: Metaphorical structures in the media coverage on Greece, Spain and Italy. *Discourse & Society, 25*(4), 424–445.

Billig, M. (1996). *Arguing and thinking: A rhetorical approach to social psychology*. Cambridge: Cambridge University Press.

Blyth, M. (2013). *Austerity: The history of a dangerous idea*. Oxford: Oxford University Press.

Bourdieu, P. (1984). *Distinction*. London: Routledge.

Bridges, L. (2012). 4 days in August: the UK riots. *Race Class, 54*(1), 1–12.

Buckley, N. (2012, June 28). Myths and truths of the Baltic austerity model. *The Financial Times*.

Clarke, I., Kwon, W., & Wodak, R. (2011). A context-sensitive approach to analysing talk in strategy meetings. *British Journal of Management, 23*(4), 455–473.

Coates, D., & Dickstein, K. (2010). A tale of two cities: Financial meltdown and the Atlantic divide. In T. Casey (Ed.), *The legacy of the crash: How the financial crisis changed America and Britain* (pp. 60–78). Houndmills: Palgrave.

De Benedictus, S. (2012) 'Feral' parents: Austerity parenting under neoliberalism. *Studies in the Maternal, 4*(2). Retrieved from http://www.mamsie.bbk.ac.uk/DeBenedictis_SiM_4_2_2012.html

Downey, J. Titley, G., & Toynbee, J. (2014, July) Ideology critique: the challenge for media studies. *Media, Culture & Society*. Retrieved from http://mcs.sagepub.com/content/early/2014/07/19/0163443714536113.full.pdf

Eddy, Melissa. (2012b, November 1). Merkel praises Irish Leader for progress against debt. *New York Times*.

Fairclough, N. (2000). *New Labour, new language?* London: Routledge.

Fairclough, I., & Fairclough, N. (2012). *Political discourse analysis.* London: Routledge.

Fowler, R. (1991). *Language in the news, discourse and ideology in the press.* London: Routledge.

Gabriel, Y. (2004). The narrative veil: Truth and untruths in storytelling. In Y. Gabriel (Ed.), *Myths, stories and organizations: Premodern narratives for our times* (pp. 17–31). Oxford: Oxford University Press.

Ghilarducci, T., & McGahey, R. (2013) *Austerity: Failed economics but persistent policy. Social Research: An International Quarterly 80*(3), Retrieved from https://epay.newschool.edu/C21120_ustores/web/product_detail.jsp?PRODUCTID=5808

Gilbert, G. N., & Mulkay, M. (1984). *Opening Pandora's box: A sociological analysis of scientists' discourse.* Cambridge: Cambridge University Press.

The global economy. Start the engines, Angela: The world economy is in grave danger. A lot depends on one woman. (2012, June 9). *The Economist.*

Hall, S. (1982). The rediscovery of 'ideology': Return of the repressed in media studies. In M. Gurevitch, T. Bennet, J. Curran, & J. Woollacott (Eds.), *Culture, society and the media* (pp. 56–90). New York: Methuen.

Hargie, O., Stapleton, K., & Tourish, D. (2010). Interpretations of CEO public apologies for the banking crisis: Attributions of blame and avoidance of responsibility. *Organization, 17*(6), 721–742.

Jensen, T. (2014). *Sociological Research Online, 19*(3), 3. Retrieved from http://www.socresonline.org.uk/19/3/3.html

Kay, J. B., & Salter, L. (2014). Framing the cuts: An analysis of the BBC's discursive framing of the ConDem cuts agenda. *Journalism, 15*(6), 754–772.

Kelsey, D. (2012). Pound for pound champions: The myth of the blitz spirit in British newspaper discourses of the city and economy after the July 7th Bombings. *Critical Discourse Studies, 9*(3), 285–299.

Kelsey, D. (2014). *The myth of the city trickster: Storytelling, bankers and ideology in the mail online. Journal of Political Ideologies, 19*(3), 307–330.

Kelsey, D. (2015a). *Media, myth and terrorism: A discourse-mythological analysis of the 'blitz spirit' in British newspaper responses to the July 7th bombings.* London: Palgrave Macmillan.

Kelsey, D. (2015b). Defining the sick society: Discourses of class and morality in British, right wing newspapers during the 2011 England riots. *Journal of Capital & Class, 39*(2), 243–264.

Kinsella, S. (2012). Is Ireland really the role model for austerity? *Cambridge Journal of Economics, 36*(1), 223–235.

Knaup, Horand, & Reiermann, Christian. (2014, October 14). Out of Balance? Criticism of Germany Grows as Economy Stalls. *Spiegel Online.* Retrieved from http://www.spiegel.de/international/germany/germany-and-finance-minister-schaeuble-under-fire-as-economy-slows-a-996966.html.

Kollewe, J. (2012, September 17). Angela Merkel's austerity postergirl, the thrifty Swabian housewife. *The* Guardian.

Krugman, P. (2013). How the case for austerity has crumbled. *The New York Review of Books,* 6. Retrieved from http://www.nybooks.com/articles/archives/2013/jun/06/how-case-austerity-has-crumbled/.

Kwon, W., Clarke, I., & Wodak, R. (2014). Micro-level discursive strategies for constructing shared views around strategic issues in team meetings. *Journal of Management Studies, 51*(2), 265–290.

Lampropoulou, S. (2014). Greece will decide the future of Europe': The recontextualisation of the Greek national elections in a British broadsheet newspaper. *Discourse & Society, 25*(4), 467–482.

Legrain, Ph. (2014, October 2013). *Sick German economy is dysfunctional, divisive and dangerous.* Center for Policy Studies. Retrieved from http://www.capx.co/germanys-sickly-economy/.

Lewis, J. (2013). *Beyond consumer capitalism: Media and the limits to imagination.* Cambridge: Wiley.

Lewis, J., & Thomas, R. (2015). More of the same: News, economic growth and the recycling of conventional wisdom. In Graham Murdock & Jostein Gripsrud (Eds.), *Money talks: Media, markets, crisis* (pp. 81–100). Chicago: University of Chicago Press.

Lugo-Ocando, J., & Harkins, S. (2014). The poverty of ideas in the newsroom. In J. Lugo-Ocando (Ed.), *Blaming the victim: How global journalism fails those in poverty* (pp. 36–59). London: Pluto Press.

Manning, P. (2013). Financial journalism, news sources and the banking crisis. *Journalism*, *14*(2), 173–189.

Mylonas, Y. (2014). Crisis, austerity and opposition in mainstream media discourses of Greece. *Critical Discourse Studies*, *11*(3), 305–321.

Olson, E. K., & Nord, L. W. (2015). Paving the way for crisis exploitation: The role of journalistic styles and standards. *Journalism. 16*(3), 341–358.

Osborne, G. (2010). Spending Review 2010: George Osborne wields the axe. *BBC News*. Retrieved from http://www.bbc.com/news/uk-politics-11579979.

Osborne, G. (2014, March 14). *The Andrew Marr show interview: George Osborne, MP Chancellor of the Exchequer*. Andrew Marr Show. Retrieved from http://news.bbc.co.uk/1/shared/bsp/hi/pdfs/1603143.pdf.

Philo, G. (2010). The Daily Politics, BBC, September 15. Retrieved from https://www.youtube.com/watch?v=Pmmf-cLnuq0.

Philo, G. (2012). The media and the banking crisis. *Sociology Review*, *21*(3).

Polanyi, K. (1944/2001). *The great transformation: The political and economic origins of our time*. Boston, MA: Beacon Press.

Radin, P. (1956). *The trickster: A study in American Indian mythology*. New York: Schocken.

Richardson, J. (2007). *Analysing newspapers: An approach from critical discourse analysis*. Basingstoke: Palgrave Macmillan.

Rojek, C. (2003). *Stuart Hall*. Cambridge: Polity Press.

Schäuble, W. (2011, September 5). Why austerity is only cure for the Eurozone. *The Financial Times*.

Schifferes, S., & Knowles, S. (2014). The British media and the 'First crisis of globalization'. In S. Schifferes & R. Roberts (Eds.), *The media and financial crises: Comparative and historical perspectives* (pp. 42–58). London: Routledge.

Schiffrin, S., & Fagan, R. (2013). Are we all Keynesians now? The US press and the American Recovery Act of 2009. *Journalism*, *14*(2), 151–172.

Schui, F. (2014). *Austerity: The great failure*. New Haven: Yale University Press.

Sommers, J., & Woolfson, C. (Eds.). (2014). *The contradictions of austerity: The socio-economic costs of the neoliberal Baltic model*. London: Routledge.

Sommers, J., Woolfson, C., & Juska, A. (2014). Austerity as a global prescription and lessons from the neoliberal Baltic experiment. *The Economic and Labour Relations Review*, *25*(3), 397–416.

Starkman, D. (2015). Wilful blindness: The media's power problem. In S. Schifferes & R. Roberts (Eds.), *The media and financial crises: Comparative and historical perspectives* (pp. 3–15). London: Routledge.

Stewart, James B. (2012a, June 15). German rectitude has its risks. *New York Times*.

Stiglitz, J. (2012a). Austerity–Europe's man-made disaster. *Social Europe Journal*, 8. Retrieved from http://www.socialeurope.eu/2012/05/austerity-europes-man-made-disaster/

Stiglitz, J. (2012b). The perils of 2012. *Social Europe Journal*, *6*(2), 5–6.

Tourish, D., & Hargie, O. (2012). Metaphors of failure and the failures of metaphor: A critical study of root metaphors used by bankers in explaining the banking crisis. *Organization Studies*, *33*(8), 1045–1069.

Vaara, E. (2014). Struggles over legitimacy in the Eurozone crisis: Discursive legitimation strategies and their ideological underpinnings. *Discourse & Society*, *25*(4), 500–518.

Wetherell, M., Stiven, H., & Potter, J. (1987). Unequal egalitarianism: A preliminary study of discourses concerning gender and employment opportunities. *British Journal of Social Psychology*, *26*(1), 59–71.

Whittle, A., & Mueller, F. (2012). Bankers in the dock: Moral storytelling in action. *Human Relations*, *65*(1), 111–139.

WILLIAM REES-MOGG: Demolished by one man and his blog. (2009, March 28). *Daily Mail*. Retrieved from http://www.dailymail.co.uk/debate/article-1165489/WILLIAM-REES-MOGG-Demolished-man-blog.html#ixzz3OAs6GG1U.

Wodak, R., KhosraviNik, M., & Mral, B. (2013). *Right-wing populism in Europe: Discourse and politics*. London: Bloomsbury Academic.

Wodak, R., Kwon, W., & Clarke, I. (2011). Getting people on board: Discursive leadership for consensus building in team meetings. *Discourse & Society*, *22*(5), 592–644.

Accounting for the banking crisis: repertoires of agency and structure

Andrea Whittle and Frank Mueller

Newcastle University Business School, Newcastle upon Tyne, UK

ABSTRACT

In this article, we conduct a discourse analysis of the testimony of the leaders of British banks during a UK public inquiry into the financial crisis. We examine the discursive devices that were used to handle the accountability of banking leaders, particularly their role in the events leading up to the collapse and subsequent state bail-out of the banks. Our analysis identifies two competing interpretative repertoires: an agentic repertoire and a structural repertoire. These repertoires are significant, we suggest, because they inform understanding of what went wrong with the banking system and what should be done to reform and regulate the sector. We conclude by calling for the notions of agency and structure to be treated as an object of study within discourse analysis rather than a form of social scientific explanation.

Introduction

There is a long-running 'yo-yo'-like movement in the social sciences between more systemic approaches and more agentic approaches to the study of social life (Wetherell, 2005). According to discourse analyst Margaret Wetherell (2005), the agency/structure debate needs a radical new approach. Rather than endlessly cycling around this fruitless debate within pre-existing binary distinctions, Wetherell argues that we need to understand how social actors *themselves* handle agency and structure – the internal and external bases of action – as part of their discursive practices. In this article, we take up Wetherell's proposal by examining agency and structure as discursive resources used by members of a particular social group in accounting for action. Our central question is this: how do members make sense of, and account for, the underlying causes of events? We propose viewing 'agency' and 'structure' as practical issues, which are central not only to scholarly theoretical debates but also to 'mundane reason' (Pollner, 1987). For example, how do members of a particular social group establish the presence of choice, freedom, will and intent? When do they invoke external determinants and constraints for their action? What practical actions are achieved in the process? And what broader patterns of culturally established sensemaking – or 'interpretative repertoires' as Wetherell and others call them (Potter & Wetherell, 1987, p. 149; Wetherell & Potter, 1988, p. 171) – are available in a culture or a community to make sense of questions of agency and structure?

We seek to advance Wetherell's agenda by exploring how agency discourse is employed in the process of accounting for the causes of the financial crisis. We examine a public hearing in the UK involving testimony by British bankers implicated in the financial crisis. We advance Wetherell's agenda by bringing together theoretical resources from a range of fields including critical sociolinguistics, analytical philosophy, ethnomethodology, discursive psychology and linguistic anthropology. Discourses of agency and structure, we show, play an integral role in the negotiation of responsibility and accountability in events such as the financial crisis, with implications for how these events are understood and acted upon.

The discourse of agency

According to Kenneth Gergen (2009, p. 79), the discourse of agency is 'significant and pervasive' in modern society, but is also historically and culturally specific. Gergen traces the debate about human agency back to Aristotle, for whom there resided an active force within each person that was responsible for decisions and actions. The modernist notion of the 'free but ultimately responsible agent' includes the 'capacity to choose' and 'direct our actions according to our decisions' (Gergen, 2009, p. 79): what Harré and Stearns (1995, p. 6) call the 'myth of the "will"'. Analytical philosophy has distinguished 'action' from an 'event' through the invocation of cognitive states such as intention, choice and purpose (Ahearn, 2001). For example, 'walking down the stairs' is seen as an 'action', whereas 'falling down the stairs' is merely an event or 'happening' (cf. Davidson, 1971). It is precisely this notion of the discrete, bounded locus of agency that has been the target of much post-structuralist critique in recent decades (e.g. Knights & Willmott, 1989). Indeed, in other systems of meaning, the 'modern' notion of the centred, intentional 'I' may well disappear: Herrigel (1953/1981), for example, describes the mastery of Zen archery in Buddhist mythology as follows:

> Is it 'I' who draws the bow, or is it the bow that draws me into the state of highest tension? Do 'I' hit the goal, or does the goal hit me? … Bow, arrow, goal and ego, all melt into one another, so that I can no longer separate them. (p. 88)

In Zen discourse, then, action no longer requires reference to an intentional agent who is purported to have degrees of 'agency'.

In this article, we approach this debate in a different way. Rather than seeking to advance the post-structuralist critique, or the philosophical debate, we instead seek to follow a more ethnomethodologically informed approach and study how the discourse of agency is deployed as part of *member's social reasoning and social practice* (Garfinkel, 1967). The 'discourse grammars' of everyday life, Harré (1995) suggests, follow typically two different types of accountability: members variously depict themselves as passive beings dictated by external influences to which they are subject (what Harré calls the 'Humean' schema), or active beings with productive capacities (what Harré calls the 'agentive' schema). For Harré, these two different schemas are alternative discursive presentations of the self that occur as part of *practical moral accountability* rather than mental mechanisms of cognitive processing – a point highly relevant to the discourse that emerged in the wake of the 2008 financial crisis.

Agency as a 'discourse grammar', we suggest, performs a number of different *social actions*, such as allocating blame, providing excuses and presenting a version of the self. For example, stressing one's agency can act as a form of expression of personal identity (Harré & van Langenhove, 1999, p. 24): presenting oneself as having *chosen* one of many possible courses of action ('I could have done X, but I chose to do Y'), where that choice displays something about the kind of person we are. Agency is emphasised by presenting the self as an 'integrated centre and originator of their actions' (Potter, Stringer, & Wetherell, 1984, p. 160). In contrast, positioning oneself as powerless and robbed of choice positions the person in terms of a lack of agency, with attendant lack of responsibility or blame. In the section that follows, we develop our theoretical position on the practical reasoning and accounting that discourses of agency and structure accomplish.

Practical reasoning and practical accounting: what discourses of agency and structure accomplish

The field of discursive psychology has been at the forefront of the development of insights into agency and structure as practical accounting procedures. Studies in this field have focused on how 'agency, intent, doubt, belief, prejudice, and so on, are built, made available, or countered "indirectly", through descriptions of actions, events, objects, persons or settings' (Potter & Edwards, 2003, p. 171). This allows us to analyse seemingly neutral descriptions of 'states of affairs' and 'events' in terms of what this does in specifying protagonists' past (and present) agency. As Tilly (2008, p. 12) notes, judging agency relies on being able to ascertain whether the action was performed 'more or less deliberately with knowledge of the likely consequences' (Tilly, 2008, p. 12). A central condition for accountability, then, is that the actor is deemed responsible within a particular moral order. The actor must be deemed conscious and competent enough to be capable of reflections on his or her own actions; and the actor must not have been caught up in external conditions that would have prevented him or her from exerting agency. Thus, moral attributions can often be accomplished 'through what look like (or are produced as) straightforward event descriptions' (Edwards & Potter, 2005, p. 242): for example, descriptions of external conditions may provide an account why a certain action supposedly fell short of certain standards.

At this point, it is worthwhile introducing the distinction drawn by Scott and Lyman (1968) between *excuses*, where the speaker concedes the moral questions about their behaviour, but seeks to avoid being attributed personal responsibility (agency), and *justifications*, where the speaker admits personal responsibility (agency) but challenges the moral critique regarding the action (see also Austin, 1970; Harré, 1995). Llewellyn and Harrison's (2006) study of corporate communications found a heavy use of a syntactic feature known as 'passive transformation' (Fowler, 1991, p. 77–78), where the object of the active verb becomes the subject. For example, rather than placing human subjects in the normal grammatical place of the subject, it was instead an institution, an abstract concept (such as 'quality') or simply a person or persons unknown in the case of agentless-passive sentences (e.g. 'New jobs will emerge and some jobs will go over the next twelve months', Llewellyn & Harrison, 2006, p. 595) that are the 'subject'. Llewellyn and Harrison (2006, p. 578) argue that these features matter because they imply that 'developments "simply happened" and were not the result of the actions of specific groups'. Most importantly, for our purposes, these discursive features also act to reduce or remove the agency of both the author(s) of the text and those on whose behalf the text was written.

The ethnomethodological study by Lynch and Bogen (1996) of the public hearings following the Iran–Contra affair also shows how agentic and structural discourse was employed by Oliver North, a US army officer at the centre of the controversy, to handle his accountability for problematic events. Lynch and Bogen show how North used a subtle rhetorical 'switch' to describe his act of shredding documents, not as a calculated decision to avoid certain documents being seized by investigators, but rather as part of normal, automatic, accepted, everyday practice by painting a 'backdrop of shredding-as-usual' (p. 173). North handled the accusation of having been conscious and strategic, i.e. having exerted 'blameworthy agency' in his shredding activity, by emphasising the structural, routine causes of his individual actions. Accordingly, due to existing routines he had 'good and sufficient reasons to destroy documents' on a daily basis, indicated by the fact that 'the government buys shredders by the tens and dozens' (p. 22). This description of events handles agency in such a way that it downplays the active agency involved in shredding documents, by presenting it as a normal part of the structure and roles of the organisation: 'what everyone does' and 'what my job demands'. In so doing, North positions his accountability as follows: I did not engage in pre-planned, strategic shredding, which would indeed be bad (excuse), I only engaged in routine shredding, which is not blameworthy (justification).

This is a practical application of a research agenda that seeks to examine the discourses people 'employ for repudiating or taking on responsibility and thus displaying our agency or lack of it' (Harré, 1995, p. 129). Indeed, descriptions can often be seen as occurring 'in the context of potential blame' raising the spectre of potential 'culpability in those events' (Edwards, 1997, p. 97). In the courtroom, a defence barrister for example makes certain inferences available to the jury by using specific, carefully chosen descriptions (Edwards & Potter, 1992, p. 50–51). In Pollner's (1987) classic study of traffic court interaction, the forms of mundane reasoning about agency (or lack thereof) employed by judges have practical consequences for the judicial outcome. For example, judges routinely employ common sense notions of probable, or typical (Schutz, 1967), intention in their reasoning about agency in order to ascertain the difference between criminal intent and an accident. The discourse of agency means that the same 'action' (such as driving on the wrong side of a divided highway) by an 18-year-old is not the same 'action' as the one performed by an 'oldster' (Pollner, 1987): the former is viewed as an outcome of criminal, intended recklessness (agentive) the latter an outcome of bad luck or circumstances (for instance, being blinded by the sun).[1]

Heritage and Clayman's (2010) conversation analytic study of the beating of Rodney King in Los Angeles in March 1991 showed that the prosecution or acquittal of the four police officers depended upon the construction of King as being portrayed as either a passive victim of police brutality (action *without* agency), or as an aggressively resistant and uncooperative suspect (action *with* agency). Small movements of the body that were captured on a video camera, such as the raising of his knee, were interpreted by the defence attorneys as indicative of a wilful move of aggression, rather than, say, a defensive move or a reflex response (Heritage & Clayman, 2010, p. 182–185). Agency (or a lack thereof) was thus constructed through the interpretative resources and descriptions brought to bear on the video recording. The 'fact' of the beating was not denied but its *blameworthiness* was denied by presenting it as a *re*action rather than an agentive and deliberately chosen *action*.

Work in the field of linguistic anthropology has revealed the operation of similar grammatical structures and linguistic features of agency discourse in other cultural contexts. In Duranti's (1990) study of Samoan society, crimes and disputes are resolved through the gathering of a 'fono', a politico-judiciary meeting where those in dispute gather in front of the 'matai', tribal leaders or titled individuals, to establish the facts and enable retributions and reparations to be administered. According to Duranti (1990), the struggle between prosecution and defence is negotiated through a linguistic exercise in agency avowal and disavowal. Those wishing to accuse a person of stealing, for instance, use grammatical features, such as transitive clauses with an explicit agent, to define the accused as a purposeful and intentional agent. Those who want to resist a particular framing of past events employ a series of grammatical strategies for mitigating agency, such as case marking, lexical choice and reported speech. Duranti (1990, p. 661–662) concludes that 'the expressing of agency is a delicate process that must be managed', with very real consequences for those involved, as the 'grammatical form of utterances becomes an integral part of the political process'.

In our study, we aim to show how discourse of agency and structure was used to account for the financial crisis – in ways that had very real implications for how the crisis was made sense of and acted upon. We will first discuss the methods and methodology employed in this study.

Methodology

The theoretical perspective we have outlined above, in particular the ethnomethodological perspective underlying work in the field of discursive psychology, involves a particular approach to data collection and analysis. First, it involves a commitment to studying naturally occurring data because it enables us to examine the accounts constructed *in situ* by those involved in the sense-making following the financial crisis. These naturally occurring materials are preferred to the kinds of *post-hoc rationalisations* produced in interviews (Potter & Hepburn, 2005). Naturally occurring accounts are important precisely because they influenced the way in which the financial crisis was both understood and acted upon. Following Brown's (2005) analysis of the reports following the collapse of Barings Bank, we view the Treasury Committee Hearings that we analyse as constituting an 'important discursive contribution to people's understanding of a significant episode in UK and global banking' (p. 1584). One limitation of this publicly available data source is that detailed Jeffersonian transcription, the established method of ethnomethodology, conversation analysis and discursive psychology, is not possible. Only the official Treasury Committee transcription was available to us, meaning complex interactional features such as pauses and overlapping talk could not be transcribed. We acknowledge this methodological limitation, but remain convinced of the overall value of analysing public texts because they show how discourse is used in 'creating, clarifying, sustaining and modifying' a particular 'version of "reality"' (Brown, 2005, p. 1584).

Second, our theoretical approach brings with it certain ontological commitments. In line with discursive psychology, we view talk as a medium of social action, rather than a reflection of inner cognitive entities, such as thoughts, memories, emotions or attitudes (Edwards, 1997, p. 90–96). Hence, the job of the analyst is not to delineate the 'true' or 'correct' account among the competing versions produced by the bankers and questioners in our study. Rather, our analysis focuses on *how* these versions are constructed to present themselves as a plausible, factual or objective version of events and, in this article specifically, the agency (or lack of) in those events. This leads us to examine the 'range of styles, linguistic resources and rhetorical devices' (Edwards & Potter, 1992, p. 28) used in this process: which we refer to simply as 'discursive devices' (Edwards & Potter, 1992, p. 68; see also Mueller & Whittle, 2011) – a term we explain in more detail shortly.

The transcript we analyse was part of a series of meetings and reports announced by the UK Treasury Committee on 25 November 2008 as part of its Banking Crisis inquiry. The inquiry involved a series of 17 oral evidence sessions, which we term 'hearings', involving banking executives, senior politicians, regulators and experts. This article focuses specifically on the hearing held on Tuesday 10 February 2009 when four former bank executives were questioned by a panel of politicians (Members of Parliament) from different political parties. The questions asked during the hearing were numbered in the publicly available transcript and are referenced accordingly (e.g. Q1570) in our discussion. A list of the participants in the hearing quoted in this article is given in Table 1.

We focus on this single hearing for one simple reason: given we are interested in how accountability and blame is managed through discourses of agency and structure, this particular hearing was where these issues were most prevalent. Other hearings involved actors whose responsibility was less the target of enquiry, such as expert academics and economists and representatives of governmental departments. Naturally, one important direction for future research would be to extend our analysis to the discourse of responsibility directed at other institutions, in the UK and beyond (see e.g. Mueller, Carter, & Whittle, 2015).

Our analysis began by identifying the linguistic features of the accounts of both the questioners (politicians) and respondents (bankers). We were guided by insights from discursive psychology to identify the forms of 'discursive devices' – turns of phrase, metaphors, pronouns, grammatical structures, linguistic techniques and so on – that were used in the accounts. Discursive devices are 'language-based tools that are employed as part of interactional business' (Mueller & Whittle, 2011, p. 188). In this case, the interactional business is one of conducting a public inquiry (the role of the politicians) and explaining past actions (the banking leaders). A discursive device can be something as simple as a collective pronoun like 'we', or a more complex linguistic

Table 1. Participants in Treasury Select Committee meeting 10 February 2009

Role	Name	Position
Questioners	John McFall	Chair of Treasury Committee
	John Mann	MP *(Labour, Bassetlaw)*
	Michael Fallon	MP *(Conservative, Sevenoaks)* (Chairman, Sub-Committee)
	Jim Cousins	MP *(Labour, Newcastle upon Tyne Central)*
	Andrew Love	MP *(Labour, Edmonton)*
	Mark Todd	MP *(Labour, South Derbyshire)*
	Graham Brady	MP *(Conservative, Altrincham & Sale West)*
Witnesses	Sir Tom McKillop	Former Chairman of RBS Group plc
	Sir Fred Goodwin	Former Chief Executive of RBS Group plc
	Lord Stevenson of Coddenham	Member of the House of Lords, Former Chairman of HBOS plc
	Mr Andy Hornby	Former Chief Executive of HBOS plc

structure or frame such as footing (Mueller & Whittle, 2011). The concept of discursive devices is a more micro concept than the concept of interpretative repertoires, which refers to the 'recurrently used systems of terms for characterizing and evaluating actions, events, or other phenomena' (Potter & Wetherell, 1987, p. 149). Discursive devices therefore provide the linguistic building blocks through which interpretative repertoires are built. Our analysis identified two competing interpretative repertoires – an agentic repertoire and a structural repertoire – from the patterns of accounting given by the politicians and the bankers, respectively. To be clear, our claim is not that these repertoires are generalisable beyond our data-set: this is a matter for future empirical research. Rather, they are repertoires identified as recurrently used within the transcripts we analysed. Issues of generality and wider relevance are discussed in more detail in the conclusion.

Agency and the financial crisis: a discursive devices analysis

In this section, we present illustrative extracts of our discourse analysis of the transcript of the Treasury Select Committee meeting on 10 February 2009. Our aim is to show the ways in which discursive devices, as summarised in Tables 2 and 3, were used to handle the accountability of the bankers, particularly their role in the events leading up to the collapse and subsequent state bail-out of the banks. We focus our analysis more closely on the way agency is handled in the responses by the bankers. While the politicians (questioners) used a range of devices to achieve agency attribution (see Table 2) – what we call the 'agentic repertoire', the bankers (respondents) used a more sophisticated array of devices to handle their agency in ways that did not concede personal responsibility (see Table 3) – what we call the 'structural repertoire'.

Table 2. The agentic repertoire: discursive devices employed in the questions posed by politicians (UK Treasury Select Committee Hearing, 10 February 2009)

Discursive devices	Description	Role in handling agency	Illustrative extract
Singular pronouns	Use of terms such as 'you' to refer to an individual rather than collective	Emphasises agency by placing locus of action within individual rather than collective	'You have destroyed a great British bank; you have cost the taxpayer £20 billion'
Hierarchical level	Reference to rights, obligations and expectations normally associated with a particular position within the organisational hierarchy. For example, the expectations placed upon junior employees is typically different to the expectations associated with senior management roles	Emphasises agency by appealing to high level of power, responsibility, decision-making rights and influence associated with a senior management role	'You were in charge of this Board'
Incumbent/ role	Invites an assessment of whether (or to what extent) a particular outcome can be attributed to the role itself (regardless of incumbent) or the particular incumbent of the role	Brings agency to the fore by inviting an assessment of the extent to which the incumbent in question is the locus of agency, or whether agency is located in the role itself, regardless of incumbent. Those in positions of hierarchical seniority may find the latter especially difficult to achieve	' ... how much worse could it have been at RBS if you had not been in charge?'

Table 3. The structural repertoire: discursive devices employed in the testimony of banking executives (UK Treasury Select Committee Hearing, 10 February 2009)

Discursive devices	Description	Role in handling agency	Illustrative extract
Plural pronouns	Use of terms such as 'we' or 'the Board' rather than I	Downplays individual agency and distributes agency to a collective	'We did in fact make a bad mistake in purchasing ABN Amro'
Nominalisation	Named subjects are replaced with nominalised verbs or objects, such as 'the bankers invented risky products' being changed to 'risky practices were invented'	Obscures agency by leaving agent unspecified	'The deal was a bad mistake'
Non-transactives	Non-transactive sentences involve one subject and imply no causal processes, e.g. 'A man aged 45 was shot' Transactive sentences, in contrast, involve one active subject and one passive subject/object, who is acted upon e.g. 'Police shot a 45 year old man'	Obscures agency by leaving cause unspecified	'The deal was a bad mistake'
Subject–object grammatical structure	Grammatical structure of causality between subject and object in a sentence, for instance 'we stopped lending' can be changed to a 'crisis of confidence led to a freeze in lending'	Presents events as caused by something (or someone) other than the speaker, removing the agency of the speaker	'… the collapse in confidence, the collapse in markets, just came round and hit us and we were caught at that point'
Passive voice	Stating 'practices were imported' rather than 'we imported practices'	Obscures role of agent by failing to specify an agent, whether singular or collective	'… a lot of these practices have come across from the United States'
Hindsight	Appeal to limited capacity to predict the future, as a reasonable human fallibility	Admits involvement but plays down culpability through appeal to universal human fallibility, suggesting a kind of 'bounded' agency: 'Yes, I knew what I was doing, but I cannot be expected to be a fortune teller/mind reader'	'At the time it did not look like that. It is easy in retrospect'
Externalisation	Locating causes outside the person, to another person, object or entity, such as 'practices from the United States'	Deflects agency onto external sources, which could be an individual, collective or abstract entity	'… the funding markets came to a complete halt post-Lehman's …'
Surprise	Emphasising the unexpected nature of events, to emphasise that they were not anticipated, to imply an absence of intention or will	Implies an absence of (intentional) agency by suggesting 'I could not have intentionally caused this to happen because it was a surprise to me'	'It was a fact, and all the more numbing, that after a rights issue, right through until the middle of September, we were moving forward positively'
Prevailing view	Appeal to a prevailing set of opinions or preferences to present action as consistent with the dominant 'view' or 'mood'	Handles agency by presenting action as following the 'view at the time', with decisions presented as not 'free' but already 'structured' by a social pattern. To do otherwise would have been to 'swim against the tide'	'I could give you many, many statements, many bits of evidence that support that …'
Higher authority	Having acted in the knowledge or approval of a higher authority, such as a regulator	Deflects agency onto a higher authority, who is given capacity for making choice and judgement	'… we received regulatory approvals …'

(Continued)

Table 3. Continued.

Discursive devices	Description	Role in handling agency	Illustrative extract
Abstract forces	Attribution of agency to abstract forces such as 'markets' or 'culture'	Moves agency to external forces over which the individual has little or no control	'It is an area where people and teams do move around the market; and if amounts are not paid and people do not feel they are appropriately remunerated they will move'
Role	Appeal to the incumbent role as the cause of conduct, as in 'any CEO would have made the same decisions'	Downplays agency through appeal to the demands of the role: 'I was just doing my job'	'I would imagine that there are others out there who think, "There but for the grace of God"'
(Bad) Luck	Appeal to luck, rather than choice or design, as the explanation for events. Can be used to explain 'bad luck' to excuse or avoid blame (e.g. 'any Bank could have needed a bail-out') or 'good luck' to avoid the appearance of arrogance or self-aggrandisement (e.g. 'I was lucky to get this promotion, there must have been a shortage of candidates')	Removes agency by presenting outcomes as random, not the result of active choices or decisions of the individual	'It could have happened to others'

Q1677 Mr Fallon: Sir Fred [Goodwin] said in October that the jury is out on ABN. Now that it appears to be back, how would you summarise it? Sir Tom, I am asking you. You were in charge of this Board. You have destroyed a great British bank; you have cost the taxpayer £20 billion; how would you now summarise that deal?

Sir Tom McKillop: The deal was a bad mistake—I have already indicated that.

Q1678 Mr Fallon: So you failed?

Sir Tom McKillop: We did in fact make a bad mistake in purchasing ABN Amro. At the time it did not look like that. It is easy in retrospect. I could give you many, many statements, many bits of evidence that support that at the time we bought that, when we made that acquisition, there was widespread support for it. Yes, there were some voices saying it was overpriced, but we received 94.5% shareholder approval; we received regulatory approvals; there was a very good financial case.

Extract 1

In this extract, the questioner Mr Fallon poses his question in terms of very *personal* responsibility and accountability. The phrase 'You were in charge of the Board' implies that McKillop, as Chairman at the time, had ultimate responsibility for the decisions of the Board: the 'buck stops here'. Fallon uses the second-person singular pronoun (see Table 2) 'You' when directly attributing blame for 'destroy[ing] a great British bank' and 'cost[ing] the taxpayer £20 billion'. Fallon makes it clear that he is using the term 'you' to refer to McKillop personally, not the institution (the bank). Harré (1995, p. 124) argues that 'one of the main ways in which we take and assign responsibility is by the use of pronouns'. In this case, the pronoun 'you' works to position agency and responsibility firmly on the shoulders of the *individual* being interrogated, McKillop. Specific agents, not the system as a whole, are held to blame.

McKillop's response re-formulates this accusation of blame using a combination of *nominalisation* and *non-transactive* sentence structure (see Table 3). Non-transactive sentences involve one subject and imply no causal processes, such as 'A man aged 45 was shot' (Potter et al., 1984, p. 91). Transactive sentences, in contrast, involve one active subject and one passive subject/object, who is acted upon, such as 'Police shot a 45 year old man' (ibid). Nominalisation refers to a similar linguistic phenomenon, the act of replacing named subjects with nominalised verbs, adjectives or adverbs to avoid mentioning those who performed the action, particularly to avoid attribution of blame or responsibility (Billig, 2008). Violent actions by police, for example, may be described in a nominalised form: 'violence was perpetrated', 'bitterness … commenced' (Wetherell & Potter, 1989, p. 210–211) to avoid mentioning the person(s) or institution(s) involved. In this case, the *personal* responsibility imputed by Fallon ('You') is replaced with an *impersonal* reference to 'the deal', a third-person inanimate noun. In so doing, McKillop not only *refuses to concede personal responsibility* but he also *diffuses and distributes agency* by referring to a 'deal' that involved many different agents, not only himself. Nominalisation can play an ideological role by obfuscating agency (Billig, 2008) and instead creating third-person entities which are said to act: 'the deal', 'the financial case'. Hence, the nominalised and non-transactive grammatical structure of McKillop's talk acts to perform *impersonalisation* and *agency distribution*.

Fallon's next question (Q1678) attempts to reverse McKillop's impersonalisation and distribution of agency by returning to the second-person singular pronoun 'you'. McKillop again rejects this attribution of personal responsibility for 'failure' by using the first-person plural pronoun 'we': he claims 'we did in fact make a bad mistake … '. *Plural pronouns* (see Table 3) such as 'we' of course work to distribute agency to a collective. Indeed, debate is ongoing within group agency theory about whether collectives such as corporations can be held to have 'agency' in the same way as individuals (List & Pettit, 2011).

McKillop then uses two further discursive devices to justify his role in the events surrounding the purchase of ABN Amro. First, he appeals to 'retrospect', the benefit of *hindsight* (see Table 3) as a justification for why the outcomes that seem so obvious today were not so obvious at the time. This was in fact a common device used by all four witnesses throughout the hearing. The terms 'retrospect', 'hindsight' and 'prophesize' were used in more than a dozen places throughout the transcript. The message suggested by these terms is that banking executives should not be expected to be 'fortune tellers' who are able to predict the future. The accusation of blame is thereby presented as an 'unfair' accusation: asking them to have done something that was humanly impossible. According to Scott and Lyman (1968, p. 48–49), this is a common form of defeasibility account where the speaker 'might excuse himself from responsibility by claiming that certain information was not available to him [sic], which, if it had been, would have altered his behaviour' (p. 48). This admits that the person had 'free will' but not complete 'knowledge' with which to exercise it. McKillop's account follows the logic of the 'gravity disclaimer' outlined by Scott and Lyman (1968, p. 48–49), where the outcome was known to be a possibility but that its *probability* was incalculable.

Another of McKillop's tactics combined an appeal to a *prevailing view* and *higher authority* (see Table 3). McKillop suggests that his agency was bounded and structured by prevailing viewpoints and opinions: the available evidence, shareholder opinions, and so on. It was not simply his choice or discretion to purchase ABN Amro, it was part of an existing momentum or flow of activity. He did not have the ability to act freely of his own volition; he was 'caught up in a wave'. His appeal to 'regulatory approvals' invokes a higher authority that can be held to share responsibility (and agency) for the decisions made. The appeal to 'officialdom' is particularly significant because it helps McKillop to present his decisions as one that met with official regulatory approval: he was not a 'lone ranger' acting alone, making decisions of his own choosing, he was only doing what others agreed with – thus there was *social legitimacy* attached to his actions. These appeals work to invoke a sense of consensus, albeit not unanimous (in the case of shareholder approval), to justify his decision and distribute agency.

Edwards and Potter (1992, p. 108) argue that 'consensus' can serve as a rhetorical device to warrant (or indeed undermine) versions of events. Witnesses in courts, for instance, often appeal to consensus across a group of observers and corroboration between independent individuals as evidence of the 'independence' and 'validity' of their accounts (ibid). The work of Pomerantz (1986) on 'extreme case formulations' (such as 'everybody knows/thinks/accepts X') is also relevant here. These formulations construct certain things as universal and normative, enabling agency to be shifted from the personal to the universal. The implication generated for McKillop is that he should not be held *personally* responsible for something that (almost) everyone agreed to: thereby diffusing agency and, in turn, responsibility and blame.

Q1696 John Mann: I am interested in the question of whether if events had gone slightly differently if there could have been others here rather than you facing the music, or whether you are particularly personally culpable?

Mr Hornby: No, I do not feel I am particularly personally culpable.

Q1697 John Mann: Sir Fred Goodwin, how much worse could it have been at RBS if you had not been in charge?

Sir Fred Goodwin: I fully accept my responsibility in the matter we are talking about. I would imagine that there are others out there who think, "There but for the grace of God". It was a fact, and all the more numbing, that after a rights issue, right through until the middle of September, we were moving forward positively. It was post-Lehman's that the collapse in confidence, the collapse in markets, just came round and hit us and we were caught at that point. It was very sudden and very sharp. It could have happened to others.

Q1698 John Mann: I keep hearing about the requirement for brilliance. People keep on telling us, and telling me all the time, "We need to attract the most brilliance". Are there people out there who are more brilliant who could have done a better job than you with RBS?

Sir Fred Goodwin: There may well be. It would seem unreasonable for me to conclude that there were not. At the time we felt that the rights issue had got the group back on track; it had dealt with the capital issue; we were moving forward; we had published our interim results; and the funding markets came to a complete halt post-Lehman's and it was a crisis of confidence that brought this about.

Extract 2

Mann's question centres on whether responsibility could (or should) be attributed to *any incumbent* of senior management, and whether Goodwin could (or should) be held *personally* responsible. The concept of *role* (see Table 3) is used here to negotiate the agency of the incumbent, Fred Goodwin. This is reminiscent of Edwards and Potter's (1992) analysis of how Thatcher handled her accountability for Lawson's resignation as Chancellor. By describing Alan Walters' (her 'inofficial' economic advisor) behaviour in such a way to make it appear as 'unremarkable, scripted … acting in role' (p. 148), the implication is that if Walters acted in role, then Lawson's resignation can only be blamed on himself.

Goodwin flatly denies the accusation of personal responsibility by stating: 'No, I do not feel I am particularly personally culpable'. Agency is attributed to the *role*, rather than the *incumbent*. Whilst Goodwin uses the phrase 'I fully accept my responsibility', the question arises whether this is a 'show concession': where an often marginal point is conceded to bolster the overall argument, making the speaker appear more reasonable and fair by conceding the validity of the counter-position (Antaki & Wetherell, 1999, p. 23). As we will discuss below, devices of externalisation are employed later on in his statement which subtly qualify his 'admission of agency'.

Goodwin refuses to be drawn into a discussion of whether he made the situation 'better' through his actions as Chief Executive of the Bank. This avoidance is significant for our purposes because it works as a refusal to assess his own agency – his capacity for action, his discretionary judgment, his ability to 'make a difference' and so on – during his tenure as Chief Executive of the Royal Bank of Scotland (RBS). To agree with the claim that he made things 'better' would run the risk of inviting ridicule: could another CEO really have caused an even greater disaster? In fact, Goodwin takes up a supposed 'modest' position of admitting that others could in fact be more 'brilliant' than him. Instead of answering the question of whether he made RBS 'better', Goodwin offers an admission of 'responsibility', even though this was not the question asked. As has been documented in studies of news interviews, respondents – just like in this extract – often refuse to directly address the question in order to reject the 'trap' set by the adversarial preface of the question (Heritage & Clayman, 2010, Ch7).

Immediately after his 'show concession' admission of responsibility, Goodwin moves on to qualify and justify the actions for which he has admitted responsibility. First, he locates the cause of the problem in the world 'out there' (the sudden 'collapse in markets'), over which he had no control, a case of *externalisation* (see Table 3). The metaphor of the 'tsunami', used by Alan Greenspan in his address to the House of Representatives Committee on Oversight and Government Reform,[2] was also used by the bankers in our case, and is a good example of such a device for externalising agency. Second, the phrase 'it could have happened to others' plays an important role in Goodwin's account. This phrase attributes the collapse of the Bank to *bad luck* (see Table 3), as opposed to decisions that could be attributed to himself and/or others. The idea that 'it could have happened to anyone' distinguishes between responsibility for an action and responsibility for an outcome. Negative outcomes are presented as bordering on 'random', removing the emphasis on agency from all those involved. This formulation presents Goodwin as being powerless to stop the crisis (he had no control over events) and no different to others (there was no reason it affected RBS as opposed to other banks).

Third, the phrase 'there but for the grace of God' is important for how it handles Goodwin's agency. Reflecting upon the possibility that others could be feeling 'lucky' not to be 'facing the music' having made the same decisions, implies that Goodwin is simply an 'unlucky' person (see Table 3): any other person in the same role could have done the same thing. His agency is presented as something common to any incumbent, not himself personally. Agency is thereby ascribed to the role position rather than the individual. We should remind ourselves that whether we emphasise commonality or difference is rhetorical work, that is, it is not stating an absolute truth but rather a position in an argument (Billig, 1987/96). For instance, one can make the point that all U.S. investment banks were caught up in the crisis; but one can also make the point that some were caught up more than others.

Fourth, a particular *subject–object* grammatical arrangement (see Table 3) is used in Goodwin's description of events, with consequences for how agency is presented. The 'collapse in confidence … hit us' presents the collapse as the *subject*, with RBS (and Goodwin himself) as the *object*. This grammatical form attributes agency to the collapse, away from himself and the bank. Consider the contrast with this subject–object arrangement: 'our actions led to a collapse in confidence'. Fifth, the emphasis on 'moving forward positively' before the collapse also acts to present the 'collapse' as something that was a *surprise* (see Table 3). Presenting events as unexpected works to create a 'sense of anomalousness' (Potter et al., 1984, p. 89): as in, 'I expected X, but instead Y happened'. This is a common linguistic strategy known as a 'contrast structure' (ibid: 88), used to present descriptions as factual by claiming they are counter-dispositional, that is, not the outcome of particular motives, biases or pre-conceptions. Contrast structures are used to make accounts more credible and have been found in stories of paranormal encounter stories, for instance (Wooffitt, 1992). In our case, presenting events as unexpected helps to downplay agency by suggesting 'if I willfully and intentionally created this situation, why was it a surprise to me?' A contrast is also made between the *ordinary* 'business as usual' ('we were moving forward positively') and the *extra-ordinary* events 'post-Lehmans' (see e.g. Edwards, 1997, p. 99; Sacks, 1992, p. 215). These constructions made it appear that events happened *to* them, not *by* them. The agency the bank claimed to have exercised pre-crisis – responsible, conscientious and prudent agency – was apparently continued post-crisis.

It is important to focus not only on how people handle accountability for reported events, but also how accountability for the *reporting itself* is handled in talk (Edwards & Potter, 1992, p. 166–167; Potter, Edwards, & Wetherell, 1993, p. 389). For discursive psychology, these two aspects of accountability are fundamentally interlinked, such that the former can be deployed for the latter, and vice versa. For example, the bankers attend not only to their accountability for past events (as senior managers within 'failed' banks), but also their accountability in the current social setting (as 'witnesses' in a public enquiry). The phrase 'unreasonable' used by Goodwin is a good example to illustrate how these two aspects of accountability relate: Goodwin is not only handling his accountability for his past actions (whether or not he did a 'good job' in his role of CEO at RBS), but also his accountability in the ongoing testimonial interaction (as someone who is a cooperative, reasonable and honest witness). Most importantly for our analysis, the latter serves to bolster his account of the former: presenting himself as a modest and reasonable character rather than a reckless and buccaneering agent.

Sir Fred Goodwin: .... As London has emerged as more and more of a global financial services centre a lot of these practices have come across from the United States. This has been a source of angst within banks if you talk to other bank chief executives who have activities in this area for years and years. It is very difficult for an individual institution to make a change unilaterally.

Q1664 Nick Ainger: It is the culture then?

Sir Fred Goodwin: It is absolutely a cultural thing. It is an area where people and teams do move around the market; and if amounts are not paid and people do not feel they are appropriately remunerated they will move. It is very much a cultural issue. I am sure Stephen Hester will explain the position tomorrow but many of the businesses within the group are doing extremely well; many businesses within GBM are doing extremely well. I do not know for a fact, but the rates and currencies businesses, for example, has probably had a record year in 2008. It is buried within all of the figures—I do not demur from your characterisation of where the bank is— and the people sitting there will be expecting to be rewarded based on their performance. That is the dilemma where Stephen and his colleagues in management and the new Board will have to square the loop.

Extract 3

Interestingly, this is one of very few instances where one of the bankers fully *accepts and agrees* with the formulation of the questioner, without significant re-formulation, avoidance or qualification of the question itself. Here, Goodwin unreservedly agrees with Ainger's formulation of the cause of the crisis lying in 'the culture'. Goodwin then appeals to the *abstract forces* (see Table 3) of 'the market' to explain the remuneration practices of the industry. Why, then, do the questioner and respondent seem to develop a shared discourse of 'structure' on this occasion? Or, to put it differently, why did Nick Ainger, who is a Welsh Labour MP, make it seemingly so easy and comfortable for Goodwin? It would be fair to assume that terms such as 'the culture' and 'the market' were so readily accepted by Goodwin because of their diffuse sense of agency and responsibility. Placing agency in the hands of abstract forces such as 'culture' and 'market' reduces the level of responsibility and potential blame attributable to individuals such as Goodwin. Individuals, according to this formulation, should not be held responsible for structural forces that are out of their hands. The individual is presented as 'passive', not an 'initiator', simply responding to external stimuli or forces (Harré, 1995, p. 128).

The phrase 'people and teams do move' is a script formulation (Edwards, 1997), which expresses some presupposed widely held 'knowledge' about some general pattern: the 'way things are'. The term 'appropriately remunerated' contains a generalised script that suggests that high performance and high remuneration are causally linked regardless of the desire or intention of the speaker: it is 'just the way the world works'. In fact, Goodwin alludes to exactly this point when he argues: 'It is very difficult for an individual institution to make a change unilaterally'. He also attributes the source of these remuneration practices to 'the United States'. Both individuals and institutions are presented as victims of *abstract forces* (see Table 3) of labour markets and cultures that have arrived from elsewhere, beyond their control.

Goodwin also uses active verbs for inanimate entities or abstractions (e.g. 'these practices have come across from the United States'). This is a grammatical pattern commonly found in scientific writing (Gilbert & Mulkay, 1984), where abstract notions are given human-like agency: 'The analysis suggests … ', 'the findings show … ', 'the hypothesis proposes' and so on. This is another instance of an impersonal construction that eliminates individual agency (*nominalisation* – see Table 3). In the case of 'practices have been imported', the *passive voice* (see Table 3) eliminates the agent(s), even though these bankers were obviously among these agents who imported these practices. The notion of culture is also subjected to nominalisation by treating it as a substance, a thing that acts. The bankers thereby claim to have been confronted by 'the systemic risks', but without being involved in creating them. While human 'practices' and 'cultures' are by definition man-made, it is noteworthy that no account is given about *who* made them.

Conclusion and theoretical implications

Notions of agency and structure, or more broadly the internal/external and subjective/objective bases of action, have an enduring presence in both classical and contemporary social scientific theory (e.g. Emirbayer & Mische, 1998; Giddens, 1984; Parsons, 1937). Yet, as Ahearn (2001) notes, the notion of agency is an academic abstraction that is generally underspecified, misused, fetishised or reified by social scientists. In this article, we have sought to approach the question of agency and structure in a very different way. By dismantling the 'inner/outer distinction' (Harré & Stearns, 1995) and other forms of reification, we instead examined 'how, on what occasions and in the service of what kinds of interactional practices discourse handles and manages its objective and subjective bases' (Edwards, 2007, p. 31). Thus, we have focused the analytic lens on how internal choices and motivations and external constraints were constructed within accounts of the banking crisis (Wetherell, 2005).

From our analysis of the testimony of senior British bankers to the UK public inquiry into the Banking Crisis, we have identified two competing interpretative repertoires. In the questions by the politicians, the bankers were positioned in an agentic repertoire as 'agents-with-agency', in line with what Harré (1995) calls the 'agentive' schema. In contrast, the responses by the bankers positioned themselves within a structural repertoire as 'agents-without-agency', in line with what Harré calls the 'Humean' schema. Our analysis has also shown the range of discursive devices through which these two repertoires were constructed. As a result, we propose viewing agency as a 'linguistic and socio-culturally mediated concept' (Ahearn, 2001, p. 115) rather than a property of social actors. Our analysis has shown that degrees of agency are the *product* of accounts, constructed in often unnoticed ways through the choice of discursive devices used and embedded within the grammatical forms of language employed.

In the sections that follow, we shall discuss the implications of our study for our understanding of the causes and consequences of the financial crisis, followed by a discussion of directions for future research.

Implications for the understanding of the financial crisis

Discursive devices are, in our view, the linguistic building blocks through which the understanding of the causes of the financial crisis was constructed. The many accounts in circulation – of which official public inquiries are significant and influential – eventually became sedimented into the widely accepted and taken-for-granted versions of 'what happened' and 'why' – part of the accepted story-line of the big crash. Those wanting to shape these accepted story-lines often, of course, have a particular stake or interest in the matter. For example, former British Prime Minister Gordon Brown (2010, p. 10) identified as the 'true cause' of the financial crisis 'recklessness and irresponsibility all too often created by greed. Money that should have capitalised the financial system went instead directly to excessive rewards.' By linking irresponsibility to rewards, the finger of blame moves away from politicians, and the regulatory bodies they oversee, and points directly and almost exclusively at bankers. Others provide a more kaleidoscopic picture of causes and corresponding institutions, policies, actions or persons that could be blamed (Davies, 2010; McLean & Nocera, 2010/2011).

An influential report written by a group of eminent British academics, in response to a question by the Queen 'why had nobody noticed that the credit crunch was on its way?', blamed a 'psychology of denial' and, more specifically, 'financial wizards' who managed to convince themselves and the world's politicians that they had found clever ways to spread risk throughout financial markets. Overall, the judgment points to a wide spreading of blame:

> the failure to foresee the timing, extent and severity of the crisis and to head it off … was principally a failure of the collective imagination of many bright people, both in this country and internationally, to understand the risks to the system as a whole.[3]

Here, the actions of specific persons (the 'wizards') are blamed as well as the very nebulous entity 'the collective imagination of many bright people'. The (lack of) agency of the signatories is excused with reference to this very convenient entity. The bankers, for their part, attempted to create a notion of agency characterised by shared suffering at the hands of what can only be described as a tsunami-like, almost natural, catastrophe: a pattern identified in other studies of the banking crisis (see e.g. Tourish & Hargie, 2012).

Many similar examples from the financial crisis could be discussed but one illuminating example can stand in for many others that could be given here. In their aptly titled *All the Devils are Here*, McLean and Nocera (2010/2011) discuss the case of Merrill Lynch, which would have collapsed if Bank of America had not rescued it. In response to the first edition of the book, two former Merrill Lynch executives in charge of the CDO business, Lattanzio and Semerci, who had been identified as blameworthy in the first edition, had complained to the authors. In a phone conversation to one of the authors, Lattanzio put his case as follows: that they had 'been singled out', because 'a convenient scapegoat' was needed. They downplayed their own agency by emphasising that 'by the time he took the reins of the CDO business, the machinery that would drive the firm's exposure into the stratosphere was already well in place, and there was little he or Semerci could do to stop it.' (McLean & Nocera, 2010/2011, kindle lines 6126–6131) Furthermore, he added that the decisive purchase of a subprime mortgage generator was decided at the 'executive-suite level – and that is where the blame belongs' (ibid). In such discourse, agency is de-personalised into the 'machinery' and shifted to other collectivities, namely the top management team.

Shared suffering is of course an ancient register that features in major world cultures and their 'stories' (Frazer, 1935, p. 372, 575). By accepting only very limited responsibility for events and pointing to structural factors that were beyond their individual agency, the bankers, just like General North's testimony analysed by Lynch and Bogen (1996) discussed above, invoke something akin to the 'Nuremberg defence' (p. 166): the defendants describe themselves as operatives with *some* but *overall very limited* responsibility for world historical events. Similarly, describing the financial crisis using the metaphor 'tsunami' (e.g. Q1899, Q1787 in the transcript we have analysed here), invokes images of the main protagonists being helpless to stop the crisis, being 'swept up' in weather-like events beyond their intention, will and control: what Hargie, Stapleton and Tourish (2010, p. 721) call the 'spectre of impersonal global events'.

Who (or what) is held as ultimately responsible? Individual traders, banks' management boards, regulators, governments? The grammatical form and discursive devices in the questions posed to the bankers in our case attributed agency squarely to the individual, as shown in Table 2. In contrast, the bankers' responses employed various discursive devices – which we present in Table 3 – in order to diffuse, deny, deflect, excuse, justify and collectivise agency in very different ways. Agency, we propose, can be understood as a *discourse grammar* – bound up in the very structure of the language used to account for events. To be clear, our argument is not that people have agency, and then attempt to deny it or 'cover it up'. Rather, the question of whether or not a person has agency is settled by participants themselves, in discourse (Potter, 1996, p. 151). According to Rom Harré,

> in an organization the person whose hand performed the deed may not be the one who is taken to be agentive in the last resort. The ordering of persons in ranks of responsibility and hence of agentiveness is a matter of discourse, of how roles in the company are defined (Harré, 1995, p. 126).

By implication, the meaning of being 'responsible' is discursively negotiable: indeed, it might be appropriate for us to think of it as a concept with *diffuse boundaries* (Wittgenstein, 1953: par. 68–71). For example, actors might accept *collective* blame but deny *individual* culpability. Actors might instead accept shared responsibility but deny sole or primary responsibility. Moreover, actors may accept responsibility for the *action*, but not for the *outcome*, like the mountaineer 'whose shout brings down an avalanche' (Frye, 1957/1971, p. 41). In the latter case, direct causality is acknowledged but almost fully detached from culpability.

While our discursive devices approach resists simplistic cause-and-effect statements, it is possible to see how certain discursive constructions of agency make certain policy responses more plausible or desirable than others. For instance, a discourse of individualised 'unbounded' agency sets up a need for regulation to contain, restrict or direct agency in certain ways. Gordon Brown (2010, p. 106), the British Prime Minister at the time the crisis was first unfolding, advocated a new balance to be struck 'between the capital that banks need, the dividends they pay, the remuneration they give employees, and the contribution they make to the public for the economic and social costs of their risk-taking.' A 'cap' on banker's bonuses, or an enforced link between pay and longer-term sustainability, are therefore plausible policy responses – and have indeed been either pro-posed or actually implemented in many countries. In contrast, a discourse of external con-straints and unpredictable events, outside the realm of human control, sets up a different kind of response: perhaps the need to stop 'the blame game' and allow a 'return to normal', perhaps with stronger oversight and regulation.[4] It is therefore clear that the dis-course of agency and structure 'makes a difference'. The version of 'what happened' clearly informs the question 'what should be done about it?'

Finally, it is important to note that discourses of agency and structure must be performed in 'situationally appropriate' ways according to 'culturally defined background expec-tations' (Scott & Lyman, 1968, p. 53). Accounts which deny, deflect or decrease claims to agency can easily be dismissed as fabrications and scape-goats intended purely to avoid blame. Accounts by politicians or policy-makers (Brown, 2010; Davies, 2010; Paulson, 2010) are primary (but by no means sole) candidates for being suspected of 'fabrications' designed to handle the author's stake and reputation. Senior managers – such as the Chief Executives of the banks in our study – are positioned in roles which make claims to be devoid of agency, or acting in an entirely random manner, particularly difficult to estab-lish. Their role bestows upon them a requirement for what Harré (1995, p. 130) calls a 'minimum discursive agentic display'. The discourse of leadership in particular implies a certain capacity to act and 'make a difference' – for why else would they be paid such vast sums to 'lead' their organizations? Employees at a lower level of the organisational hier-archy, on the other hand, may legitimately be able to claim to have virtually no capacity for agency, appealing to their role as 'functionaries' within a wider system. In the story of the Enron collapse, for instance, the role of blame (and villain) was allotted to many parties: the US government, Enron executives, auditors, or sometimes all of them (Czarniawska, 2004, p. 9). What is clear in our case, however, is that a great deal rests on which story (either politicians or the bankers) becomes embedded in our society's 'repertoire of legiti-mate stories' (Czarniawska, 1997, p. 16). This is where non-discursive forms of power will undoubtedly also enter the equation, influencing which stories become dominant.

Future research directions

In terms of a future research agenda, our article has opened up space for a new research agenda directed towards studying the discursive devices (micro-linguistic tools) and inter-pretative repertoires (general culturally acceptable patterns of talking and making sense) employed to account for agency and structure during periods of social crisis and trans-formation. Future research could usefully be directed towards mapping the repertoires of agency and structure used by other actors implicated in the banking crisis and sub-sequent 'era of austerity'. This could take the form of studying the accounts employed to justify austerity by politicians and policy-makers, accounts employed to legitimate or de-legitimate proposed reforms in banking practices and regulatory regimes, accounts made by civil society and social movements (e.g. UK Uncut) to question austerity econ-omics, and accounts in the media regarding the economic policies that followed the banking crisis and the subsequent budget deficit reduction plans.

Another related avenue for future research would be to explore the links between the social, political and legal context and the discourse of agency and structure. For instance, how are the changing legalistic notions of responsibility linked to changes in our understanding of who (or what) can be said to have 'agency'? One interesting avenue for pursuing this further could be to track the broader shift from the structural level (holding the corporation liable for, say, serious health and safety breaches) to the individual level (CEO's can now be jailed for such offences) within contemporary legal discourse. Another set of research questions arises from the political context around how responsibility for austerity is allocated within post-crisis discourse, particularly how responsibility for deficit reduction is discursively allocated between actors such as the State, corporations, employees and welfare recipients. Notions of who (or what) caused the crisis – which individual *agentic* acts and which broader *structural* systems – are clearly going to be bound up with notions of who has to 'pay'. In the context of the kind of austerity economics across Europe and beyond, where ordinary citizens rather than banking institutions are being asked to bear the brunt of budget cuts and deficit reduction programmes, the topic of discourses of agency and structure is particularly relevant for future analyses. What this article has contributed is a first step in viewing agency and structure as a discursive process, with implications for understanding how issues of accountability and blame are managed, and tracing the socio-economic consequences that follow.

Notes

1. In some criminal justice systems, this distinction is expressed for example through distinctions between 'culpable homicide', 'manslaughter' and 'murder'.
2. 'Financial crisis "like a tsunami"'. BBC News. Thursday, 23 October, 2008.
3. 'This is how we let the credit crunch happen, Ma'am'. http://www.guardian.co.uk/uk/2009/jul/26/monarchy-credit-crunch. Heather Stewart, economics editor and The Observer, Sunday 26 July 2009. and http://www.ft.com/cms/s/0/7e44cbce-79fd-11de-b86f-00144feabdc0.html#ixzz1NMU2DK26.
4. http://www.ft.com/cms/s/0/d4f02d66-1d84-11e0-a163-00144feab49a.html#ixzz1KFg6Sc5e: "Diamond says time for remorse is over": "There was a period of remorse and apology; that period needs to be over" - Bob Diamond, quoted in Financial Times, 11 January, 2011.

Disclosure statement

No potential conflict of interest was reported by the authors

References

Ahearn, L. M. (2001). Language and agency. *Annual Review of Anthropology, 30*, 109–137.

Antaki, C., & Wetherell, M. (1999). Show concessions. *Discourse Studies, 1/1*, 7–27.

Austin, J. L. (1970). A plea for excuses. In J. O. Urmson & G. J. Warnock (Eds), *Philosophical papers* (pp. 175–204). Oxford: Oxford University Press, 1st ed., 1961; 2nd ed., 1970.

Billig, M. (1987/1996). *Arguing and thinking: A rhetorical approach to social psychology*. Cambridge: Cambridge University Press.

Billig, M. (2008). The language of critical discourse analysis: The case of nominalization. *Discourse & Society, 19*, 783–800.

Brown, A. D. (2005). Making sense of the collapse of Barings bank. *Human Relations, 58*(12), 1579–1604.

Brown, G. (2010). *Beyond the crash: Overcoming the first crisis of globalization*. London: Simon & Schuster.

Czarniawska, B. (1997). *Narrating the organization: Dramas of institutional identity*. Chicago: University of Chicago Press.

Czarniawska, B. (2004). *Narratives in social science research*. London: Sage.

Davidson, D. (1980/1971). Agency. In D. Davidson (Ed), *Essays on actions and events* (pp. 43–61). Oxford: Clarendon Press.

Davies, H. (2010). *The financial crisis: Who is to blame?* Cambridge: Polity Press.

Duranti, A. (1990). Politics and grammar: Agency in Samoan political discourse. *American Ethnologist, 17*, 646–666.

Edwards, D. (1997). *Discourse and cognition*. London: Sage.

Edwards, D. (2007). Managing subjectivity in talk. In A. Hepburn & S. Wiggins (Eds.), *Discursive research in practice: New approaches to psychology and interaction* (pp. 31–49). Cambridge: Cambridge University Press.

Edwards, D., & Potter, J. (1992). *Discursive psychology*. London: Sage.

Emirbayer, M., & Mische, A. (1998). What is agency? *American Journal of Sociology, 103*, 962–1023.

Fowler, R. (1991). *Language in the news: Discourse and ideology in the press*. London/New York: Routledge.

Frazer, J. G. (1935). *The golden bough: A study in magic and religion*, Volume 1, Part 1. Forgotten Books.

Frye, H. N. (1957/1971). *Anatomy of criticism: Four essays*. Princeton: Princeton University Press.

Garfinkel, H. (1967). *Studies in ethnomethodology*. Englewood Cliffs, NJ: Prentice-Hall.

Gergen, K. J. (2009). *Relational being, beyond self and community*. New York: Oxford University.

Giddens, A. (1984). *The constitution of society. Outline of the theory of structuration*. Cambridge: Polity.

Gilbert, N., & M. Mulkay. (1984). *Opening Pandora's box: A sociological analysis of scientists' discourse*. Cambridge: Cambridge University Press.

Hargie, O., Stapleton, K., & Tourish, D. (2010). Making sense of CEO public apologies for the banking crisis: Attributions of blame and avoidance of responsibility. *Organization, 17*(6), 721–742.

Harré, R. (1995). Agentive discourse. In R. Harré & P. Stearns (Eds.), *Discourse psychology in practice* (pp. 120–136). London: Sage.

Harré, R., & van Langenhove, L. (1999). The dynamics of social episodes. In: R. Harré & L. Van Langenhove (Eds.), *Positioning theory: Moral contexts of intentional action* (pp. 1–13). Oxford: Basil Blackwell.

Harré, R., & Stearns, P. (1995). Introduction: Psychology as discourse analysis. In R. Harré, & P. Stearns (Eds), *Discursive psychology in practice* (pp. 1–8). London: Sage.

Heritage, J. and Clayman, S. (2010). *Talk in action. Interactions, identities and institutions*. Oxford: Wiley-Blackwell.

Herrigel, E. (1953/1981). *Zen in the art of archery*. New York: Pantheon Books/Random House.

Knights, D., & Willmott, H. (1989). Power and subjectivity at work. *Sociology, 23*(4), 535–558.

List, C., & Pettit, P. (2011). *Group agency: The possibility, design, and status of corporate agents*. Oxford: Oxford University Press.

Llewellyn, N. & Harrison, A. (2006). Resisting corporate communications: Insights into folk linguistics. *Human Relations. 59*, 567–597.

Lynch, M. & Bogen, D. (1996). *The spectacle of history: Speech, text, and memory at the Iran-contra hearings*. Durham, NC: Duke University Press.

McLean, B., & Joe Nocera, J. (2010/2011). *All the devils are here: The hidden history of the financial crisis*. Viking edition.

Mueller, F., Carter, C., & Whittle, A. (2015). Can audit (still) be trusted? *Organization Studies, 36*(9), 1171–1203.

Mueller, F., & Whittle, A. (2011). Translating management ideas: A discursive devices analysis. *Organization Studies, 32*(2), 187–210.

Parsons, T. (1937). *The structure of social action*. Glencoe, IL: The Free Press.

Paulson, H. (2010). *On the Brink: Inside the race to stop the collapse of the global financial system*. New York: Hachette Book Group.

Pollner, M. (1987). *Mundane reason: Reality in everyday and sociological discourse*. Cambridge: Cambridge University Press.

Pomerantz, A. (1986). Extreme case formulations: A new way of legitimating claims. *Human Studies, 9*, 219–230.

Potter, J. (1996). *Representing reality: Discourse, rhetoric and social construction*. London: Sage.

Potter, J., & Edwards, D. (2003). Rethinking cognition: On Coulter on discourse and mind. *Human Studies, 26*(1), 165–181.

Potter, J., Edwards, D., & Wetherell, M. (1993). A model of discourse in action. *American Behavioral Scientist, 36*(3), 383–401.

Potter, J., & Hepburn, A. (2005). Qualitative interviews in psychology: Problems and possibilities. *Qualitative Research in Psychology, 2*, 281–307.

Potter, J., Stringer, P., & Wetherell, M. (1984). *Social texts and context: Literature and social psychology*. London: Routledge.

Potter, J., & Wetherell, M. (1987). *Discourse and social psychology: Beyond attitudes and behaviour*. London: Sage.

Sacks, H. (1992). *Lectures on Conversation*, Volumes I and II. Edited by G. Jefferson with Introduction by E. A. Schegloff. Oxford: Blackwell.

Schutz, A. (1967). *The phenomenology of the social world*. Evanston, IL: Northwestern University Press.

Scott, M. B., & Lyman, S. M. (1968). Accounts. *American Sociological Review, 23*, 46–62.

Tilly, Ch. (2008). *Credit and blame*. Princeton: Princeton University Press.

Tourish, D., & Hargie, O. (2012). Metaphors of failure and the failures of metaphor: A critical study of the root metaphors used by bankers in explaining the banking crisis. *Organization Studies, 33*(8), 1045–1069.

Wetherell, M. (2005). Unconscious conflict or everyday accountability? *British Journal of Social Psychology, 44*, 169–173.

Wetherell, M., & Potter, J. (1988). Discourse analysis and the identification of interpretive repertoires. In C. Antaki (Ed.), *Analysing everyday explanation: A casebook of methods* (pp. 168–183). Newbury Park, CA: Sage.

Wetherell, M., & Potter, J. (1989). Narrative characters and accounting for violence. In J. Shotter. & K. Gergen (Eds.), *Texts of identity* (pp. 206–219). London: Sage.

Wittgenstein, L. (1953). *Philosophical Investigations (PI)*, 1953, G.E.M. Anscombe and R. Rhees (eds.), G. E.M. Anscombe (trans.), Oxford: Blackwell.

Wooffitt, R. (1992). *Telling tales of the unexpected: The organization of factual discourse*. Hemel Hempstead: Harvester Wheatsheaf.

PROTESTING TOO MUCH
Alastair Darling's constructions after the Financial Crash

Catherine Walsh

How did UK political elites publicly represent the economy after the Financial Crash? In his budget speeches, Chancellor of the Exchequer, Alastair Darling (2007–2010), talked about finance and mortgages much more, and taxation much less, than one would expect by comparing him to other chancellors. With his rhetoric he constructed a vigorous defence of the financial sector and mortgage market, and described limited technical reforms comfortably. But as well as avoiding taxation as a topic, he appeared less comfortable and more inconsistent defending his taxation policies. Refusing to increase corporate or capital-gains taxes, he argued instead that top-percentile earners, banks, and tax evaders should pay more tax. Coming many months before Occupy would encamp at St. Paul's, these are surprising characterizations of top-earner and financial taxation from an elite orator. I argue that Darling understood the power of anti-elite critique, and so was willing to criticize some limited and select elements of financial activity and taxation in order to protect more fundamental aspects of the financial system, particularly the capital upon which it depends. Via an appropriation of critical language about finance and the Crash, his elite rhetoric defensively protected owned-capital and corporate profit from other claims.

Introduction

How did the UK chancellor publicly construct the economy after the Financial Crash, and why might he have chosen such representations? Much has been written about how elites publicly presented antecedents, explanations, and prescriptions, and many have argued that elites created discursive frameworks to protect established neo-liberal projects and themselves. In this paper I drill deep down within the discursive – all the way down to the rhetorical – and uncover more detail about how elite rhetoric worked, in the operational sense. I investigate an emblematic sample of the British Minister of Finance's description of the economy, considering what sorts of materials he used and how he assembled them. Understanding how Alastair Darling constructed the post-Crash world between 2007 and 2009 illuminates which kinds of strategies elites can and do use to understand, express and protect themselves in uncertain times.

In many ways, Darling constructed the sort of vigorous defence of finance, mortgage access, and capital taxation that one would expect of a G7 Minister of Finance post-2008. He argued that the financial sector was a public good, that mortgage access must be guaranteed, and that capital gains and corporate profits should not increase. Darling was broadly reluctant to discuss taxation at all, as a recession took hold, and as a general election loomed. But the Crash had amplified critiques of finance and its elites in the public sphere, and Darling was compelled to respond to vigorous public challenges to the *status quo*. With his rhetoric Darling strategically utilized those critiques of finance and of elites by calling for (very limited) reform of the financial sector, emergency measures for the mortgage market, and increases in income taxation for the top one-, two-, and five-per cent of earners. In order to improve the credibility of his account, Darling made anti-elite concessions to criticism in finance and taxation. I argue that this credibility was not only politically useful for Darling, but had political-economic use as well, because it sacrificed small amounts of elite privilege to protect fundamental aspects of the financial system, specifically the owned capital upon which so much debt was secured. Darling responded to external challenges to finance and elite taxation by incorporating that criticism into his constructions, sacrificing smaller matters in order to defend more fundamental issues. His defensive constructions appropriated incomplete, limited, and closely controlled popular arguments *against* finance and *against* unequal wealth, better to protect capital assets.

Finance, the Crash and the UK State

Elite representations of the causes and consequences of the Financial Crash have largely involved technocratic fixes that support the maintenance of the financial system. Englen et al. (2011) have argued that policy-makers and academics adjudicated on the crisis as either: (1) accidental structural failures between complex systems, or (2) political and economic elites driven by self-interest, or (3) an intermediate position, in which agents took relatively innocent decisions within which unforeseen risks lay. They have also observed that experts recommended technical fixes rather than addressed broader challenges. Whittle and Mueller (2011) have proposed two main public narratives of Treasury Committee questioners and UK banking executives: bankers as villains causing the Crash vs. bankers as victims who had been doing their best to create prosperity. Riaz, Buchanan, and Bapuji (2011) have found that academic and financial elites have recommended technical changes in either government policy or in banking practices, respectively, while regulatory elites mostly recommended maintaining the existing system, and all three groups implied tacit support of existing institutions. Other political economists have gone further, arguing that the established neo-liberal order that had benefited elites for decades has not only endured the Crisis, but prospered in its wake (Crouch, 2011; Mirowski, 2014).

We may take two proxies to gain some insight into the criticisms of finance specifically and capitalism in general, post-Crash. The first is academic criticism of the growing dominance of finance over other types of economic activity, which had existed before but gained a wider audience now. Scholars like Lapavistas (2008), Skidelsky and Joshi (2008), and Shiller (2009) wrote in broadsheets like *The Guardian* and *The Financial Times* not only that financial regulation was poor, but that finance had de-coupled from the real economy in destructive ways, that inequality and debt could be detrimental to economic growth, and that economic stimuli other than tax cuts were needed now. The second proxy is the Occupy movement, which arose formally more than a year after Darling left post, but reflected ideas that had circulated prior. Echoing the aforementioned economists, Occupy protesters would soon demand more wealth equality (Holmer Nadeson, 2013), especially a more equitable system of taxation (Barnes, 2013) and an economy that did not rely so heavily on mercurial finance (Ho, 2012).

The intense and symbiotic relationship between the UK Treasury and the UK state has been well-argued for decades (Fine & Harris, 1985; Glyn, 2006; Ingham, 1984). Strange (1988) defined the financial system itself as the interdependency and, ultimately, cooperation, between banks, markets, and the fiscal and financial arms of the state (particularly the Treasury and central bank). Financialization – the rise and rise of finance since the 1970s – has brought new challenges for politics and economics, as finance has become socially privileged over other economic activities. During this epoch states and banks cooperatively innovated to expand credit (Konings, 2011; Schwartz, 2008), increasing numbers of people participated in mundane finance, via savings and debt (Langley, 2008), and governments successfully reaped both economic and political rewards of their participation (Seabrooke, 2006). While finance has become a more powerful elite domain, its ubiquity has also widened the stakes for all, and its Crisis has invited widespread criticism.

The tumultuous financial events that dominated Darling's chancellorship also deserve brief review. In Summer 2007 the US mortgage-securitization market came unglued, and in September 2007 Darling rescued UK bank Northern Rock from a run, first by granting it emergency funds, then by nationalizing it (Shin, 2009). By Autumn 2008 Darling had rescued four more banks and announced the availability of a £25 billion recapitalization fund (UK Parliament 8 October 2008). In January 2009 Darling authorized the Bank of England to create liquidity by exchanging bonds for bank assets (Bank of England, 2010). Despite widespread calls for financial-sector reforms, fundamentally very little changed in terms of the Government's macro-economic policies, the structure and governance of financial institutions, or the instruments that financial instruments were permitted to sell (Froud, Johal, Montgomerie, & Williams, 2010; Hodson & Mabett, 2009). But a lingering consequence of the Crisis was the effect it had on state balance sheets. By late 2009 at least £850 billion had been spent by HM Treasury to support UK banks, a tally which *did not* include quantitative easing activity at the Bank of England (National Audit Office, 2009), which by February 2010 had spent £200 billion purchasing (mostly) UK government gilts from UK banks (Joyce, Lasaosa, Stevens, & Tong, 2010). Thus, by the end of Darling's tenure, over a trillion pounds had been extended by the UK government to the financial sector, and the Bank's balance sheet was three times its pre-Crisis size as a proportion of GDP (Cross, Fisher, & Weeken, 2010).

How does criticism of finance, and elite response to it, fit into this larger political-economic picture? For an explanation I draw on *The New Spirit of Capitalism* (2005) in which Luc Boltanski and Éve Chiapello have posited a model for the evolution of modern capitalism through mechanisms of political and civil feedback, arguing that anti-capitalist critique has contributed to the vibrancy and resilience of contemporary capitalism. According to Boltanski and Chiapello, capitalism has responded to popular challenge by either evading or absorbing critique, proving resilient to challenge via adapting to *select* social challenges. In their analysis, French capitalism responded to the 1968 students' strikes in part by incorporating a language of 'freedom' and 'creativity' into capitalist discourses, and subsequently a 'creative class' into elite ranks, which allowed an evasion of the critique of workers' pay and thereby foiled that threat to accumulation. In this paper I will argue something similar, but on a much smaller scale: after the Crash Alastair Darling used popular criticism of the financial system and financial elites in his rhetoric, and actively responded to it, such that the fundamental base of the financial system – asset capital – was protected.

Investigating Budget Rhetoric

According to the Treasury's own publicity, 'chancellors use the Budget statement to update Parliament and the nation on the state of the economy, on the public finances and on progress against the Government's economic objectives' (HM Treasury, 2013). These two audiences – Parliament and the nation – (themselves not even distinct) are comprised of as many sub-audiences as one might like to define. Darling speaks to all these audiences simultaneously, as well as international markets and policy-makers, but he is speaking to and for other elites especially, building an account for and about them. I believe this partly because Darling and his Treasury aides are elites themselves, creating meaning from their own experiences, but also because empirical studies suggest that budget statements should be especially meaningful for other elites (Hellwig & Coffey, 2011; Schneider & Jacoby, 2005). For all audiences, budget statements deliberately communicate the Government's preferred economic narrative and accompanying judgements, as progress towards preferred objectives is defined by the chancellor.

As rhetoric analysis is necessarily detailed and intense, I must select text carefully. In order to select distinctive text, I use a computer-based quantitative content analysis to determine how Darling's budgets were most dissimilar from the chancellors whom preceded and succeeded him. The annual budget statements delivered between 1976 and 2013 (see Table 1 for chancellors, prime ministers, and political parties) makes a corpus of 396,328 words, and I investigate it using *Antconc 3.2.4w*, (Anthony 2013) a free-ware, UNIX-based corpus analysis application, developed by Dr Laurence Anthony of Waseda University, Tokyo, Japan, who holds copyright. This allows me to identify n-grams (words and phrases) in Darling's budget statements that have an unusually high or low frequency in comparison with other budgets. From a much larger list of n-grams associated with finance, fiscal matters, monetary measures, industry, and employment, I determined which shared n-grams (n-grams that every chancellor said at least once) appeared much more or much less often in Darling's budgets.

Table 1. UK Chancellors of the Exchequer, 1976–present

Chancellor	Years in post	Serving Prime Minister	Political Party
Denis Healey	1976–1979	Jim Callaghan	Labour
Geoffrey Howe	1979–1983	Margaret Thatcher	Conservatives
Nigel Lawson	1983–1989	Margaret Thatcher	Conservatives
John Major	1989–1990	Margaret Thatcher	Conservatives
Norman Lamont	1990–1993	John Major	Conservatives
Kenneth Clarke	1993–1997	John Major	Conservatives
Gordon Brown	1997–2007	Tony Blair	Labour
Alastair Darling	2007–2010	Gordon Brown	Labour
George Osborne	2010–present	David Cameron	Conservatives

My rhetoric analysis is based on constructivist frameworks, in which rhetoric is employed to build credible and robust representations of reality. Following Herrick's (2009) indications, I think of rhetoric as: (1) planned, (2) adapted to an audience, (3) a revelation of motives of both speaker and audience, (4) responsive, response-making, and response-inviting, (5) a seeking to persuade, through argument, appeal, arrangement, and aesthetics, and (6) an address to issues of contingency and deliberation. I then draw on work studying rhetoric as a matter of constructing credible accounts that can compete successfully against alternate accounts (Antaki & Horowitz, 2000; Billig, 1996; Edwards & Potter, 1992) and especially Jonathan Potter's conception of rhetoric as 'discourse used to bolster particular versions of the world and to protect them from criticism' (1996, p. 33) and 'a feature of the antagonistic relationship between versions: how a description counters an alternative description, how it is organized, in turn, to resist being countered' (1996, p. 108). My rhetoric analysis, then, is the analyst's act of scrutinizing how descriptions are organized to make them seem the more credible and objective to audiences than other versions.

Following Potter (1996), rhetoric often recommends an action, if only an active agreement with the speaker's version of reality, what he calls its action-orientation. This may be done by explicitly asking, instructing, declaring, or demanding, but the more sensitive the suggestion, the more likely it is to be made by inference, implying a next best action. If there is a 'dilemma of stake', that compromises speaker trustworthiness, it is common to attempt to manage that appearance. A speaker may also suggest an action through a categorization that maximizes, minimizes, or normalizes an object, while categorizations of 'normal' and 'routine' can be used to obscure speaker agency or environmental change. Or a description may suggest an action by selectively managing the terrain of description, so that only some objects are admitted but not others, an 'ontological gerrymandering' (Woolgar & Pawluch, 1985) that shapes what is problematic and what is not. Rhetoric also has an epistemological-orientation, which builds an account as credible. The appearance of self-interest must be managed so that the account looks independent of vested interests, or true in spite of them. Here Potter has borrowed Goffman's (1979) notion of footing, how closely/distantly a speaker presents himself or herself to the account, to build the appearance of veracity through accountability or to dodge blame. Rhetoric often uses empiricist discourse, and here Potter has borrowed Gilbert's and Mulkay's (1984) list of empirical features in scientific accounts: impersonal grammar, the primacy of data, and presenting procedural rules that appear universal. Speakers may make claims of consensus or corroboration, or vivid detail may be employed to make accounts appear more factual. Alternatively, detail may be left vague so that the account is harder for others to undermine. Narrative order can build an account by implying causation and temporal order. Potter has noted that some of these procedures can work against one another and require trade-offs; perhaps worst of all for politicians, many of the procedures that heighten veracity also heighten accountability (see also Stapleton & Hargie, 2011). In the upcoming evidence sections, I will use these ideas to assess Darling's rhetoric.

Other published work in discourse studies will be helpful here. Firstly, Antaki and Wetherall (1999) have proposed that 'making a show' of conceding by a well-structured sequence of proposition–concession–reassertion can strengthen a speaker's relative offensive position in an argument. Show concessions do rhetorical work by introducing caricatures of the opposition's case, or by reasserting the proposition as a reversal of the concession, or by devaluing some aspect of the proposition with the concession as a dismissive reassertion. '[B]y making a show of the concessionary gift the speaker corrupts it' (Antaki & Wetherall, 1999, p. 24), and this can help protect the perceived stake or interest of a speaker such as Darling. Secondly, Finlayson (2006) conceptualizes political rhetoric in terms of setting the definition of problems and advancing arguments based on ideas, beliefs, and meanings. Darling certainly constructs problems with his budget statement rhetoric, although I emphasize only how he sets problems in order to manage problem-setting that he himself did not generate. Thirdly, Fairclough and Fairclough (2011) have analysed the UK Treasury's 2008 Pre-Budget report in terms normative judgements of what politicians and audiences believe and want. We share related data sets, but I rely less than they on whether the audience follows a rational progression in practical reasoning just as the speaker intended, in part because this is something that I simply cannot know. Instead I keep my focus on my speaker's constructions, what versions of reality he was likely countering, and what his motivations may have been for doing so.

Finance and Mortgages

Darling spoke of finance more than any of the other post-1976 chancellors (see Figure 1), almost twice as often as either Brown or Osborne, and Darling's 95% confidence interval clears all other error margins except John Major's. (Major is an anomaly among post-1976 chancellors as he only delivered one budget; his confidence intervals tend to be quite wide, so this should not be over-interpreted.) The shared n-grams are 'interest rates', 'market(s),' 'bank(s)', 'shares', 'investors', 'mortgage', 'housing', 'debt', 'credit' (not 'tax credit'), 'capital', 'equity', 'finance' (not 'finance bill'), and 'financial' (not financial year). Given the unsettled financial climate that Darling finds himself in, it is unsurprising that the n-gram list method generates this difference between Darling and other chancellors.

Darling's 2008 budget speech addressed finance with text approximately one-fifth the size of comparable text in 2009 or 2010, but still his commitment to the financial sector is clear. He said that 'we have maintained confidence and stability in the banking system' (UK

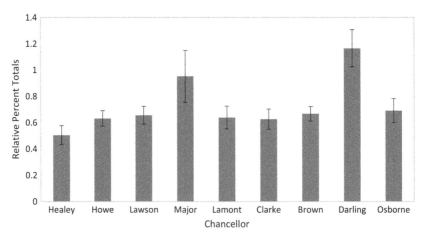

Figure 1. Total relative per cent frequencies of shared finance n-grams (error bars indicate 95% confidence)

Parliament, 2008a) and that 'we want to bring together investors and lenders with the Treasury, the Bank [of England] and the Financial Services Authority to find market-led solutions to strengthen these funding markets further' (UK Parliament, 2008b). Finance had not yet come under widespread criticism, but Darling was clear in his support. In April 2009, with a well-publicized Financial Crash in the recent past, constructions that address perspectives critical of finance begin to enter Darling's budget, alongside his established defence. The financial sector was still a crucial public good, but now one in need of reform:

> A successful economy needs a strong financial sector. We do not want to throw away the many advantages that come from our position as a world centre for finance. I intend that we retain that position. Hundreds of thousands of jobs across the United Kingdom depend on it. We need to build trust in the banking system, and harness the strengths of the financial services sector for the benefit of society. Crucial to this is financial regulation (UK Parliament 22 April 2009a).

The significant new claim in this account is that finance has great social worth, is for the 'benefit of society', is crucial to hundreds of thousands of jobs. Darling implicitly admitted that trust has been lost and now promised to restore it with financial regulation. He responded to widespread criticism of the sector – criticism that he does not explicitly cite, only implies – by incorporating its remedies into his description. He sets the problem in terms of popular criticisms, but his account is tightly constricted by a larger insistence that banking is central, vital, and good.

In 2010 Darling's defence of banking only grew stronger in the face of implied criticism:

There can be no return to business as usual for the banks, but we also must remember that their success is vital not just for the global economy but for Britain's future. London is the world's leading financial centre. Across the country, the sector supports over a million jobs including in Edinburgh, Leeds, Manchester, Cardiff, and other cities. A healthy, strong financial services industry is essential for our long-term prosperity (UK Parliament 24 March 2010a).

Darling alluded to criticisms of finance, but then immediately described how important the financial sector was, for a 'million jobs' throughout Britain, responding to an implicit criticism that finance only benefited London. Darling responded not just to calls for reform, but also to concerns about bankers' bonuses and the cost of bank rescues for the public accounts:

> We will sell our shares in RBS and Lloyds, as well as Northern Rock, in a way that maximizes value for the taxpayer and recoups the money we invested. We intend to get all taxpayers' money back. In the meantime, I can tell the House that the Treasury has already received over £8 billion in fees and charges from the banks, in return for our support. At the time of the pre-Budget Report I put in place a one-off 50% tax on the excessive bonuses of bankers. I made it clear that banks had a choice of whether to pay bonuses or not – but if they did, given the amount of taxpayer support that had been provided, I believed it was right that the country as a whole should benefit. I can tell the House that that tax has raised £2 billion – more than twice as much as was forecast. (UK Parliament 24 March 2010b).

In this construction, taxpayers are told that they will recoup on an investment, while banks have received the same funding as 'support'. Darling repeated the framework he had offered the year before, in which he chided the banks while insisting that they must be supported. He was also careful to say 'fees' and 'charges' (not a tax) for banks, while bankers were paying a 'one-off 50% tax' (not a charge or fee), making a clear distinction between language for institutions and employees. Note that this one-off tax is on individual income, not owned assets or institutions. Darling worked hard to give the impression that he was responding to challenges, while changing very little indeed.

Darling was eager to talk about mortgages, again an expected reflection of elites' fears for the housing market after the Crash. Figure 2 shows that Darling spoke of mortgage(s) significantly more often than all other post-1976 chancellors (CI > 95%, save Norman Lamont, who presided over his own era of repossessions).

Most of this attention was bestowed in 2009, when Darling described the repossession fears of mortgagees and announced that the state would pay mortgage interest in cases of unemployment. Unspoken were lenders' fears of mass defaults, but I argue that Darling was also responding to their concerns, implicitly. Darling continued to say that 'the housing market is also being held back by a lack of mortgage credit', and that:

> The recession and the credit crunch have made it much harder for people to take their first step on the housing ladder. This is not just difficult for those involved, but also undermines the entire housing market. So, to help, I have decided to extend the stamp duty holiday on properties sold for less than £175,000 until the end of the year. Sixty per cent of residential properties will continue to be exempt, which will encourage modest and middle-income home buyers (UK Parliament 22 April 2009b).

Darling's construction takes into account criticisms from people who cannot afford mortgages, as well as home-owners worried that mass defaults would damage their own net worth, as 'the entire housing market' is undermined. Explicitly, he was happy to state the case for protecting the housing market, despite acknowledging those who felt 'shut-out'. More importantly, he in no way challenged the financial trade in mortgage credit or house prices, which had grown to many multiples of income in the decade before. These would be sustained via state subsidy as necessary. Again, Darling responded to criticisms, but only with small technical changes that maintained the market, and asset prices, while decreasing taxation on owned capital.

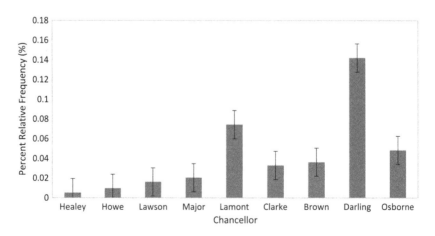

Figure 2. Per cent relative frequencies for 'mortgages(s)' (error bars indicate 95% confidence)

Taxation

Darling exhibited a precipitous drop in tax talk, as demonstrated by Figures 3 and 4, before talk of taxation returned to typical levels under Osborne. Taxation (a word that Darling did not say once in three speeches) is a fundamental topic for budget speeches, so Darling's reticence to speak about taxes is quite striking.

In 2008 Darling made an emphatic defence of 'non-doms', wealthy UK residents who were not deemed resident for tax purposes in the UK:

> We welcome the contribution made by people born outside the UK who choose to come and work here. They are an important and central contributor to our economy's growth and prosperity. They pay taxes on their earnings here; they also pay tax on money they bring into the country from abroad. But for those non-domiciled individuals or families who have chosen to make Britain their home, I believe that it is right and fair that they should, after 7 years, pay a reasonable charge to maintain the right to be taxed differently from other UK residents. Beyond that, as I have said before, we will not seek to charge UK tax on offshore income or capital gains that are not brought into the UK. This new charge will be implemented from April. There will be no further changes to this regime for the rest of this Parliament or the next [Interruption] (UK Parliament 12 March 2008c).

The fact that Darling meets the criticism of non-doms' favourable tax status not by direct citation but implicit construction makes the policy's contentiousness clear. Even the *Parliamentary Hansard* recorder indicated the controversial nature of Darling's decision by recording an 'interruption' in the House. Darling defined the terrain of the debate by categorizing the Treasury's compensation for offering this favourable tax status as 'reasonable', just as he declined to characterize the 'charge' as a 'tax'. He makes a second categorization, suggesting with the phrase 'no further changes' that his decision was routine. He maintained a distant footing throughout by separating 'I' and 'we' from 'they', 'those', and 'their', a choice which manages his dilemma of stake as an elite, and his appearance of interests as the Chancellor. Of the 150 words in this short passage, Darling spent the first 66 defending why the UK needs the 'contribution made' by non-doms 'who choose to come and work'. Crucially, the tax status of non-doms did not fundamentally change, only a smaller adjustment was made.

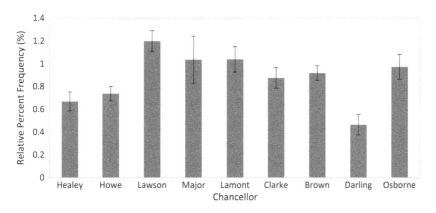

Figure 3. Per cent relative frequencies 'tax(es)' (error bars indicate 95% confidence)

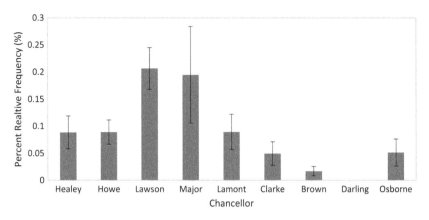

Figure 4. Per cent relative frequencies for 'taxation' (error bars indicate 95% confidence)

In 2009 Darling's reluctant tax talk started to qualitatively change, as he began to characterize taxation as matter of top and bottom segments:

> I believe that it is fair that those who have gained the most should contribute more. Only those with incomes over £100,000 a year – or 2% of the population – will be affected. In November, I announced a new rate of income tax of 45% on incomes above £150,000 – the top one per cent of taxpayers. In order to help pay for additional support for people now, I have decided that the new rate will be 50%, and will come in from next April – a year earlier (UK Parliament 22 April 2009c).

Darling implicitly responded to criticism of elite taxation by stating that 'those who have gained the most should contribute more'. He named the top one- and two-per cent, gave great detail, and arranged the narrative so that first gains are cited, then penalties, making the case that this was 'right' with narrative order. Thus, two-and-a-half years before the Occupy movement's high-profile occupations began, Darling publicly constructed income taxation in terms of top-percentages.

This trend only grew stronger in 2010, as Darling described taxpayers as top one-, two-, and five- per cent of earners:

> The 50% rate of income tax will come in next month, but only affects those with earnings over £150,000 a year, the top 1% of earners. For people with incomes over £100,000 a year, the top 2%, we will gradually remove the value of their personal allowances. Tax relief on pensions will be restricted from next year, but again only for those with incomes above £130,000 a year. Looking across all the tax rises since the beginning of this global crisis, 60% of them will be paid for by the top 5% of earners. We have not raised these taxes out of dogma or ideology. We are determined to ensure our overall tax regime remains competitive. But I believe those who have benefited the most from the strong growth in incomes in past years should now pay their fair share of tax (UK Parliament 24 March 201c).

Here Darling cited dogmatism, and that explicitness indicates that, in truth, the charge did not trouble him too deeply; in contrast, as he employs the euphemism of 'competitiveness' to defend the existing low-tax system. Corporation and capital gains tax remain untouched again in 2010, but small concessions were made in terms of the top-percentages of earners. While income tax for top-percentiles was rising, taxes on owned capital were remaining the same, or decreasing.

In 2010 Darling brought banks, as institutions, into his tax talk for the first time, explicitly reassuring his audience that the banks would be taxed worldwide, eventually:

> We cannot continue with a situation where the banks are rewarded for creating excessive risk, but the taxpayer foots the bill when things go badly. More countries now agree on the need for an international systemic tax on banks. This must be brought forward quickly, as I will urge international Finance Ministers in Washington next month. I agree with all those who think that such a tax should be internationally co-ordinated. Going it alone, as some have suggested, would cost thousands of jobs, not just in London, but across the whole country (UK Parliament 24 March 2010a).

This is significant, because Darling was now willing to concede that banks as institutions may need to pay more tax. But I interpret this as a hedged bet: while taxation is promised, international coordination on international taxation agreement is beyond Darling's control. This is corroboration, but not as a reason to do something, rather as a reason to do nothing. Darling's capacity to act domestically is not acknowledged in this account, he only alludes to the constraints of acting globally. Similarly, tax evaders were in his sights, but international cooperation was needed:

> While people are suffering hardship, it is all the more unfair that some are escaping their tax obligations. I am determined to continue our successful drive to prevent avoidance and evasion. Measures in this Budget will bring in additional tax worth half a billion pounds each year, while protecting £4 billion worth of revenues by 2012–2013. These steps include tax agreements like that already signed with Liechtenstein, which is expected to bring in around £1 billion of extra revenue. I can also now tell the House that we are ready to sign tax information exchange agreements with three additional countries – Dominica, Grenada, and Belize (UK Parliament 24 March 2010d).

Darling constructed himself as tough on tax evaders and tax avoiders, but constrained by lack of international agreement so far. His footing was close, he categorized 'our successful drive' as potent and intentional, and he promised that he was 'ready to sign' so that more could be done. I argue that he could safely construct himself as active because nothing would actually happen to assets because of his speech. What needed no international agreement, what he could actually change – capital and corporate tax rates within the UK – he would not raise in his budget speech of 2010.

Discussion

Finance and the asset values that underpin the system are staunchly protected in Darling's budgets, while critique is only admitted in a very limited fashion. In 2008 he insisted that the financial sector would be protected and the global system maintained. As the Financial Crisis worsened, Darling never retreated from this explicit position, instead he widened his defence of finance to include expressions about employment, the regions, and the public good. But by 2009 he added limited, controlled, criticism, specifically the incorporation of a message of regulatory reform. Like finance in general, mortgages in particular were protected. Darling constructed mortgage jeopardy – that many mortgage holders were holding debt they struggled to pay – and characterized this explicitly as an anxiety for all property owners. He answered criticism not with any suggestion that the housing market might be over-valued, but instead as a clear case for state support. The construction of taxation also protected owned wealth, by sacrificing limited top-percentile income taxation. Darling talked little about taxation, indicating that interventions in taxation – whether increasing or decreasing – were not his desire amidst financial upheaval. In 2008, Darling's construction of non-domiciled residents was very much defensive, a response to criticism but not a very conciliatory one. But by 2009 Darling began to admit criticism of elite taxation into his account of tax, but only implicitly, and only in terms of income tax. Again in 2010, even though top-percentile earners and tax evaders were to pay more, capital gains tax and corporate tax were barely mentioned, and rates remained the same. Darling was willing to admit criticism of the top-percentiles of earned capital, but owned wealth was protected by being almost entirely omitted from the construction of tax.

There were other options, most easily seen in terms of the things I have argued Darling was reacting against. The state could have significantly re-regulated the financial sector, with the division between retail and investment banking re-instated. Instead of cutting stamp duty in the first-time home-buyer's range, the government could have accepted that the UK housing market was over-valued and allowed market-forces to correct this. Doing so arguably would have done as much for first-time buyer access. The government could have administered a Tobin tax to retard the rates of financial transactions, as some EU leaders were advocating, or re-valued the council tax system, or levied a mansion tax (still an elusive policy measure at the time of writing). Great lip-service was paid to supporting the 'real economy' in the wake of the Crash, but very little was done, as the Brown Government still did not like to 'pick winners', despite re-energized Keynesians inside the Labour Party. Darling's increases in top-earner taxes did not amount to a significant redistribution of wealth: owned wealth was untouched, offshore wealth was untouched, and there was no distribution from, say, earners between 95% and 33% of incomes to the lowest third. When Darling set the problems of finance, mortgages, and taxation, his answers were like his rhetoric: measured, controlled, and of no significant challenge to elite constituencies.

Following Potter (1996) I argue that allowable criticisms built veracity in Darling's account, made his account palatable for a range of audiences, and constructed elites as sensible and responsive to subaltern criticism. Incorporating criticisms into constructions that supported the *status quo* was a tactic to soften accounts of contentious issues. His incorporation of criticisms of finance, mortgages, and especially taxation were attempt to inoculate himself against his stake as an elite, to increase his own appearance of trustworthiness, and construct himself as a vested interest only up to a defined point. He managed his appearances of agency, accountability, and activism with this tactic, and in turn attempted to manage the expectations of multiple audiences about what he could and would do. The criticisms are softened by the fact that they remain largely allusions in the text, rather than being explicitly defined. This softening helps Darling build a picture of consensus within his account, regardless of how much or little audience members agree on the role of finance, the mortgage market, or taxation in the Financial Crash. Admitting these criticisms also facilitates 'ontological gerrymandering' (Woolgar & Pawluch, 1985), as Darling constructed particular financial, mortgage and taxation activities as problematic while remaining silent on other activities. Darling worked hard at these accounts, constructing his own activism and agency through categorization, close footing (Goffman, 1979, 1981), detail, and narrative order where he wanted to construct his own agency. Conversely, he used a lack of consensus and empiricist repertoire

(Gilbert & Mulkay, 1984) where he wished to look less culpable, especially in terms of tax talk. While this is problem-setting (Finalyson, 2006), it is not a setting of Darling's choosing, rather these are responses that he was uncomfortably forced to make. Darling made show concessions, specifically what Antaki and Wetherall (1999) have called a 'sting in the tail', in which Darling acknowledged a criticism (typically implicitly), and then addressed it with a very limited response.

With this rhetoric, Darling implicitly acknowledged criticisms of finance, including sub-altern criticisms of elite taxation, yet financialized elites were reassured that fundamental change would not happen. I argue that he sacrificed smaller issues of regulation in order to protect more fundamental aspects of how the financial system operated, specifically the capital value of assets upon which it is based. In sociological terms, Boltanski and Chiapello (2005) have suggested that by incorporating selected critiques, capitalism has evaded other, more challenging critiques, and that this adaptive tendency has helped make capitalism robust. I suggest here that Darling's speeches after the Financial Crash can be viewed in a similar light, that his response to the Financial Crash was an observable example of a political elite enacting what Boltanski and Chiapello recognized as a broader historical trend. Darling incorporated criticism into his constructions, but he simultaneously placed constraints around critiques of financialized capitalism. Owned capital was protected and top-percentile earned income sacrificed; house prices would be protected even if mortgage payments had to be socialized; the banks should be re-regulated, but finance would remain central to the economy. In short, Darling incorporated allowable critique in hopes of maintaining some control over larger and more fundamental narratives. And this makes perfect sense, in light of the long-standing relationship between the UK Treasury and the City (Ingham, 1984; Seabrooke, 2006; Strange, 1988), another example of the way that the state protects finance and financial capital, a system in and for which it is integral itself.

Conclusion

Alastair Darling's constructions after the Financial Crash were extraordinary in terms of how often he spoke about finance, mortgages, and taxation, and how he responded rhetorically to the challenges of the Financial Crash. Darling protected finance and capital, but he was willing to construct finance as in need of reform, and even to penalize top-percentile earners. He admitted critiques of finance, mortgage provision, and taxation into his constructions as a means of building his own credibility and the credibility of his solutions. My findings suggest that after the Crash elites incorporated in rhetoric select elements of criticism of finance and even themselves in an attempt to influence how the Crash and its criticisms were framed in public debate. Alluding to limited criticism provided 'cover' for more fundamental issues, and provided 'balance' that attempted to appeal to a wide range of audiences, all while carefully managing expectations about the degrees to which finance would be reformed.

Affirming previous empirical findings about limited technocratic responses to the Financial Crash in terms of institutional reform, I add the observation that political elites are willing to sacrifice select elements of elite privilege in order to limit consideration of fundamental reforms to the economy. I, too, find that Darling sought to defend what he described as the fundamental worth of finance, while recommending that the Crash be remedied through technological improvements to the existing architecture. What I add with my analysis is that Darling utilized a dynamic criticism of financial, mortgage, and taxation activity in order to make the case that he was implementing remedies, and did so in a way that preserved these systems from fundamental critique within his account. He was compelled to respond to the Financial Crash in some way, publicly, and he navigated this difficult problem by admitting criticisms, often implicitly, and always in a limited manner. In providing a budget narrative, Darling provided leadership to other elites, suggesting how they might present themselves, recommending that concessions to critique might be necessary in this new post-Crash epoch. My findings suggest that political elites are part of what Boltanski and Chiapello (2005) have described as capitalism's ability to respond to and incorporate selected critiques while evading others, and that it may be political elites, rather than financial elites, who have been key. Future work should consider this possibility more fully by comparing the two, as well as compare the rhetoric of Chancellors Brown and Osborne, who flank Darling in history but did not have to deal with an immediate, catastrophic, and high-profile financial crisis.

References

Antaki, C., & Horowitz, A. (2000). Using identity ascription to disqualify a rival version of events as 'interested'. *Research on Language & Social Interaction*, *33*(2), 155–177.

Antaki, C., & Wetherall, A. (1999). Show concessions. *Discourse Studies*, *1*(1), 7–27.

Anthony, L. (2013). *AntConc 3.2.4w*. Retrieved May 4, 2013, from www.antlab.sci.waseda.ac.jp/antconc_index.html

Bank of England. (2010). Extract from the red book: The Bank's current operations in the sterling money markets. *The red book, chapter VIII: quantitative easing*. Retrieved July 14, 2013, from http://www.bankofengland.co.uk/markets/Documents/money/publications/redbookqe.pdf.

Barnes, W. (2013). We are the 99 percent: Occupy and the economics of discontent. In R. Guarriello Heath, C. V. Fletcher, & R. Munoz, (Eds.), *Understanding occupy from Wall Street to Portland: Applied studies in communication theory* (pp. 17–34). Lanham, MD: Lexington Books.

Billig, M. (1996). *Arguing and thinking: A rhetorical approach to social psychology*. (2nd ed.). Cambridge: Cambridge University Press.

Boltanski, L., & Chiapello, É. (2005). *The new spirit of capitalism*. London: Verso.

Cross, M., Fisher, P., & Weeken, O. (2010). The bank's balance sheet during the crisis. *Quarterly Bulletin of the Bank of England*, *50*(1), 34–42.

Crouch, C. (2011). *The strange non-death of neoliberalism*. Cambridge: Polity Press.

Edwards, D., & Potter, J. (1992). *Discursive psychology*. London: Sage.

Englen, E., Froud, J., Johal, S., Leaver, A., Moran, M., Nilsson, A., & Williams, K. (2011). *After the great complacence: Financial crisis and the politics of reform*. Oxford: Oxford University Press.

Fairclough, I., & Fairclough, N. (2011). Practical reasoning in political discourse: The UK Government's response to the economic crisis in the 2008 budget report. *Discourse & Society*, *22*(3), 243–268.

Finalyson, A. (2006). What's the problem?: Political theory, rhetoric and problem-setting. *Critical Review of International Social and Political Philosophy*, *9*(4), 541–557.

Fine, B., & Harris, L. (1985). *The peculiarities of the British economy*. London: Lawrence & Wishart.

Froud, J., Johal, S., Montgomerie, J., & Williams, K. (2010). Escaping the tyranny of earned income?: The failure of finance as social innovation. *New Political Economy*, *15*(1), 147–164.

Gilbert, G. N., & Mulkay, M. (1984). Experiments are the key: Participants' histories and historians' histories of science. *Isis*, *75*(1), 105–125.

Glyn, A. (2006). *Capitalism unleashed: Finance, globalisation, and welfare*. Oxford: Oxford University Press.

Goffman, E. (1979). Footing. *Semiotica*, *25*(1–2), 1–30.

Goffman, E. (1981). *Forms of talk*. Philadelphia: University of Pennsylvania Press.

Hellwig, T., & Coffey, E. (2011). Public opinion, party messages, and responsibility for the financial crisis in Britain. *Electoral Studies*, *30*(3), 417–426.

Herrick, J. A. (2009). *The history and theory of rhetoric: An introduction*. Boston, MA: Pearson.

HM Treasury. (2013). *Budget*. Retrieved March 5, 2013, from http://www.hm-treasury.gov.uk/budget.htm

Ho, K. (2012, May 15). Occupy Finance and the Paradox/Possibilities of Productivity. *Fieldsights – Theorizing the Contemporary, Cultural Anthropology Online*, Retrieved February 19, 2015, from http://www.culanth.org/fieldsights/340-occupy-finance-and-the-paradox-possibilities-of-productivity

Hodson, D., & Mabbett, D. (2009). UK economic policy and the global financial crisis: Paradigm lost? *Journal of Common Market Studies*, *47*(5), 1041–1061.

Holmer Nadeson, M. (2013). Neofeudalism and the financial crisis: Implications for occupy wall street. In R. Guarriello Heath, C. V. Fletcher, & R. Munoz (Eds.), *Understanding occupy from Wall Street to Portland: Applied studies in communication theory* (pp. 35–52). Lanham, MD: Lexington Books.

Ingham, G. (1984). *Capitalism divided? The City and industry in British social development*. London: Macmillan.

Joyce, M., Lasaosa, A., Stevens, I., & Tong, M. (2010). *The financial market impact of quantitative easing (Bank of England Working Paper No. 393)*. Retrieved August 6, 2013, from http://ssrn.com/abstract=1638986

Konings, M. (2011). *The development of American finance*. Cambridge: Cambridge University Press.

Langley, P. (2008). *The everyday life of global finance: Saving and borrowing in Anglo-America*. Oxford: Oxford University Press.

Lapavistas, C. (2008, October 2). No private matter. *The Guardian.*. Retrieved February 19, 2015, from http://www.theguardian.com/commentisfree/2008/oct/02/creditcrunch.marketturmoil

Mirowski, P. (2014). *Never let a serious crisis go to waste: How neoliberalism survived the financial meltdown*. London: Verso.

National Audit Office. (2009). Maintaining financial stability across the United Kingdom's banking system. *Report by the comptroller and auditor general: HC 91, Session 2009–2010*. Retrieved July 18, 2013, from http://www.nao.org.uk/wpcontent/uploads/2009/12/091091es.pdf

Potter, J. (1996). *Representing reality: Discourse, rhetoric and social construction*. London: Sage.

Riaz, S., Buchanan, S., & Bapuji, H. (2011). Institutional work amidst the financial crisis: Emerging positions of elite actors. *Organization*, *18*(2), 187–214.

Schneider, S. K., & Jacoby, W. G. (2005). Elite discourse and American public opinion: The case of welfare spending. *Political Research Quarterly*, *58*(3), 367–379.

Schwartz, H. M. (2008). Housing, global finance, and American hegemony: Building conservative politics one brick at a time. *Comparative European Politics*, *6*, 262–284.

Seabrooke, L. (2006). *The social sources of financial power: Domestic legitimacy and international financial orders*. Ithaca, NY: Cornell University Press.

Shiller, R. (2009, March 8). A failure to control animal spirits. *Financial Times*. Retrieved February 19, 2015, from http://cachef.ft.com/cms/s/0/453e55ca-0c0c-11de-b87d-0000779fd2ac.html#axzz3SCy9kqfT.

Shin, H. S. (2009). Reflections on Northern Rock: The bank run that heralded the global financial crisis. *Journal of Economic Perspectives*, *23*(1), 101–119.

Skidelsky, R., & Joshi, V. (2008, November 11). A dangerous free for all.. *The Guardian*. Retrieved February 25, 2015, from http://www.theguardian.com/commentisfree/2008/nov/11/global-economy-banking-reforms

Stapleton, K., & Hargie, O. (2011). Double-bind accountability dilemmas: Impression management and accountability strategies used by senior banking executives. *Journal of Language and Social Psychology*, *20*(10), 1–24.

Strange, S. (1988). *States and markets*. London: Pinter.

Whittle, A., & Mueller, F. (2011). Bankers in the dock: Moral storytelling in action. *Human Relations*, *65* (1), 111–139.

Woolgar, S., & Pawluch, D. (1985). Ontological gerrymandering: The anatomy of social problems' explanations. *Social problems*, *32*(3), 214–227.

Parliamentary Hansard.

UK PARLIAMENT HC Deb 12 March 2008a vol 472 c286.

UK PARLIAMENT HC Deb 12 March 2008b vol c295.

UK PARLIAMENT HC Deb 12 March 2008c vol. 508 c292.

UK PARLIAMENT HC Deb 8 October 2008 vol 480 c278.

UK PARLIAMENT HC Deb 22 April 2009a vol 481 cc245–246.

UK PARLIAMENT HC Deb 22 April 2009b vol c241.

UK PARLIAMENT HC Deb 22 April 2009c vol 481 c244.

UK PARLIAMENT HC Deb 24 March 2010a vol 508 c251.

UK PARLIAMENT HC Deb 24 March 2010b vol 508. c250.

UK PARLIAMENT HC Deb 24 March 2010c vol 508 cc255–256.

UK PARLIAMENT HC Deb 24 March 2010d vol 508 c262.

Evaluating policy as argument: the public debate over the first UK austerity budget

Isabela Fairclough

School of Journalism, Language and Communication, University of Central Lancashire, Preston, UK.

ABSTRACT

This article aims to make a methodological contribution to the 'argumentative turn' in policy analysis and to the understanding of the public debate on the UK Government's austerity policies. It suggests that policy arguments are practical arguments from circumstances, goals and means–goal relations to practical conclusions (proposals) that can ground decision and action. Practical proposals are evaluated in light of their potential consequences. This article proposes a deliberation scheme and a set of critical questions for the evaluation of deliberation and decision-making in conditions of incomplete knowledge (uncertainty and risk). It illustrates these questions by analysing a corpus of articles from five newspapers over the two months following the adoption of the first austerity budget in June 2010. It also suggests how analysis of 'frames' and 'framing' can be integrated with the evaluation of deliberation and decision-making.

1. Introduction

The austerity policies initiated in 2010 by the UK's Conservative and Liberal-Democrat coalition government have so far involved a systematic programme of public spending cuts and tax rises aimed at reducing the budget deficit and helping Britain recover from the effects of the financial crisis. In this paper,[1] I will focus on the way in which the argument for austerity made by George Osborne in his first Budget speech (22 June 2010) was received by economic analysts and journalists in a range of daily newspapers, at the time when it was first made. With the benefit of hindsight, it is always possible to say that a course of action which seemed reasonable at some point in the past, in light of everything that was known or could have been known at the time, was not in fact reasonable. This is different from a situation when a course of action turns out to have been unreasonable in light of facts that could and ought to have been known at the time but were ignored or disregarded (e.g. arguably, Britain's participation in the invasion of Iraq). It is only in the former situation that the fallibility of human knowledge can be legitimately invoked as an excuse. This analysis addresses the public debate on austerity at a time when there was no hindsight, which is the typical context for practical decisions, namely a situation of incomplete knowledge – uncertainty and risk – when practical proposals have to be assessed on the basis of their *potential* consequences, given all the knowledge available to the deliberating agents.

'Uncertainty' means that it is genuinely impossible to predict how things will turn out (i. e. there are 'unknown unknowns' that will interfere with the most carefully planned out course of action). 'Risk' means that the possible outcomes are known in principle, but which outcome will materialize is hard to predict. Uncertainty cannot be reduced to risk, as risk presupposes some calculation is possible. As Keynes (1971–89 cited in Parsons, 2012) warned, economic policy involves primarily uncertainty rather than risk, as it unfolds against a background of unknown future events and developments about which little, if any, calculation of probability can be made. This notwithstanding, he argued, under pressure to act, agents often go ahead on the assumption that uncertainties *are* risks, that the future can be predicted in terms of what we know about the past, often with disastrous consequences – as the financial crisis has itself shown.

In addition to being an empirical study, this article develops the analytical framework for the evaluation of practical arguments in political discourse presented in Fairclough and Fairclough (2012), where a more systematic 'argumentative turn' was advocated for the field of critical discourse analysis. It thus aims to make a methodological contribution to the 'argumentative turn' in policy studies (Fischer & Gottweis, 2012) by proposing a set of critical questions for the evaluation of practical arguments in deliberative activity types. It also briefly indicates how the concept of 'framing' relates to the evaluation of argument.

For the purpose of this analysis, 461 media texts, published over the interval 15 June–15 August 2010, were selected from *The Guardian* (121 articles), *The Daily Telegraph* (105), *The Daily Mail* (93), *The Financial Times* (92) and *The Sun* (50), with a combined total of around 315,000 words.[2] The first section briefly introduces the concepts of practical argumentation, deliberation and critical questioning. The second provides a brief illustration of the way in which each critical question was used in the media debate on austerity in June–August 2010. The third section looks at a selection of data in more detail, in relation to one critical question, and shows how frame analysis can fit into analysis and evaluation of argumentation.

2. Critical questions for the evaluation of policy as practical argument

In discussing the public response to austerity policies, I start from the practical argument scheme originally defined by Walton (2006, 2007a, 2007b), which I am re-expressing as argumentation from circumstances, goals and a means–goal relation (Fairclough & Fairclough, 2011, 2012):

> The agent is in circumstances C.
> The agent has a goal G (generated by a particular normative source.)
> Generally speaking, if an agent does A in C, then G will be achieved.
> Therefore, the Agent ought to do A.

I suggest the following situation as a starting point: an (individual or collective) agent having a stated goal G in a set of circumstances C, proposing a course of action A (or several such proposals), that would presumably transform their current circumstances into the future state-of-affairs corresponding to their goal G. (The goal is underlain by a concern for the realization of some value, desire, obligation, etc.) Based on all the knowledge available, the agent is conjecturing that they ought to do A_1 (or A_2 or A_3 ...) to achieve G in circumstances C. In order to decide rationally, the agent should subject

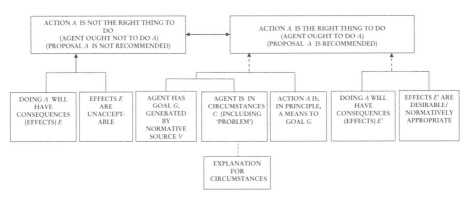

Figure 1. Proposal for the structure of practical reasoning in deliberative activity types

each of these alternatives (hypotheses) to critical testing, trying to expose potential negative consequences of each. A pragmatic argument from negative consequence (left-hand
side of Figure 1) can potentially rebut the practical proposal (conclusion) itself, whereas
challenges to the validity of the argument or to the truth of the premises cannot show
that the proposal is unreasonable but merely that it does not follow from the premises.
The pragmatic argument from negative consequence has this form:

> If the agent does A (adopts proposal A), consequence (effect) E will follow.
> Consequence E is unacceptable.
> Therefore, the agent ought not to do A (adopt proposal A).

Van Eemeren (2010, pp. 138–143) distinguishes among abstract *genres* (e.g. deliberation), *activity types* (e.g. parliament or policy debate) and concrete *speech events* (e.g. particular examples of such debates). Deliberation is a genre common to many activity types
whose intended outcome is a normative–practical conclusion that can, in principle,
ground decision and action. I suggest that argumentation in deliberative activity types
can be succinctly represented as follows (Figure 1), where the conclusion of the practical
argument from goals and circumstances (centre) is tested by a pragmatic argument from
consequence (left). Any action has both intended and unintended consequences, and the
latter may be foreseeable or not. From a critic's perspective, the foreseeable unintended
effects (consequences) can be such that the action had better not be performed, even
if the intended effect can be achieved by doing A. The intended effect (i.e. the goal)
itself can be unacceptable. If either of these is the case, a *critical objection* to A has
been exposed and the hypothesis that the agent ought to do A has been refuted
(rebutted). However, if the negative consequences, while unacceptable in principle, do
not constitute critical objections against A (this could be because there is some 'Plan B'
or mitigating strategy in place, or because they can be traded off against positive consequences), then the conclusion in favour of A may still stand, in spite of these counter-
considerations.

Practical claims can also be supported by arguments from positive consequence. The
argument from goals can itself be seen as an argument from positive consequence. Positive consequences also include desirable side effects that are not explicitly intended (are
not goals that agents start from), but can be predicted to occur. The right-hand side of

Figure 1 represents the arguments from (intended or unintended) positive consequence (E′) that allegedly count in favour of the conclusion. Figure 1 is a development of the schema proposed in Fairclough and Fairclough (2012), connecting two argument schemes, the practical argument from goals and the pragmatic argument from consequence; it also shows how explanations may be related to the argument.[3]

The decision to adopt proposal A is reasonable if the hypothesis that A is the right course of action has been subjected to critical testing in light of all the knowledge available and has withstood all attempts to find critical objections against it. By critical objection, I understand an overriding reason why the action should not be performed, that is, a reason that is not overridden by another reason that has normative priority in the context, in the process of 'weighing' reasons that characterizes deliberative activity types. The primary point of critical questioning is not to narrow down a range of alternative proposals to the one and only 'best' one, but to eliminate the clearly unreasonable ones from a set of alternatives. The underlying conception is a critical rationalist view of the function of argument and of rational decision-making (Miller, 1994, in press).

Walton (2007b) talks about three ways of challenging a practical argument: challenging the premises, the conclusion and the inference. In the set of questions suggested below, some critical questions (CQ4 and CQ5) attempt to test the practical proposal (conclusion) and may indicate that it is unreasonable and ought to be abandoned. Other questions (CQ1–CQ3) attempt to undermine the premises of the argument from goals, questioning their rational acceptability ('truth' for short, here). Finally, CQ6 attempts to defeat the inference from premises to conclusion, by indicating that there may be other facts that can be added to the premise set in light of which the conclusion no longer follows.

The following questions (Table 1) should be asked from the perspective of the critic, as antagonist, in order to evaluate a practical proposal (and the argument that allegedly supports it) being put forward by an arguer (as agent, or on behalf of an agent), as protagonist. The numbering of questions from 1 to 6 should not be taken to mean that they need asking in this strict order, that is, CQ1–CQ3 *before* CQ4–CQ6, as the questions are of three different types.[4]

Critical questioning in the format above integrates deliberation about means and deliberation about goals within a single recursive procedure. A successful challenge will redirect the deliberative process to some antecedent stage or to the starting point. If the foreseeable side effects are unacceptable, then a new practical proposal has to be made and the testing procedure will start again. If the goal itself is unacceptable, then deliberation may want to start again with a revised goal, prior to making a new conjecture about the right means to deliver it. The arguer (agent) may of course deny that any of these critical

Table 1. Critical questions for the evaluation of practical arguments

Challenging the rational acceptability ('truth') of the premises
CQ1 Is it true that, in principle, doing A leads to G?
CQ2 Is it true that the Agent is in circumstances C?
CQ3 Is it true that the Agent actually has the stated goals and values (motives)?
Challenging the reasonableness of the conclusion
CQ4 Are the intended consequences of A (i.e. the goal) acceptable?
CQ5 Are the foreseeable unintended consequences (e.g. risks) of A acceptable?
Challenging the inference
CQ6 [Among reasonable alternatives,] is A comparatively better in the context?

challenges have been successful. For example, s/he may deny that doing A will have the predicted side effects E or that those effects would be on balance unacceptable (e.g. on balance undesirable or normatively inappropriate).

3. Challenging and defending austerity

All of the above lines of criticism were pursued from the start in the public media debate on austerity policies in the months of June, July and August 2010. One line of attack implicitly challenged the means–goal premise (CQ1), with economists, journalists and politicians questioning the government's apparent belief in the possibility of economic recovery by means of spending cuts. Bringing examples from the Great Depression and Japan's history of stagnation, some argued that austerity, as means, always fails to deliver the intended goals. In other words, based on all available information about particular cases in the past – which indicates that, in similar situations, by killing demand, austerity has always worsened the economic situation – it is not rationally acceptable that austerity can in principle deliver economic recovery. In the *Financial Times*, Wolf (2010b) argued that 'in the current circumstances, the belief that a concerted fiscal tightening across the developed world would prove expansionary is, to put it mildly, optimistic', if not 'heroic' – a 'mythical belief' in the 'confidence fairy', according to Krugman (2010a), in the *New York Times*. Others claimed, on the contrary, that it is perfectly possible for austerity to lead to recovery. 'Austerity drives can unleash confidence' and 'there is every chance growth can resume even as cuts take hold'; 'though seemingly a paradox, expansionary fiscal contractions are not a figment of economists' imagination' and can be illustrated with successful examples from recent history – Denmark and Ireland in the 1980s (Monson & Subramanian, 2010).

Whether or not the means–goal premise is acceptable depends on how convincing is the evidence that supports it, and the evidence was interpreted in radically different ways. In the *Austerity* debate hosted by the *Financial Times* in July 2010, those who argued for immediate fiscal retrenchment on the basis of alleged evidence for 'expansionary fiscal contraction' were accused of misinterpreting the evidence or 'rejecting the counsels of history' (DeLong, 2010), but so were those who advocated postponing the cuts until growth had resumed. While, for Ferguson (2010), all the evidence pointed to the incorrectness of the Keynesian position ('today's modern Keynesians have learnt nothing'), for Skidelsky and Kennedy (2010), Keynes was right to argue that 'the boom, not the slump, is the right time for austerity at the Treasury'.

If the argument does not survive critical questioning at this stage (CQ1), the arguer is expected to revise the means–goal relation, which may mean either choosing an alternative means or combining the chosen means with some other, if in itself it is insufficient in view of the goal. In the *Financial Times*, for example, Sachs (2010) argued that, while austerity is not sufficient for recovery, it should not be abandoned, but should be coupled with other policies – with 'long-term investments in physical and human capital as the proper way back to sustained growth'. 'Fiscal adjustment and higher medium-term growth' should be 'twin policy goals' (El-Erian, 2010).

CQ2 amounts to asking whether the circumstances (including the 'problem') are as they are being described. Commentators both agreed and disagreed with the government's representation of the current situation in Britain: a situation of national 'emergency', an economy in ruins ('the ruins of an economy built on debt'), facing threats of insolvency similar to ones faced by Greece, where the state is 'crowding out' the private sector and the financial sector is disproportionately large compared to manufacturing. The associated explanation for the current state of affairs (it was all Labour's fault) was accepted by some and rejected by others. In *The Guardian*, Freedland (2010b) argued that the case against austerity would not be made convincingly until Labour managed to 'win the blame game' and explode the 'myth ... that Brown, not bankers, caused our economic woes'. The real cause of the deficit, he said, was the bank bailout, the 'colossal borrowing Labour had to undertake in order to prevent the crash of 2008 engulfing the entire economy'; ultimately, the cause was 'the larcenous greed of bankers'.[5] On the contrary, according editorial in *The Sun* (The Sun says, 2010) on the day of the Budget speech, 'the nation is clear who it blames for Britain's debts: LABOUR'. The crisis was caused by excessive consumption, living on borrowed money and by irresponsible state spending on a welfare system that rewards only those who prefer 'wallowing in state-sponsored idleness' (Randall, 2010, in *The Daily Telegraph*).

The stated motives of action were also questioned (CQ3). Normally, it is taken for granted that a proposal is based on the stated goals and values. But sometimes arguments are *rationalizations*: the overt, stated reasons are not the real reasons, and there are other, covert reasons driving the proposed action (Audi, 2006). It was argued that austerity policies are in fact ideology-driven: 'the real reason has to do a lot with ideology: the Tories are using the deficit as an excuse to downsize the welfare state' while using the 'the official rationale' that 'there is no alternative' (Krugman, 2010b). The government's 'real goal' is, allegedly, to 'complete the demolition job on welfare states that was started in the 1980s' (Elliott, 2010a).

According to the Budget speech, the government was committed *both* to being effective in reducing the deficit *and* to doing so in a way that was fair to the population. Constant invocation of this double (and often triple) commitment ('responsibility, freedom, fairness') implied that the proposal being presented to the public as the result of deliberation was informed by all these normative sources, that none had been sacrificed. However, many journalists cited the Chancellor's expressions 'tough but fair' and 'we are all in this together' in order to question that fairness was a genuine concern – see the *Guardian* headlines: 'Osborne's claims of fairness are now exposed as a fraud' (Milne, 2010) or 'Rooted in deficit-slashing superstition, this budget will hit the poor hardest: The fairness Osborne trumpets is skin deep' (Freedland, 2010a). This is Polly Toynbee's comment, in *The Guardian*, on the morning after the Chancellor's Budget speech:

> The word 'progressive' crossed the floor yesterday and entered the lexicon of the right. If these were the promised 'progressive cuts', then the word vanished into the realm of double-think. True, some Lib Dem yellow ribbons decorated the handle of the axe, but they barely impeded the swing of the executioner's arm. [...] 'Fairness' repeated over and over will not make it so. [...] The coalition has opted for cuts far beyond anything the markets expected or demanded. Why? The reason can only be ideological. (Toynbee, 2010)

Overall, *The Guardian's* verdict was that the Budget was 'Tough but Unfair' (headline), 'regressive' rather than 'progressive', 'a classic Tory budget of broken promises and unfairness'. By contrast, *The Sun* tended to agree that 'the pain has been spread fairly, with the better-off hit hard while those at the bottom are protected', and cited a YouGov poll according to which 57% of the respondents thought Osborne had made the right decision, with only 27% thinking the Budget was unfair.[6]

Appeals to fairness were used in very different ways: for some arguers, fairness genuinely informed action; for others, it manifestly did not but ought to have done. This is to say that the argument either did or did not pass the test of CQ3. In addition to challenging fairness as a genuine motive (CQ3), the austerity budget was challenged in light of how its consequences would affect the government's institutional *obligation* to act fairly, in the process of weighing reasons (CQ5). According to the critics, fairness was being sacrificed in the process of pursuing the goals; this was advanced as a very strong argument against austerity by those who took the government's commitment to fairness to be non-overridable (an institutional constraint on action). More often, though, fairness was understood according to a meritocratic, 'desert' conception – one that accords with popular common sense – and not in relation to justice or equality. This may explain the general acceptance of cuts in the welfare budget on the strength of the argument (made by *The Daily Telegraph*, *Daily Mail* or *The Sun*) that welfare spending cuts have to be made *for the sake of* fairness: 'we must all bear our fair share of the burden of paying off the deficit', 'it is only fair the unions accept the need for efficiencies', and the 'state's disgraceful indulgence of welfare-guzzling layabouts' has to come to an end. This argument said that fairness was not being sacrificed, thanks to the government's efforts to 'spread the pain fairly', protect the worst-off and demand more from those with the 'broadest shoulders'. Though rarely, the argument was also heard (in *The Daily Telegraph*) that fairness *had to* be sacrificed because there was no alternative.[7]

Questions 1–3 challenge the truth of the premises (indicating they may need revising) but leave the proposal (conclusion) itself intact: a satisfactory answer to these questions does not mean that the proposal itself is reasonable. By comparison, CQ4 and CQ5 can rebut the conclusion of the argument. CQ4 asks whether the stated goal (as intended consequence) is, on balance, acceptable, and CQ5 asks whether the foreseeable unintended consequences (risks, side effects) are, on balance, acceptable, as far as they can be foreseen, based on all the facts at the critics' disposal. Critical testing at this stage can yield critical objections that cannot be overridden, thus indicating that the proposal ought to be abandoned. Once a proposal is conclusively rejected, deliberating agents would need to return to the starting point and start testing another proposal (alternative).The question is: which considerations (reasons) can and ought to override others in evaluating a particular alternative? The political field, as an institutional order, is the realm of *deontic* reasons for action (Searle, 2010) – rights, obligations, commitments, entitlements, authorizations and prohibitions. These function as external (desire–independent) constraints on action and cannot be easily overridden: political actors are expected to act in a certain way whether they want to or not (Fairclough & Fairclough, 2012, 2013).

Criticism of practical proposals on the grounds of their likely undesirable consequences (CQ4, CQ5) was widely used in the aftermath of the Budget speech. While some of the Chancellor's long-term stated goals (a 'fairer Britain … where prosperity is shared among all sections of society and all parts of the country') were hard to challenge, critics of austerity called for a fundamental redefinition of what they saw as the immediate goals of action, for a new political vision. According to Caroline Lucas, instead of 'slashing public spending in the hope of resuming business as usual', the government should 'seize this opportunity to reconfigure the deeply unsustainable economic system which has helped push us towards financial meltdown' (Elliott, 2011). If the goal was a return to business-as-usual, to the same system that had caused the crisis, as the 'soft touch approach to the City' (Elliott, 2010b) seemed to indicate, then austerity was in need of radical transformation at the level of goals (i.e. it failed CQ4).

Regarding the unintended consequences (CQ5), opponents of austerity pointed to the likely catastrophic consequences of cutting expenditure too soon and too quickly, for example a surge in unemployment, particularly among young people. Not only would austerity fail to realize its own stated goals (because a combination of low growth in tax receipts and high growth in welfare spending would require more borrowing, which would only increase the existing debt), but it would clash with existing political commitments (institutional facts) – it would be unjust, it would damage lives – and there-fore with concerns that the government was expected to have. In *The Daily Telegraph*, for example, Mary Riddell (2010) warned that 'the very fabric of society will be put at risk by this unfair Budget' and that 'directing savage spending cuts at the young is a dangerous course for any government to pursue', forcing them 'down the long road to perdition'. In turn, defenders of austerity pointed to the likely catastrophic consequences of *failing* to deal with the debt: loss of business confidence, a downgrade of Britain's credit rating, leading to higher interest rates, which would increase the existing debt. In both cases, the argument was that the anticipated consequences would undermine the government's stated goals (to reduce the debt) and other widely accepted, legitimate goals (keeping unemployment down, retaining business confidence), as well as going against a range of reasons which, depending on which conclusion was defended, were deemed to be in principle non-overridable: existing commitments to fairness or justice, to financial responsibility and the national interest. For example, in warning that '[the Liberal Demo-crats] pick up an axe that will inflict great pain on those they once vowed to protect', Freedland (2010a) was not only referring to potentially unacceptable consequences ('great pain') but also at the same time making it clear that, in his view, the promises that the Liberal Democrats had made during the electoral campaign gave them non-over-ridable deontic reasons for action which their current action placed them at odds with.

It is also possible to conclude that the potential side effects of a policy proposal would be in principle unacceptable, but do not constitute critical objections to it (i.e. the case for austerity stands in spite of counter-considerations). This could be for several reasons, all making implicit or explicit reference to a notion of strategy. It may be the case that an effective way of dealing with the side effects (should they arise) has already been ident-ified: there is a 'Plan B' that the agent can switch over to, if faced with negative feedback. There may also be a broader strategy in place, involving actions whose role is to *mitigate* the negative effects of doing A. For example, while austerity is increasing unemployment, the government could be simultaneously engaging in a job-creation strategy; or while the state sector is being shrunk, the private sector could be encouraged to grow to compen-sate. It is also possible to reasonably persist in doing A in the face of emerging negative feedback if it can be reasonably argued that more time is needed before the benefits begin to appear. On this view, the unacceptable side effects are outweighed by the long-term benefits, or are merely temporary, and the situation 'needs to get worse before getting better'. Finally, it is also possible to answer CQ5 in the negative and, although no 'Plan B' or mitigation strategy are in place, still decide to go ahead with A, thereby taking the risk of an unacceptable outcome. In this situation, there is a rationality deficit, and deciding to do A is similar to a gamble.

The critics and defenders of austerity exploited all these possibilities. Early in 2011, as austerity was already on its way, a fall in GDP for two consecutive quarters prompted the government's critics to call for a 'Plan B'. From a critical rationalist perspective, it is rational to take a negative outcome into account as a real possibility and prepare for it, not to have blind confidence in a positive outcome. The fact that the Chancellor did not seem willing to change course was taken by his critics as a failure of rationality. A *Guardian* editorial (Spending cuts, 2010) cited Osborne's reply to the Treasury select committee, who had asked 'what his back-up plan actually was'. He said: 'The plan is to have confidence in the British economy', prompting the editor's comment that 'crossing one's fingers is not a plausible strategy for the man running the British economy'. The economic strategy was called into doubt by those who argued that the government was not sufficiently stimulating alternative sectors that could provide employment and growth, and was defended by those who argued that it was in fact creating favourable conditions for the private sector to compensate for public sector cuts, as well as mitigating the impact on the poor (e.g. taking more people out of taxation). Austerity was also defended in spite of the potential high costs, by seeing the costs as temporary and over-ridable in view of the benefits ('short-term pain for long-term gain', according to *The Sun*). 'If bitter deficit reduction medicine may push economically weak countries into recession, so be it', wrote Feldstein (2010) in the *Financial Times*, and 'a double dip is a price worth paying', on balance, if this sets the UK on the path to stable recovery. Austerity was also seen as a dangerous 'gamble' (Stephens, 2010; Wolf, 2010a) – a serious challenge to the rationality of action, in view of the stakes involved. To conclude, defenders of austerity denied that, on balance, the potential consequences constituted critical objections against the strategy, either because spending cuts were allegedly part of a coherent strategy whose other components were designed to compensate, or because negative consequences could not be declared unacceptable within a short time frame, or because such consequences were essentially overridable in view of the goals and the even more serious consequences of not acting as proposed.

A proposal for action that undermines its own stated goals is clearly unreasonable in an instrumental sense (if not downright irrational). In the words of Elliott (2010c) in *The Guardian*, 'Slash and burn is Osborne's cunning plan: Blackadder's Baldrick would be proud of the reasoning behind the austerity budget … Like Baldrick, George Osborne has a cunning plan. It involves growing the economy through cuts'. This is to say that the chosen action will not achieve its goal because it is in principle impossible to achieve the goal by means of such action (the means–goal premise is false, the argument fails CQ1), or that in the process of pursuing the goal, side effects are generated that undermine the possibility of achieving the goal (the proposal fails CQ5). From a non-instrumental perspective, one that evaluates the goals themselves, an action may be instrumentally adequate in view of its stated goal but may be wrong (unacceptable), either because the stated goal itself is unacceptable (the proposal fails CQ4) or because the action has unacceptable unintended consequences – for example, it clashes with other agents' legitimate goals, or goes against constraints on action (socially accepted values, institutional facts) which are arguably, on balance, non-overridable (it fails CQ5).

For example, according to Vince Cable, the way in which the financial crisis was dealt with, that is, with 'the reckless and incompetent … being rewarded, [and] the prudent and socially responsible punished', was 'a blow to the underlying value system, the social contract' (Cable, 2009, pp. 127–128). Similarly, for Martin Wolf, one aspect of the failure of the Western political elites to handle the crisis, which 'undermines the sense of fairness that underpins the political economy of capitalism', was their incapacity to prevent those 'parts of the elite most associated with the crisis [from becoming] richer than before' (Wolf, 2014a, p. 352). The 2010 Budget was often criticized along these lines: making the poor pay for the crisis caused by the banks was fundamentally *unjust* (Milne, 2010; Toynbee, 2010), as it went against existing *commitments* and *publicly recognized, legitimate values*. It was also pointed out that the coalition government did not in fact have a *democratic mandate* for such an economic programme, that is, there were legitimate non-overridable constraints on what the government was entitled or authorized to do. As such (deontic) reasons were not being taking into account, or were being overridden, the proposed action was arguably unreasonable (it failed either CQ4 or CQ5).

Rejecting a proposal on the basis of unacceptable consequences will return the arguer to the starting point, where an alternative line of action should be chosen. In spite of the government's insistence that 'Labour's legacy of waste' made austerity unavoidable ('this is the unavoidable Budget', Osborne, 2010), many arguably better means to deficit reduction were proposed from the start: structural economic reform, investment in green industries, a wholly new taxation system, including successfully pursuing tax evasion and tax avoidance (Elliott, 2011). The 'necessary' (unavoidable) character of austerity was thus challenged: if there are alternatives, a proposal cannot be 'necessary'. In the *Financial Times*, Brittan (2010) asked: 'are these hardships necessary?'; 'the real argument … should be whether we need unparalleled fiscal austerity or not'. Similarly, Wolf (2010a), calling the 2010 Budget 'savage', noted that 'the government must now win the argument that this tightening was essential'. The necessary character of austerity was by no means self-evident to him, in light of the alternatives available, for example, continued borrowing, or a more 'aggressive monetary expansion' policy, only followed by contraction when growth has resumed (Wolf, 2010b).

Finally, the last question (CQ6) cannot rebut the proposal but amounts to asking whether there are no *other relevant facts* about the context, which have not been taken into account, in light of which the conclusion does not follow (i.e. adding these facts to the premise set will invalidate or defeat the argument). For example, if there are facts about the context that make a proposal impossible to achieve, or if there are better means that have not been considered, then, however reasonable the proposal may be in principle, and even if it cannot be rebutted in light of its negative consequences, the argument in its favour will be defeated. It will not follow that the agent ought to do A, though neither will it follow that he ought not to do A. At this stage, critical questioning can help choose – *from a set of reasonable alternatives that have survived criticism in light of their intended and unintended consequences* – a proposal which is more easily feasible or preferable in the context. For example, without objecting to the reasonableness of austerity, Jeremy Warner asked in *The Daily Telegraph* whether it would be *possible* to implement it in the context:

> The other main risk is that the spending cuts envisaged simply won't be achievable, involving as they do a complete reversal of the public sector expansion that took place under the last Government. […] Mr Osborne can talk tough, but can he execute? (Warner, 2010a)

This suggested a negative answer to CQ6. This last question is designed to choose, from among reasonable and contextually feasible alternatives, a comparatively better alternative, one that best corresponds to a particular agent's *de facto* overriding concerns. For example, the Chancellor defended a particular distribution of the financial consolidation: 80% of the savings were to come from spending cuts, while 20% from tax rises. It can be argued, even by defenders of austerity, that this ratio could have been different, while still being reasonable from the government's point of view. In the context, however, the 80:20 split was justified by a *de facto* concern for increasing Britain's attractiveness for business, which this particular split would presumably achieve more *efficiently* than others.

How have these arguments fared since 2010? Following a return to growth in 2014, the government took credit for having set the country on the road to recovery, and Britain's recession was officially declared over in July 2014. Together with a record fall in unemployment (under 2 million, i.e. pre-crisis levels, in October 2014), the recovery seemed to refute the critics' objections and provide conclusive evidence that the government's plan was working. However, according to some critics the 'wrong kind of recovery' is currently taking place, an 'unbalanced' one, dominated by the service industries (including the financial sector), by consumer spending and the housing market, not by manufacturing (Vince Cable cited in Wintour, Elliott, & Allen, 2014). Moreover, the return to growth is not being translated into increases in wages: a 'jobs-rich but pay-poor recovery', according to a Bank of England chief economist, where many jobs are only part-time, on 'zero-hour contracts', or poorly paid. Although the budget deficit decreased between 2010 and 2012, it is still high, while the UK national debt has grown every year, thus clearly defeating the George Osborne's (2010) targets of having 'a balanced budget and falling national debt by the end of this Parliament', that is, 2015. The argument has also been made (by Elliott, 2015 and others) that the Chancellor in fact abandoned his original Plan A sometime in 2012 and reverted to the plans inherited from the Labour Chancellor, Alistair Darling, hence the incipient recovery.

For political scientist Mark Blyth (2013), 'austerity doesn't work'. There are no genuine cases of expansionary fiscal contraction in periods of economic slump, and austerity will always make the debt bigger, not smaller, as historical evidence shows. In his view, there was nothing inevitable about austerity, there were alternatives. One, preferable in retrospect, would have been not to bail out the banks. A solution now would be a renewed effort to collect taxes on a global scale – taxing the rich and the banks, the beneficiaries of the bailout (Blyth, 2013, pp. 229–244).

4. Framing austerity: negative consequences as salient premises

In this section, I will draw selectively on work in progress on the corpus, focusing on just a few keywords and their associated semantic fields.[8] My primary purpose is to suggest an argumentative conception of 'framing' and illustrate how analysis of framing can be integrated with the analysis and evaluation of argumentation.

The concept of 'framing' is widely used in political communication and media studies, as well as in cognitive linguistics, psychology, sociology and anthropology. There is little consensus on how to define and operationalize 'frames' (D'Angelo & Kuypers, 2010; Entman, 1993; Reese, Gandi, & Grant, 2007), yet there is some consensus that exposure to alternative arguments in public deliberation can weaken 'framing effects', the cognitive or decision bias induced by alternative ways of 'framing' an issue (Sniderman & Theriault, 2004).

In another paper, I have proposed an argumentative definition of *framing* that is compatible with Entman's (1993) classic definition of framing in terms of 'selection and salience'.[9]

Not all framing occurs within deliberative, decision-making processes (there is, for example, narrative framing, underlain by a different genre). When decision-making is involved, however, framing can be viewed as the selective salience given to certain premises in a deliberative process, intended to direct an audience towards a particular conclusion (and potentially towards a particular decision and course of action). Any practical reasoning premise (goals, values, consequences, circumstances and means–goals relations) can be made selectively more salient in the attempt to direct the audience towards a preferred con- clusion. The practical claim (proposal) itself can be made more salient by redefining it in a way that suggests it either should or should not be adopted. In this process, metaphors, ana- logies and 'persuasive definitions' (i.e. rhetorically biased definitions, Walton, 2007a) may be used to redefine facts in rhetorically convenient ways and thus lend support either to the practical claim that A should be performed or that it should not.

The way in which the financial crisis was 'framed', for example, as a crisis of overspend- ing (by making salient the alleged explanation for the circumstances) supported a particu- lar solution: spending cuts. Similarly, the Chancellor's comparison between the UK economy and that of a household (making salient a particular definition of the circum- stances of action) argued in favour of clearing debts as solution. Successful challenges of such definitions, metaphors and analogies can defeat the arguments in which they function as premises. National economies, for example, are not really similar to house- holds. For a family or individual business, it makes sense to cut costs, but if national econ- omies try to cut costs, this will shrink demand and damage growth. In other words, 'an individual may not spend all his income. But the world must do so' (Wolf, 2008).

While the primary mechanism of framing, on this account, involves making a particular premise more salient and potentially overriding, a second, additional mechanism seems to be at work whenever framing involves metaphors (X is Y), analogies (X is like Y) or persua- sive definitions (X is a kind of Y). In such cases, two frames, corresponding to the target and source domains, are mapped onto one another, so that the entailments of the source domain can be used to reason about the target domain (Fairclough & Mădroane, in press). This section illustrates the first mechanism, the next one illustrates the second.[10]

One way of making the negative consequences salient in the austerity debate was in (non-metaphorical) terms of 'risk' (a total of 217 relevant occurrences) (Table 2 - the use of the asterisk, e.g. risk*, is explained in note 6). The 'risks' of a 'double-dip recession'

Table 2. Negative consequences as 'risks'

Newspaper	Risk*	Examples
The Guardian	72	'George Osborne's austerity budget has increased the risk of Britain sliding back into recession'; 'the risk is you derail the recovery and that means your borrowing in the longer term will be higher'
The Daily Telegraph	40	'The Liberal Democrats now agree with the Conservatives that the balance of risk favours early action'; 'Britain remains at risk of a rating downgrade'; 'this Budget risks tearing society apart'
The Daily Mail	30	'Britain is so far into the red that we risk losing the confidence of the financial markets'; 'the scale of the budget deficit risks causing a major crisis in our economy'; 'Osborne is risking a double-dip recession'
Financial Times	70	'There is a risk that synchronised fiscal adjustment across several major economies could adversely impact the recovery'; 'Fiscal consolidation will bring with it the risk of a temporary decline in economic activity and a rise in unemployment'; 'the risk of a second Great Depression'
The Sun	5	'[Labour warned that the Budget] would put recovery at risk'

Note: The use of the asterisk, e.g. risk*, is explained in note 6.

(58 occurrences) of 'choking off the recovery' (7) or of 'stagnation' (9) are potential consequences that need to be averted and result from various probability judgements based on
known facts. For the defenders of austerity, failing to deal with the deficit is the main
source of risk: Britain may lose fiscal credibility, which can lead to a downgrade in credit
rating, hence to spiralling borrowing costs, a fall in investor confidence and so on. Austerity will actually reduce risk: 'the economic gamble is much exaggerated', 'the cuts aren't
that deep' and their effect is to reduce the 'possibility [of a fiscal crisis] from probable
to most unlikely' (Warner, 2010b, *Daily Telegraph*). For the critics, the austerity agenda
itself is the source of risk. In particular, high risk arises from proposed action that is not
accompanied by a 'Plan B' and seems immune to falsification in light of available knowledge (knowledge about past crises, economic theory) which should be used to test its
reasonableness. There are 15 occurrences of 'Plan B' in the corpus, for example, 'What's
the plan B if the cunning plan goes wrong? The answer is simple: there is no plan B
because the Treasury believes the need for one will not arise' (*The Guardian*). For some
critics, this makes the risks unacceptable ('Overzealous cuts risk a double-dip recession
and will fall disproportionately on the small people', *Financial Times*); for others, the
risks are outweighed by the fact that any alternative would be worse ('There is a perfectly
reasonable justification for taking this sort of risk: the alternative – a failing to tackle the
deficit – is even more dangerous', *The Daily Telegraph*).

Besides emphasizing negative consequences as serious risks, usually seen as critical
objections against the proposed action, a variety of metaphors were used to strengthen
the case for or against austerity, by lending support to the claim that the consequences
were, on balance, acceptable or not. I will now turn to a few cases of such metaphorical
framing.[11]

5. The argumentative function of metaphors in framing the austerity debate

Austerity as policy proposal was 'framed' in various ways. A particularly striking definition
was that of the June 2010 Budget as a 'gamble' (43 relevant occurrences in the corpus).
According to *The Guardian*, Osborne's Budget was 'in reality … the budget of a
gambler', 'a gamble on a monumental scale', 'a gamble with the livelihoods and living
standards of millions of people' (21 occurrences). Readers were told that 'Osborne has
gambled that early toughness will yield later peace' and 'if Osborne's gamble pays off,
it is Thatcherism's finest hour'. In addition, the policy was described as 'deficit-slashing
superstition' and 'deficit fetishism', suggesting a deficit of rationality and irrational risk-
taking and lending argumentative support to the conclusion that austerity is not the
right policy. According to the *Financial Times*, 'this gamble has now defined the government. If it is seen to have failed, it will be finished'. ('Gamble' occurs 10, 4, 6 and 2
times in the *Financial Times*, *Daily Telegraph*, *Daily Mail* and *Sun*, respectively.) The
Budget was also said to be a 'bet' (nine occurrences in the corpus): 'Mr Osborne is
taking a big bet that the economy will come right through market forces … and he
does not have a safety net in case his bet sours'; 'all is bet on the heroic assumption
that the economy comes good, growth is miraculously quick and the pain was worth it'.
If austerity is a gamble, then by entailment[12] it involves unjustifiable, even irrational
risk. This feeds into an argument against austerity: because austerity is similar to a

gamble, the potential consequences are unacceptable and the proposal fails to survive CQ5 (the outcome could be disastrous and there is no way of mitigating or redressing it).

In addition to metaphors suggesting extreme reckless or irrational behaviour ('gambling', but also 'lunacy': 'the lunatics are back in charge of the economy and they want cuts, cuts, cuts', Elliott, 2010a), metaphors suggesting extreme violence towards the population seem to predominate in framing austerity policies. For example, there are over 83 occurrences of 'axe' in the corpus: 'axing spending', 'where the axe will fall', a 'repeat of the heartless axe-wielding of the Thatcher years', 'some Lib Dem yellow ribbons decorated the handle of the axe, but they barely impeded the swing of the executioner's arm', 'the axe-man' [i.e. Osborne]. The Budget is also described as an 'assault' ('the biggest sustained assault on the public sector since the war'), an 'attack' ('attacks on public services, pay and pensions'), a 'war' ('an ideological war against the public sector'), and a 'slash-and-burn' approach. In the *Financial Times*, Martin Wolf (2010a) uses 'bloodbath' as a metaphor for the Budget ('this was a bloodbath none was prepared for'); there are 14 occurrences of 'bloodbath' in total.

Other metaphors support the opposite conclusion. Framing the Budget as 'surgery' (*The Daily Telegraph*: 'painful surgery', 'the surgeon-Chancellor was gentler than many expected') suggests that it will restore Britain's economy to health (will have positive consequences), and therefore austerity is, on balance, the right policy. Surprisingly, defining austerity as a bloodbath sometimes supports the same conclusion in favour of austerity. In an article entitled 'Britons Back Tough George', *The Sun* claimed that 'George Osborne's bloodbath Budget is a shock hit with voters'. This reflects a particular way of weighing reasons, in which the impact of austerity is outweighed by its alleged benefits.

Framing austerity as a 'gamble' (or as 'surgery' or 'execution') achieves two things: (1) it maps two frames onto one another, i.e. the POLICY frame is mapped onto the GAMBLE frame, and the entailments of the latter are then used to reason about the former; (2) it gives prominence to a particular premise within the deliberation scheme (in this case, a premise within the argument from negative consequence) so as to direct the audience towards a particular conclusion. If austerity is adopted, then the consequences (i.e. very high risks) will be unacceptable, *because the policy is similar to a gamble*; therefore (unless these potential consequences can be overridden), it follows that the policy should not be adopted.[13]

Figure 2 suggests where such metaphors or definitions are embedded in the overall argument ('austerity as a gamble' or 'bloodbath' in the argument from negative consequence on the left, and 'austerity as surgery' in the argument from positive consequence on the right).

The consequences of austerity are also frequently expressed in metaphorical terms of 'pain' (Table 3), part of the wider framing of austerity in terms of metaphors of violence. *The Guardian* speaks about 'the unjust distribution of pain', generally questioning the claim that 'the rich will feel more pain than the poor' or that 'the pain would be borne equally' and warning that that 'the pain will fall on the poorest people in the poorest regions'. *The Daily Mail* argued that 'Without pain, there will be no recovery' and the 'Budget pain can make Britain stronger' (headlines), that the 'painful Budget' was 'unavoidable if Britain is to prevent the money markets imposing a Greek-style crisis on this country'. This suggests that the potential negative consequences have been weighed against other reasons in favour and have been overridden: pain is necessary and

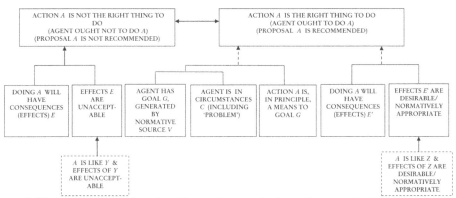

Figure 2. The argumentative function of metaphors, analogies and persuasive definitions

unavoidable if the goals are to be achieved and even more serious consequences are to be avoided. Similarly, *The Daily Telegraph* claimed that 'some pain today would avoid more pain tomorrow' and 'to be radical, in the current situation, means to perform painful but life-saving surgery on the British economy', that is, alternatives to 'pain' are worse ('pain' is overridden or outweighed).

To a much greater extent than the other newspapers, *The Sun* viewed pain as a necessary consequence, and one that was overridden by other reasons. As the headline: 'Worth the Pain. Tough measures get thumbs-up' suggested, the benefits of austerity were worth the suffering. 'If, out of the ashes of Labour, Mr Osborne creates a self-reliant nation freed from the shackles of benefit addiction, he will have ensured yesterday's pain was not in vain'. According to *The Sun*, the Budget 'has to hurt', and it 'has to be so tough it brings tears to our eyes'. Thus, a late-June Yougov poll allegedly showed that Britons gave the Chancellor a 'vote of confidence' and indicated 'strong support for many of the other pain doses', particularly the cap on housing benefits (with 70% in favour). In addition, austerity's effects on the poor had allegedly been carefully mitigated: 'the pain has been spread fairly, with the better-off hit hard while those at the bottom are protected'; 'like a dentist with a pain-killing injection, Mr Osborne will ease the misery by taking nearly a million low-paid workers out of income tax altogether'. Austerity cannot, therefore, be faulted and successfully survives critical questioning in light of its consequences (withstands both CQ4 and CQ5).

Table 3. Negative consequences as 'pain'

Newspaper	Pain*	Examples
The Guardian	47	'Pain now, more pain later'; the 'debatable claim' that 'the rich will feel more pain than the poor'; 'the unjust distribution of pain'; 'unnecessary pain', 'severe pain', 'painful spending cuts'
The Daily Telegraph	28	The Chancellor 'delivered the bad news about painful surgery'; 'everyone had to share the pain to repair the ruins of the economy'; 'the pain has been spread proportionately'
The Daily Mail	44	'painful public spending cuts'; 'a Parliament of pain'; 'making sure that the pain will be evenly shared between rich and poor'; 'ease the pain of a bloodbath package'
Financial Times	35	'Mr Osborne believes the fiscal pain now will pave the way for recovery'; 'for all that the government claims it wants the pain to be evenly spread, the less well-off and the poorest regions will suffer most'; 'a painful Budget'
The Sun	35	'Worth the Pain'; 'Pain today rather than more pain tomorrow'; 'Britain braces itself for five years of pain'; 'George Osborne vowed to ease the pain of cuts'; 'his painful national belt-tightening was right'; 'painful but unavoidable job losses'

The way in which the 'pain' metaphor is used in the five newspapers is apparently similar (similar collocations: 'spread the pain', 'inflict pain', 'ease the pain' and 'share the pain') but, from an argumentative perspective, very different. Almost without exception, *The Guardian* talks about 'pain' as an unacceptable consequence that ought not to be overridden by other reasons (i.e. the goal does not justify the means). At the other end of the spectrum, again almost without exception, *The Sun* predominantly views pain as fundamentally overridable concern, in light of the greater benefits to be obtained and of the efforts being made to mitigate or 'ease the burden' on the population. Two fundamentally different arguments are being made in these articles. One is an attempt to conclusively reject austerity, on the grounds of failing CQ5, admitting it has survived CQ4. The other supports it, for allegedly answering both CQ4 and CQ5 in a satisfactory manner: the negative consequences do not, on balance, constitute critical objections, in light of mitigation strategies in place and because they are outweighed by greater benefits.

To conclude, negative consequences (as premises) were made more salient (and thus presumably expected to direct the audience towards a particular view of austerity) either with or without the help of underlying metaphors, analogies or persuasive definitions. In both cases, the framing process was accompanied by a weighing of reasons (the essence of deliberation). In some cases, the negative consequences were deemed to be on balance unacceptable, thus indicating that austerity was not a reasonable policy and ought to be abandoned; in others, they were allegedly overridden or outweighed by other premises and did not succeed in rebutting the conclusion. Rhetorically powerful metaphors (austerity as 'gamble' or 'bloodbath') were used by the critics of austerity to persuade audiences that the consequences should on balance be viewed as unacceptable, that they cannot overridden by any other reasons (i.e. they are critical objections), and thus to direct the audience towards rejecting austerity.

6. Conclusion

I have illustrated the way in which the austerity policies initiated by the UK government in 2010 were evaluated in a range of newspapers in the two months that followed the 2010 Emergency Budget. In proposing a deliberation scheme and set of critical questions, I have tried to offer a means of analysing and evaluating any deliberative activity type that ends in a practical proposal for action. My main purpose was to offer a framework for analysis and evaluation, usable primarily by policy and discourse analysts, but also potentially by policy-makers, political activists, journalists and other actors in the political field. I have also shown how 'framing', which is only vaguely, if at all, related to analysis of argumentation in the literature, is best seen as contributing premises in a deliberative and decision-making process and thus shaping the inferential process towards a particular conclusion.

I have drawn (admittedly, to a limited extent) on Corpus Linguistics methods in order to analyse concordance lines and keywords, but I have done so primarily in order to facilitate analysis of argumentation. I have placed keywords within argument schemes, in the premises and conclusions of arguments. The analysis has shown not only that there is no straightforward correspondence between the concept of consequence and its linguistic realizations, *but that one needs to have a concept of consequence first, as a premise in an argument scheme*, and an understanding of what the public debate is about, in order to start looking for the linguistic realization of this premise with the help of computer software. It has also shown that the same reasons (premises) are weighed differently by different arguers, leading to different conclusions. Generalizations about the way different newspapers position themselves in relation to austerity are thus impossible to make on the basis of judgements of keyness alone: the arguments themselves must be carefully unpacked.

The austerity agenda has been criticized by economists, political scientists and NGOs (NEF, Compass, Tax Research UK, etc.). However, apart from the Occupy movement and a number of other protests and strikes, austerity has not been challenged significantly by the broad UK public. This may be due in part to the way in which, in framing the crisis as one of state overspending, the government has successfully enlisted common sense on its side: a common sense view of the economy (a 'household' that must pay off its debts and 'live within its means'), of acceptable solutions ('no pain, no gain', 'you cannot cure debt with more debt') and of fairness (it is not fair that working people should support people who choose to live on benefits). It has also been suggested that, by activating a 'logic of resentment', and 'drawing a line of antagonism' between 'hard-working' people and 'scroungers' or 'skivers', the government has managed to create a broad acceptance of the austerity agenda by the population, in spite of its harsh impact (Seymour 2014, p. 158). Possibly, another cause is the failure of the main parliamentary opposition, Labour, to develop a real alternative to austerity.

All of the arguments for and against austerity that are being heard at the end of 2014 were already present in the public debate on austerity that took place in the summer of 2010. Neither the supporters nor the critics of austerity seem at the moment willing to withdraw their original arguments in the face of emerging evidence, which continues to be interpreted in ways that support their original standpoints. For the Chancellor, a return to growth and high employment figures indicate that austerity is working. For his opponents, austerity's clear failure to reduce the debt and the weakness of the recovery indicate it ought to be abandoned. Not only have the intended goals not been achieved (instead, what high-income countries are now experiencing is a 'truly extraordinary state of managed depression', according to Wolf, 2014b), but the impact on other legitimate goals (living standards, in the UK and throughout Europe) has been severe, hence some alternative arguably has to be found. It may be that, as Blyth (2013, p. 244) argues (in defending taxation as a reasonable solution), austerity will be abandoned eventually, though 'not because [it] is unfair, which it is', but primarily because, from a purely instrumental perspective, 'austerity simply does not work'.

Disclosure statement

No potential conflict of interest was reported by the author.

Notes

1. This paper started as a keynote at a conference entitled *The discourse of austerity: Critical analyses of business and economics across disciplines*, hosted by Newcastle University in September 2013. I am grateful to the conference organizers and participants, particularly to Darren Kelsey and Majid KhosraviNik, as well as to David Miller, Norman Fairclough, Sheryl Prentice and two anonymous reviewers for valuable comments and suggestions.

2. These were selected with the help of LexisNexis database (except for the *Financial Times*), using 'Budget' and 'Osborne' or 'cut*' as search terms, from a total of 973 articles (in all UK national newspapers). This corpus was then restricted to 4 national newspapers (461 articles). The *Financial Times* corpus was compiled separately, using two separate searches in the *FT* archive, one among 'articles', using the pre-defined search terms 'United Kingdom', 'George Osborne' and the relevant time period, and another one with 'cut*' and 'austerity', to select other pieces which were not classified as 'articles', for example, the July 2010 'Austerity Debate'. These two searches yielded a total of 92 articles between the same dates. The analysis was assisted by Antconc, a Corpus Linguistics software (Anthony 2014).

3. Argument schemes are basic patterns of human reasoning, empirically derived inferential structures that underlie everyday argumentation. Their structure creates possibilities for critical questioning, in the form of finite sets of critical questions attached to each scheme. These may be actually asked by participants in everyday argumentation or they may not. It is the task of the analyst to bring the normative template of the deliberation scheme to bear on the systematic evaluation of public debate, by asking all the relevant questions that the template makes possible (normative critique), as well as inquiring into why some of these questions are either not asked or answered in a satisfactory manner, if that is the case (explanatory critique). For the distinction between normative and explanatory critique, see the Introduction to Fairclough (2014).

4. There does not seem to be a way of ordering CQ1–CQ3 among themselves; however, CQ4–CQ6 do enable a progressive narrowing down of alternatives.

5. According to Blyth, the 'opportunistic rebranding' of private-sector debt as public debt and the attribution of its causes to excessive public spending was 'the greatest bait and switch in modern history'. The correct explanation was this: 'Bailing led to debts. Debt led to crisis. Crisis led to austerity' (Blyth, 2013, pp. 73, 231).

6. *Fair* (fair, fairness, unfair, and any other derived forms) is one of the main keywords; there are 99 relevant occurrences of *fair* in *The Guardian*, 59 in *The Daily Telegraph*, 31 in *The Daily Mail*, 31 in the *Financial Times* and 29 in *The Sun*. 'Progressive' (68 occurrences) and 'regressive' (32 occurrences) are used similarly.

7. A concern for fairness is an *internal* reason, a motive for action. A commitment to fairness, creating an obligation to be fair, is an *external* reason (part of the circumstances of action, as an institutional constraint) that ought to motivate agents, although it does not always do so. External reasons may be internalized, turned into motives or not, but agents continue to *have* them as reasons, even when they do not act on them (obligations do not disappear just because we choose to ignore them) (Fairclough & Fairclough, 2012, pp. 69–73; see Searle, 2010).

8. The lexical items I am looking at (*fair*, pain*, risk*, hit*, ax*, gambl* and bloodbath) all occur with the first 500 keywords of the corpus (out of 8777) and have very high keyness values. Judgements of keyness initially emerged from reading a smaller version of the corpus (250 texts, 50 for each newspaper) in its entirety; these initial impressions were then tested by comparing the keyword list with the Brown corpus keyword list, available on the Antconc website, which was used as reference.

9. 'To frame is to select some aspects of a perceived reality and make them more salient in a communicating text, in such a way as to promote a particular problem definition, causal interpretation, moral evaluation, and/or treatment recommendation for the item described' (Entman, 1993, p 52).

10. I am proposing a new view of the *framing* process, not of *frames*. Regarding frames, I take the Fillmorian view that they are systems of related concepts – for example, the RISK frame (Fillmore & Atkins, 1992), involving an agent, a proposed action, potential harm, intended gains, etc. The argumentative scheme for deliberation can be used to define a DECISION-MAKING frame in Fillmorian terms, involving an agent proposing a course of action amongst possible alternatives, in view of certain goals and values, with potential consequences.

11. In the corpus, negative consequences are expressed in both metaphorical and non-metaphorical terms, for example, verbs such as 'suffer' or 'hit' and nouns like 'impact', 'effect', 'consequence', 'burden'. There are 290 relevant occurrences of 'hit*' ('[The Budget will] hit the

poorest hardest, while barely inconveniencing the rich') and 68 of 'suffer' ('the poor will suffer the most from the budget').

12. Entailment is a logical relation between sentences, where the truth of one requires the truth of the other: if something is a gamble, then it is risky.

13. It is possible to see such arguments from analogy or definition as directly supporting the practical claim via their entailments. However, I am representing them as subordinated to the arguments from positive or negative consequence because this shows more clearly that: (a) it is in virtue of the known effects of 'gambling', 'execution' or 'surgery' that austerity itself becomes acceptable or unacceptable; (b) it is in virtue of the redefinition present in these supporting premises that the consequences can emerge as non-overridable in the process of weighing reasons. This also shows why it is possible to use a metaphorical redefinition of austerity as 'bloodbath' *in favour of* austerity (as in the *Sun* example): through its entailments, the metaphor will still support the counter-claim (austerity is not the right policy) via the premise which says that the consequences are unacceptable, but the weight of the latter is apparently overridden here by other reasons (the positive consequences).

References

Anthony, L. (2014). *AntConc (Version 3.4.3w) [Computer Software]*. Tokyo, Japan: Waseda University. Retrieved from http://www.antlab.sci.waseda.ac.jp/

Audi, R. (2006). *Practical reasoning and ethical decision*. London: Routledge.

Blyth, M. (2013). *Austerity. The history of a dangerous idea*. Oxford: Oxford University Press.

Brittan, S. (2010, June 18). Are these hardships necessary? *Financial Times*. Retrieved from www.ft.com

Cable, V. (2009). *The storm. The word economic crisis and what it means*. London: Atlantic Books.

D'Angelo, P., & Kuypers, J. A. (Eds.). (2010). *Doing news framing analysis. Empirical and theoretical perspectives*. New York, NY: Routledge.

DeLong, B. (2010, July 23). Trichet rejects the counsel of history. *Financial Times*. Retrieved from www.ft.com

van Eemeren, F. H. (2010). *Strategic maneuvering in argumentative discourse*. Amsterdam: John Benjamins.

El-Erian, M. (2010, June 24). Beyond the false growth vs austerity debate. *Financial Times*. Retrieved from www.ft.com

Elliott, L. (2010a, June 14). UK economy: The deficit hawks need their talons clipped: Sadly, the Lib Dems are unwilling to challenge these cuts that risk returning us to recession – Or worse. *The Guardian*, p. 26.

Elliott, L. (2010b, June 22). Budget 2010: The axeman cometh. *The Guardian*. Retrieved from www.theguardian.com

Elliott, L. (2010c, July 19). Slash and burn is Osborne's cunning plan: Blackadder's Baldrick would be proud of the reasoning behind the austerity budget. *The Guardian*, p. 22.

Elliott, L. (2011, January 25). Britain's shrinking economy: Panel verdict. *The Guardian*. Retrieved from www.theguardian.com

Elliott, L. (2015, February 15). Labour must push what Milliband has got right on the economy in election runup. *The Guardian*. Retrieved from www.theguardian.com

Entman, R. M. (1993). Framing: Toward clarification of a fractured paradigm. *Journal of Communication, 43*(4), 51–58.

Fairclough, N. (2014). *Language and power* (3rd ed.). London: Routledge.

Fairclough, I., & Fairclough, N. (2011). Practical reasoning in political discourse: The UK government's response to the economic crisis in the 2008 pre-budget report. *Discourse & Society, 22*(3), 243–268.

Fairclough, I., & Fairclough, N. (2012). *Political discourse analysis*. London: Routledge.

Fairclough, I., & Fairclough, N. (2013). Argument, deliberation, dialectic and the nature of the political: A CDA perspective. *Political Studies Review, 11*(3), 336–344.

Fairclough, I., & Mădroane, I. D. (in press). An argumentative approach to policy 'framing'. Competing 'frames' and policy conflict in the Roşia Montană case. In B. Garssen & A. F. Snoeck Henkemans (Eds.), *Proceedings of the 8th conference of the international society for the study of argumentation*. Amsterdam: SicSat.

Feldstein, M. (2010, July 22). A double dip is a price worth paying. *Financial Times*. Online edition, www.ft.com

Ferguson, N. (2010, July 19). Today's Keynesians have learnt nothing. *Financial Times*. Retrieved from www.ft.com

Fillmore, C. J., & Atkins, B. T. (1992). Toward a frame-based lexicon: The semantics of risk and its neighbours. In A. Lehrer & E. F. Kittay (Eds.), *Frames, fields, and contrasts: New essays in semantic and lexical organization* (pp. 75–102). Mahwah, NJ: Erlbaum.

Fischer, F., & Gottweis, H. (Eds.). (2012). *The argumentative turn revisited*. Durham: Duke University Press.

Freedland, J. (2010a, June 23). Rooted in deficit-slashing superstition, this budget will hit the poor hardest. *The Guardian*, p. 31.

Freedland, J. (2010b, October 20). Osborne will escape public wrath if labour lets him win the blame game. *The Guardian*, p. 31.

Keynes, J. M. (1971–89). *XIV: The general theory and after: Part II, in The Collected Writings, volumes I to XXX*. London: Macmillan & Cambridge University Press for the Royal Economics Society.

Krugman, P. (2010a, July 2). Myths of austerity. *The New York Times*. Retrieved from www.nytimes.com

Krugman, P. (2010b, October 21). British fashion victims. *The New York Times*. Retrieved from www.nytimes.com

Miller, D. (1994). *Critical rationalism: A restatement and defence*. Chicago, IL: Open Court.

Miller, D. (in press). *Deductivist decision making*. Unpublished MS.

Milne, S. (2010, June 24). Budget 2010: Osborne's claims of fairness are now exposed as a fraud. *The Guardian*, p. 33.

Monson, G., & Subramaniam, S. (2010, July 27). Austerity drives can unleash confidence. *Financial Times*. Retrieved from www.ft.com

Osborne, G. (2010). *2010 Budget – Responsibility, freedom, fairness: A five year plan to re-build the economy*. HM Treasury. Retrieved from http://webarchive.nationalarchives.gov.uk/20130129110402/http:/www.hm-treasury.gov.uk/2010_june_budget.htm

Parsons, W. (2012). Keynes and the utility of policy-relevant knowledge. *Critical Policy Studies, 6*(3), 223–242. doi:10.1080/19460171.2012.704978.

Randall, J. (2010, June 18). Budget 2010: The days of spend now and pay back later are over. Later is now. *The Daily Telegraph*, p. 28.

Reese, S. D., Gandi, S. D., & Grant, A. E. (Eds.). (2007). *Framing public life: Perspectives on media and our understanding of the social world*. Mahwah, NJ: Erlbaum.

Riddell, M. (2010, June 22). Budget 2010: The very fabric of society will be put at risk by this unfair Budget. *The Daily Telegraph*, p. 20.

Sachs, J. (2010, July 21). Sow the seeds of long-term growth. *Financial Times*. Retrieved from www.ft.com

Searle, J. R. (2010). *Making the social world. The structure of human civilization*. Oxford: Oxford University Press.

Seymour, R. (2014). *Against austerity*. London: Pluto Press.

Skidelsky, R., & Kennedy, M. (2010, July 27). Future generations will curse us for cutting in a slump. *Financial Times*. Retrieved from www.ft.com

Sniderman, P. M., & Theriault, S. M. (2004). The structure of political argument and the logic of issue framing. In P. M. Sniderman & W. E. Saris (Eds.), *Studies in public opinion: Attitudes, nonattitudes, measurements, error and change* (pp. 133–155). Princeton, NJ: Princeton University Press.

Spending cuts: No way to run an economy (2010, July 21). *The Guardian*, p. 30.

Stephens, P. (2010, June 22). True-blue cuts will test the coalition. *Financial Times*. Retrieved from www.ft.com

The sun says: Owed Labour (2010, June 22). *The Sun*, p. 8.

Toynbee, P. (2010, June 23). Lib Dem ribbons decorated the axe – But didn't impede the executioner. *The Guardian*, p. 1.

Walton, D. (2006). *Fundamentals of critical argumentation*. New York, NY: Cambridge University Press.

Walton, D. (2007a). *Media argumentation*. New York, NY: Cambridge University Press.

Walton, D. (2007b). Evaluating practical reasoning. *Synthese, 157*, 197–240.

Warner, J. (2010a, August 14). Osborne hit the ground running, but can he stay the distance? *The Daily Telegraph*, p. 20.

Warner, J. (2010b, June 24). Get a sense of proportion – The cuts aren't that deep. *The Daily Telegraph*, p. 5.

Wintour, P., Elliott, L., & Allen, K. (2014, January 28). Vince cable undermines chancellor with 'wrong sort of recovery' message. *The Guardian*, p. 2.

Wolf, M. (2008, December 23). Keynes offers us the best way to think about the financial crisis. *Financial Times*. Retrieved from www.ft.com

Wolf, M. (2010a, June 22). A bloodbath none was prepared for. *Financial Times*. Retrieved from www.ft.com

Wolf, M. (2010b, June 23). Why it is right for central banks to keep printing. *Financial Times*. Retrieved from www.ft.com

Wolf, M. (2014a). *The shifts and the shocks*. London: Allen Lane.

Wolf, M. (2014b, October 9). An extraordinary state of 'managed depression'. *Financial Times*. Retrieved from www.ft.com

How Malthusian ideology crept into the newsroom: British tabloids and the coverage of the 'underclass'

Steven Harkins[a] and Jairo Lugo-Ocando[b]

[a]Department of Journalism Studies, University of Sheffield, Sheffield, UK; [b]School of Media and Communication, University of Leeds, Leeds, UK

ABSTRACT

This article argues that Malthusianism as a series of discursive regimes, developed in the Victorian-era, serves in times of austerity to reproduce an elite understanding of social exclusion in which those in a state of poverty are to blame for their own situation. It highlights that Malthusianism is present in the public discourse, becoming an underlining feature in news coverage of the so-called 'underclass'. Our findings broadly contradict the normative claim that journalism 'speaks truth to power', and suggest instead that overall as a political practice, journalism tends to reproduce and reinforce hegemonic discourses of power. The piece is based on critical discourse analysis, which has been applied to a significant sample of news articles published by tabloid newspapers in Britain which focussed on the concept of the 'underclass'. By looking at the evidence, the authors argue that the 'underclass' is a concept used by some journalists to cast people living in poverty as 'undeserving' of public and state support. In so doing, these journalists help create a narrative which supports cuts in welfare provisions and additional punitive measures against some of the most vulnerable members of society.

Introduction

Contrary to the normative claim that 'journalism speaks truth to power' (Nichols, 2014), an important body of scholarly research shows that overall the mainstream news media tends to reproduce prevalent discourses of power (Dijk, 1988; Hackett, 1984). This is more often than not the case of news reporting of poverty and social exclusion in which the narratives tend to refer to people in a state of poverty as 'others' who are often blamed for their own condition supposedly because they lack the skills, the knowledge and sometimes even the will to drive themselves out of destitution (I Campos, 2014, p. 13). We argue that journalists tend to undertake this approach as they operate within the boundaries of the newsroom's specific discursive regimes. These regimes underpin news narratives within an ideological framework from which journalists develop the deontology that they use to assess and later frame news articles on poverty from an ethical point of view. For us, the prevalent discursive regimes are characterised by a Malthusian ideology 'which focuses on scarcity of resources instead of unequal wealth distribution and which emphasises the need to further private property to maximise the efficiency of economic growth' (Ross, 1998, p. 2).

As a result of these discursive regimes, news media – generally speaking- tends to represent poverty at the margins of society and, since the end of the Cold War, increasingly more as a natural and unavoidable phenomenon. Therefore, the news stories reported by journalists are not only framed by these particular discursive regimes but enhanced by the political economy of the news media outlets –dependent on commercial revenues-, which requires invisibilising structural explanations such as 'inequality' within media narratives. Indeed, media outlets depend on advertising revenue from companies, corporations and governments that are institutionally committed to preserve the status quo, all of which creates a specific dynamic and rationale across the different newsrooms. Therefore, in order to deal with these contradictions, journalists working for these news media outlets have to create a social reality in which poverty is seen as marginal to mainstream society.

Another key feature of these discursive regimes is the need to displace responsibility from structural conditions towards the individual. To be sure, individualising poverty has been an elite response to the problem since the days of Thomas Robert Malthus (1766–1834). Malthus argued that as 'hard as it may appear in individual cases, dependent poverty ought to be held disgraceful' (1996). For him and many of his contemporaries and followers the poor lacked the intelligence and ability to control their needs or drive themselves out of poverty.

It is in this context that we have looked at the notion of the 'underclass' as one of the most important rhetorical devices to convey a specific meaning of poverty to general audiences. As a language resource, the notion of the underclass allows journalists to consider poverty from a non-structural perspective. This notion provokes then a different rationality of poverty among the public by means of displaying emotions such as pettiness, irony and even contempt towards those in a state of poverty. This creates a space between the spectator and the person who suffers. A process often referred to as a 'regime of pity' (Boltanski, 1999; Chouliaraki, 2013) in which spectators encounter those who suffer in the media space. Chouliaraki describes how within this regime news consumers themselves are 'part of the news narrative' however 'their emotions are, in fact, shaped by the values embedded in news narratives about who the "others" are and how we should relate to them' (2013, p. 11). This regime ultimately confers and reinforces a sense of power to the viewer (Lugo-Ocando, 2015, p. 173).

In the context of Malthusianism, immigrants and benefit claimants in London, for example, are blamed in the journalistic narratives for the shortage of houses instead of a critical review of the privatisation of social housing during and after the Thatcher era. Those claiming disability benefits are often presented in these same newspapers as 'abusers of the system', instead of examining the shortages in the health system to diagnose and support those with disabilities that potentially could allow them to go back to work. Political and media discourses have also portrayed single mothers as a burden on society because they are linked to dysfunctional behaviour, receiving welfare and producing children who are portrayed as being likely to turn into criminals (Silva, 1996, p. 178).

Consequently, our research has examined news coverage of poverty since the 2007/ 2008 financial crash by some key British tabloids and the use of the term 'underclass' by journalists. This research examines how the use of the 'underclass' by journalists has a historical precedent in news coverage of poverty. We argue that its use is mostly defined in terms of Malthusianism and through the idea of the 'undeserving poor' that dates back to the pre-industrial era.

The article is contextualised by outlining the political debates of these eras and how these discursive regimes have survived over the years, while exploring how they relate to contemporary debates about domestic issues such as welfare reform. The findings of this study suggest that the reporting of poverty presents it as an individual issue rather than a by-product of structural forces. In carrying out this analysis, the research offers a critique of the way in which journalistic narratives legitimise and support discourses of power in relation to poverty. Indeed, the paper builds on this evidence to argue that these representations are bound up with the dominant political and economic paradigm that journalists work in, which is confined to specific discursive regimes.

Background

Our main claim is that the notion of the 'underclass' inscribes itself foremost within a Malthusian-inspired worldview that is adopted by journalists. The media use Malthusianism as a rhetorical device in order to reconcile contradictions between normative claims of journalism as an activity that holds power to account and the political economy that defines and censors the possible narratives that journalists are allowed to express. This might appear paradoxical to many as hardly any journalists would have read in their lives the original works of Thomas Robert Malthus (1766–1834). However, in reality prevalent discourses become widely disseminated and embraced by journalists (Fowler, 1991), without them necessarily accessing the original sources. Instead, these discourses are often adopted in the newsroom as explanatory frameworks in order to facilitate reductionist approaches that support existing views within the editorial policy of the news media or set by what has been referred to as 'news cultures' (Allan, 1999).

This, we argue, became particularly evident after the collapse of *Lehman Brothers* and the subsequent financial crisis of 2007/8, mainly because of the need to justify programmes of austerity that placed most of the burden and sacrifices on the most vulnerable, together with the perpetuation of irrational rewards systems to financiers, bankers and elites alike. It was a rhetorical exercise that required a type of rationale in which the blame for the crisis could be displaced to the 'others'. It is in this context that the 'underclass' as a notion that has been embraced as a convenient language device to bring a type of emotionality into the public that could facilitate advancing a non-structural logic in the analysis of both the events and subsequent policies that took place afterwards.

While Malthusian ideology has been one of the guiding principles of how poverty is framed in the newsroom since the nineteenth century (Lugo-Ocando & Harkins, 2015, p. 40), there is also the long standing social classification of the poor into categories of 'deserving' and 'undeserving'; formalised through the Elizabethan poor laws (Boychuk, 1998, p. 8) and which has been a predominant feature of the way journalism represents poverty in Britain (Golding & Middleton, 1982).

In this context and by conceptualising poverty as a problem of scarce resources and overpopulation, Malthus was able to argue against poor relief for the 'able bodied'

(Avery, 1997, p. 62), (Daunton, 1995, p. 447). This was to become a common stance within news discourses of the Victorian-era which argued that helping the 'undeserving poor' would lead to laziness, moral decline and degeneration (Serr, 2006). This is a discourse that has been carried out all the way into the twenty-first century and that now translates in our times in calls for necessary cuts and reforms to the welfare system to make sure that the money goes to 'worthy' recipients of benefits who can 'earn' what they get from society.

It is important to fully appreciate the profound impact of Malthusianism in all areas of public life during the Victoria-era. For example, Charles Darwin (1809–1882) acknowledged in his own autobiography (1876) the influence that Malthus' had on his work:

In October 1838, that is, fifteen months after I had begun my systematic inquiry, I happened to read for amusement Malthus on Population, and being well prepared to appreciate the struggle for existence which everywhere goes on from long- continued observation of the habits of animals and plants, it at once struck me that under these circumstances favourable variations would tend to be preserved, and unfavourable ones to be destroyed. The results of this would be the formation of a new species. Here, then I had at last got a theory by which to work. (1958)

Nevertheless, the use of evolutionary theory to explain differences in human society was not done by Darwin himself but by others, most notably Herbert Spencer (1820–1903). The general notion of evolution was appropriated to explain why some people were wealthy and others were poor and why some societies succeeded while others failed. All these factors were explained through a concept which was to become known as 'social Darwinism' (Marks, 2007, p. 151). Social degeneration, for example, was one of the key tropes linked to Spencer's thinking; this idea is clearly expressed in this passage from his 1851 book *Social Statistics* where he argued that:

Blind to the fact, that under the natural order of things society is constantly excreting its unhealthy, imbecile, slow, vacillating, faithless, members, these unthinking, though well meaning, men advocate an interference which not only stops the purifying process, but even increases the vitiation … And thus, in their eagerness to prevent the really salutary suf-ferings that surround us, these sigh wise and groan foolish people bequeath to posterity a continually increasing curse. (1851, p. 323–324)

This line of 'arch-individualist' thinking (Willson, 1950, p. 359), placed responsibility for poverty at the level of the individual while complementing the laissez-faire economic lib-eralism of the Victorian-era. The influence of these ideas was clearly summed up in 1914 by William Graham Sumner, the first professor of sociology at Yale, when he said:

Let it be understood that we cannot go outside of this alternative: liberty, inequality, survival of the fittest; not-liberty, equality, survival of the un-fittest. The former carries society forwards and favours all its best members; the latter carries society downwards and favours all its worst members. (Ruse, 2009, p. 116)

To be sure, the ideology of social Darwinism stemmed from a Malthusian premise and served to justify the legacy of inequality that had developed following the expansion of the British Empire and the subsequent industrial revolution that stood on the shoulders of slavery proceedings. As a discursive regime, it shaped the views of many and framed the most prominent news stories published by newspapers in Britain until well into the inter-war period and after.

Despite common assumptions, the horrors of the Nazi concentration camps did not seem to curb the appetite for Malthusianism; although it did tone done some of its more explicit manifestations such as Eugenics. The post-second World War II settlement meant that Keynesianism and 'welfare consensus' would dominate policy-making (Harvey, 2005; Hutton, 1996) and public discourse until the 1970s as there was the need to articulate constantly a propagandistic response to Soviet menace during the Cold War. Throughout this period, Malthusianism was less appreciated in the context of laissez-faire thinking and instead adapted to the state-interventionist mode of the era, while surviving in the discourses of 'development' and 'progress' which demanded population control of those in the Global South (Connelly, 2008; Kasun, 1988).

However, following the economic crisis of the 1970s which led to the breakdown of the welfare consensus, Malthusianism in the public discourse was re-appropriated by those voices embracing classical economic thinking now in the face of neo-liberalism (Cockett, 1994). This consequently had a profound effect on the overall approach that journalists undertook for the following decade. As some authors point out, 'free market ideas have been the main driving force shaping media policy since the early 1980s' (Steel, 2012, p. 167).

Described by critics as a period of neo-liberal hegemony, the 1980s and 1990s were characterised by 'privatisation, deregulation and cuts to government services' (Klein, 2007, p. 444). This can be seen by examining one of the key political debates during the neo-liberal period which has centred around the public crisis of welfare expenditure (Golding & Middleton, 1982). Indeed, as some have highlighted, social policy usually only becomes news when there is a political or economic crisis (Franklin, 1999, p. 1). These changes led to 'pressures to cut welfare and state benefits that had provided a safety net for the victims of economic change' (Critcher, 2003, p. 64). In this context, Critcher argues that this caused widespread insecurity amongst benefit recipients and 'many of the moral panics that accompanied these profound social changes could well be interpreted in terms of the politics of anxiety' (2003, p. 64).

According to Peter Golding, the media have subjected unemployed people in the UK to 'more blitzes than the Luftwaffe could ever have imagined possible' (Golding in Franklin, 1999, p. 147). Golding and Middleton's seminal study into media coverage of poverty described the first of these 'blitzes' as a 'welfare backlash of cruel and massive proportions'. They argue that the economic crisis had led to a culture of 'indicting welfare and convicting the poor for the crisis of economic fortune' (Golding & Middleton, 1982, p. 3). The 1970s 'scroungerphobia' backlash set the 'rhetoric and vocabulary' for future reporting of welfare stories (Golding in Franklin, 1999, p. 147).

Moreover, these media campaigns against welfare at this time were used as 'the occasion for a social derision of the poor so punitive in its impact' that it was to 'threaten the very props of the modern welfare state' (Golding & Middleton, 1982, p. 5). Stanley Cohen argues that 'cutbacks in welfare state provisions during the Thatcher years were accompanied by the deliberate construction of an atmosphere of distrust' (Cohen, 2011, p. xi–xxi). He uses 'dole cheats' and 'welfare scroungers' as examples of 'fairly traditional folk devils' (Cohen, 2011, p. xxi). Deacon argues that the intensity of hostility towards abuse of the benefits system was greater than at any time since the Great Depression era (1978, p. 1). According to Deacon, official government investigations into abuse of the welfare system 'unearthed virtually no abuse' and he adds that 'the costs of one inquiry into fraudulent claims for dependant's benefits were eight times the amount discovered in over-payments' (1973, p. 346).

Other authors have argued that media attacks on 'scroungers' serve to 'transform the social problem of unemployment into a public crisis, if not moral panic, about welfare scroungers' (Franklin, 1999, p. 2). These voices underline the fact that the contemporary understanding of welfare is based partly on 'the pathology of individual inadequacy as the cause of poverty' (Golding in Franklin, 1999, p. 146), as it is far less painful to recognise poverty as a structural phenomenon in which there is collective responsibility. Indeed, this view that people 'seek individualised, rather than structural explanations for poverty' was also evident in the *Joseph Rowntree* Foundation's 2008 report into the way poverty is represented in UK media (McKendrick et al., 2008).

The discourses of the 'undeserving poor' in the USA and UK have, since the late 1970s, morphed into a discussion about the existence of an 'underclass' (Gans, 1995; Katz, 1995; Lister, 2004). The 'underclass' was created as a 'creature of journalism' and a great section of the media have frequently used the term as a synonym for poverty, thereby stigmatising the poor (Lister, 2004, p. 107–109). The term 'underclass' is used by many journalists to describe a group of people who pose a threat to society, by arguing that they are 'immoral' and 'violent' (Gans, 1995; Katz, 1995; Lister, 2004). Indeed, poverty discourse from the 1980s onwards became dominated by the idea of a growing 'underclass' (Katz, 1990, p. 185). One of the reasons was that in the 'culture of capitalism' people were increasingly judged in terms of 'their ability to produce wealth and by their success in earning it' (Katz, 1990, p. 7).

In the 1980s and 1990s, the hostile media campaigns were broadened to include single mothers as well as unemployed and homeless people (Franklin, 1999; Jones, 2011, p. 67). Throughout the 1980s culminating in a peak of hostility in the early 1990s, single mothers also became 'folk devils' and were constructed as a 'potent moral threat' (Cohen, 2011, p. xxi). In this sense, Cohen argues that the demonisation of single mothers is central to the theory of the 'underclass':

> 'Feckless mothers' get pregnant to obtain state welfare; they raise children who will be criminals of the future; absent fathers are present somewhere, unemployed and also living off the state. (2011, p. xxi)

In fact, this idea of the 'underclass' as a 'menace' would become a key definer in journalistic narratives from the 1990s onwards. Indeed, Kendall argues that media portrayals of welfare recipients and homeless people frequently present them in terms of posing a threat to middle-class values (Kendall, 2005). Social class plays a strong role in framing stories about poverty. In the USA, for example, women receiving welfare are often 'stereotyped as lazy, disinterested in education, and promiscuous' (Bullock, Fraser Wyche, & Williams, 2001, p. 230). Furthermore, Baumann argues that the rise of the 'underclass' theory coincided with the end of the Cold War. The 'underclass' was used to fill the void that had been left by no longer credible theories of a foreign revolution (Bauman, 1998, p. 67). This idea that the 'underclass' represents a threat to the rest of us is common throughout the literature on the subject (Bauman, 1998; Lister, 2004).

It is in this context that the notion of the 'underclass' in journalistic narratives needs to be understood as an enduring legacy of Malthusian ideas, which the mainstream news media tends to use to 'support and propagate the aspect of neo-liberal ideology concerning poverty and welfare' (de Goede, 1996, p. 352). That, as we argue here, is the basis for the resilient presence of the Malthusian paradigm in the newsroom of today.

Methodology

This study used the *Nexis* database to search for national press articles containing the word 'underclass' for a five-year period between the 9th August 2007 and the 9th August 2012. The original date was chosen because it represented the beginning of the 'credit crunch' (Leader, 2012). A five-year period was selected because it allows us to study the transition between New Labour (which stayed in power between 1997 and 2010) and a new government formed by a coalition of the Conservative and Liberal Democrat parties. The sample encompasses 285 articles which were selected for a close reading to examine how the concept of the 'underclass' fitted into the wider ideology of the newsroom.

The main reason we have focussed on tabloid newspapers in our research is due to the fact that these media outlets play a pivotal role in shaping both the news agenda and public opinion in Great Britain, particularly in regards to popular culture (Conboy, 2002) and worldviews on poverty. Indeed, as some authors have pointed out, British tabloids have been able to create imaginary communities across their audiences in which people see the world in terms of 'outsiders' and 'insiders' and extend their influence beyond the boundaries of print (Conboy, 2006).

In the context of discourses of poverty and the underclass, the tabloids have played historically one of the most important roles in telling people what to think about. For example, some research on tabloids in the UK has highlighted how important they have been in perpetuating for years notions such as that of the 'underclass' by using alternative language such as 'chav' in order to reinforce historical social classification of a certain type among the public (Hayward & Yar, 2006, p. 9). It is precisely because of this double role of being agenda shapers and public opinion definers that we have chosen to work with the tabloids in order to understand how public discourses on poverty have been articulated in the media.

The following table shows the way these articles were spread across different tabloid platforms: (Table 1)

The spread of these articles suggests that the concept of the 'underclass' is more likely to be employed by the newspapers who lean politically to the right rather than the left. The sole left leaning tabloid in this sample is the *Mirror* a newspaper which employs this discourse much less often than the other three newspapers. The volume of underclass articles in the *Daily Mail* also suggests that this concept is a key part of that newspapers ideology.

An analysis was carried out on these articles focussing specifically on the subject of the underclass and the research aimed to tackle three key questions about this group. The main purpose of this analysis was to examine the 'influential role of ideology' (Fernández Martínez, 2007, p. 1).

(1) The first question we asked was, who are the 'underclass'? That is to say, who do the news media describe and define as 'underclass'?

Table 1. 'Underclass' articles in the British tabloid press

Newspaper	Number of articles
Daily Mail and *Mail on Sunday*	135
Daily and Sunday Express	77
Sun, News of the World and *Sunday Sun*	54
Daily and Sunday Mirror	19

(2) The second question asked was, how do the news media describe the social problem of the 'underclass' and how it relates to the discursive regime of Malthusianism?

(3) Finally the study examines the solutions expressed by journalists to solve the 'underclass' problem in the context of their own ideologies and discursive regimes.

By examining the notion of 'underclass' we aim at answering these questions, which we hope will lead to a better understanding of how poverty is articulated in the public discourses expressed in the media in the context of Malthusianism. Although we are unable to present here the full range of articles analysed for this study, we can confirm that cases cited here are widely representative of the coverage of the underclass in the *Sun*, *Sunday Sun*, *News of the World*, the *Daily Mail* and the *Mail on Sunday* and the *Express* and *Sunday Express*. This type of story about the 'underclass' is much rarer in the *Mirror* and *Sunday Mirror* even within the much smaller sample of articles that were found in these two last publications.

Findings

One of the most important findings is that the British tabloid press has used the underclass label as a highly malleable label to describe 'jobless young men', 'single mothers',[1] 'the unemployed'[2] and 'delinquent youths'[3] who are described as 'young thugs'[4] or 'teen yobs'.[5] The label is also used –although far less often- to describe 'illegal immigrants'[6] and children who are falling behind in school who are referred to as part of the 'educational underclass'.[7] Overall, the underclass is mainly articulated as a pejorative term to describe both welfare recipients and criminals, who too often are also reported as being the same.

The language used is highly problematic as tabloid journalists describe the 'underclass' as 'feral',[8] 'white chavs',[9] 'chav types',[10] 'a thuggish, feral underclass',[11] who are part of 'the chav class, the great unwashed', 'freeloaders', 'scrounging on the dole', who according to these reports 'keep pushing out their soon-to-be-feral offspring'.[12] In the words of journalists writing these stories or their editors, members of the underclass are 'parasites', 'second- and third-generation scum',[13] the 'feral, the feckless and the freeloaders', are also 'slappers – useless, ugly freeloaders'.[14] They are represented as living in 'chaotic families that loaf away their days on easy welfare benefits',[15] being 'irresponsible and useless',[16] 'depraved and sick', and their voices are portrayed as coming from the 'ugly mouths of the vile underclass',[17] for whom, we are told, 'unemployment, drug addiction, under-age sex and truancy are an everyday way of life'.[18] They are constructed as 'feral', 'scroungers' who sleep 'in their stinking pits'.[19]

There is also a clear trope that marks the underclass as a lazy group that 'refuse to work'.[20] They are described as 'welfare scrounging'[21] ... baby machine(s)',[22] and constructed through these news discourses as a 'huge, idle underclass for whom work is a dirty word'.[23] These news discourses stigmatise people by describing them as the 'the feral, the feckless and the long-term useless [who] could breed with impunity. Usually after several cans of Stella while us hardworking, tax-paying mugs picked up the bill'.[24] They are exemplified as 'a feckless underclass who don't work and lay slumped in front of the TV stuffing their faces with deepfried lard'.[25] While developing a reputation for being lazy the underclass are also 'terrorising communities across Britain'.[26]

The use of particular brands of lager (Stella) and types of cooking (deepfried lard) create a vivid image which has a clear dimension of class prejudice. Slavoj Zizek argues that the process of creating these modern images started during the 'back to basics' campaign of the Conservative Government that followed the 'black Wednesday' crash of September 1992, where the image of the single mother on benefits was used as an embodiment of 'all the evils of society' to used symbolically as a 'singular cause of all social ills' (Zizek 2006 p. 41).

The link between individuals who commit criminal acts and the underclass is made repeatedly across these news stories. They are described as being an underclass 'whose depravity goes so low, the extent of their evil often goes undetected'.[27] The conflation between criminals and welfare recipients as members of an underclass allows the British tabloids to select specific cases to criminalise whole communities of benefit recipients. Descriptions such as 'feral', unacceptable if they were targeting almost any other social group, nonetheless are openly used as a metaphor to blur any distinction between crime and welfare. This discourse allows tabloid newspapers to describe the unemployed or single mothers in the same terms as they would describe a child murderer or a wild animal out of control. This link is made explicitly in the following article:

> And that's what we have to address now-this underclass, this group of deviants who've been allowed to take root in this country and who kill, maim and torture without guilt. These are people who have sponged off the welfare state their whole lives and who believe nothing is their responsibility, their fault or their problem. For too long we've tap-danced around these people because of political correctness. The problem was too sensitive to talk about-let alone handle. But handle it we must, because if we don't this underclass will become even more savage, more Feral-and more innocents will die.[28]

This link between individuals who commit criminal acts and the underclass is made repeatedly. The sample shows an overall Malthusian discursive regime among the tabloids in the articulation of news. In these stories we find expressions about how an overgenerous welfare system has led to a 'mushrooming underclass',[29] which in itself is presented as a threat that is magnified by the underclass association with 'rampant violent crime'.[30] Following the Malthusian rationale that charity towards the poor –welfare in this case- only perpetuates the problem. The British tabloids tend to conclude that the most serious political challenge facing the UK is 'rooting out the persistent underclass'.[31] Indeed, the development of an 'underclass' is explicitly linked in these news stories to welfare provision, when these newspapers state that 'we only have an underclass because we fund it with handouts'.[32]

According to these news reports, the 'generous welfare payments', also referred to as 'the poverty trap', have led to a situation where 'billions more [are] spent, insanely, making benefits more lucrative than a pay cheque'.[33] These individuals are presented by the media as 'a problem we can no longer ignore, because the future prosperity of this country relies on the ability of generations to come making a valuable contribution'.[34]

Other articles bring back the notion of deserving and undeserving poor when they touch on unemployment by arguing that 'in a country where the dole figure has just passed 2.2 million ... scroungers can rot in their stinking pits, only stirring to pick up the next benefit cheque or breed the next member of the feral underclass'.[35] This line of argument suggests that the problem with the underclass is that they are inherently lazy while ignoring structural issues with high unemployment. Wright-Mills offered a critique of this line of thinking on unemployment when he argued:

> When, in a city of 100,000, only one man is unemployed, that is his personal trouble, and for its relief we properly look to the character of the man, his skills, and his immediate opportunities. But when in a nation of 50 million employees, 15 million men are unemployed, that is an issue, and we may not hope to find its solution within the range of opportunities open to any one individual. (1959, p. 9)

The tabloid press has inverted this logic by blaming high unemployment on the personal characteristics of the 'underclass'. In so doing, the tabloid press has created a narrative paradox where the 'underclass' problem is due to the fact that 'the unemployed have become the unemployable'.[36] Here the Malthusian paradigm is used to solve this paradox by highlighting the 'inferiority' of those in welfare as it points out that they are 'unemployable' because they are not fit, which leads to calls to curb their numbers. Because of this pre-conception, the 2007/8 crises presented a unique opportunity to reintroduce more draconian narratives against those in benefits that echo the core of classical Malthusianism. Indeed, one proposed solution to the crisis made by the tabloids was to present benefit claimants with a stark choice of 'sterilisation or no more benefits', which echoes fully Malthusianism.[37]

For the tabloid press, their work ethics have been destroyed by an 'overdeveloped welfare state',[38] which threatens the whole nation, as the *Daily Mail* questions,

> How much longer can we survive and prosper as a nation of bankers, lawyers, architects and theatrical designers, picking up the social bills for an unemployable underclass.[39]

Other similar articles go on to describe a 'submerged underclass' of 'ill-educated, ill-disciplined, near illiterate and innumerate unemployables' who are portrayed as 'living better than the working families next door'.[40]

In many of these reports, New Labour is presented as being responsible for creating the underclass,

> For all Blair's words about Asbos, tags and banning orders, he created a benefit culture where the Feral, the feckless and the long-term useless could breed with impunity.[41]

The story of Karen Matthews[42] is repeatedly used in order to make the case for welfare reform, for example, an article in the *Sun* explains how:

> Britain's benefits culture has spawned an underclass of kids brought up on welfare. They include evil mum-of seven Karen Matthews, who was caged for eight years for kidnapping her daughter Shannon. She pocketed £350 A WEEK.[43]

Benefit recipients are described in one article as being the 'Karen Matthews brigade',[44] public authorities are criticised for carrying out a 'Karen Matthews test' to 'skew resources further towards the underclass'.[45] Matthews is also described as a 'one-woman advertisement for urgent welfare reform'.[46] She is also constructed as being 'part of the chav class',[47] which reinforces historical notions of class hierarchy (Hayward & Yar, 2006, p. 9). The argument is that she is part of an 'underclass' who are represented as being able to 'get more by scrounging on the dole rather than working'.[48] Journalists such as Fraser Nelson from *the Sun* have argued that the 'underclass' had developed precisely because 'Britain is rich enough to keep them on benefits.'[49] The key point made by these stories is that the 'underclass' exist only because they can withdraw money from the state.

The *Daily Mirror* and *Sunday Mirror* is the only publication in our sample that offers a critical perspective on the existence of an underclass. *UNITE* union's general secretary Len McCluskey is quoted in an article arguing that the language of the 'feral underclass' was likely to create 'widening divisions in society'. McCluskey asks of the political class, 'what are they doing about the feral ruling class, who have ripped us to shreds?'[50] However, such critical perspectives are rare and almost exclusive to the left leaning *Daily Mirror* and *Sunday Mirror*. These rare narratives, however, do help us to highlight the ideological and editorial nature of the use of the terms 'underclass' in the journalistic narratives.

Another important finding in our research is that US style welfare reforms -echoing Bill Clinton's approach in 1996- are broadly supported by the British tabloids. These reforms, under the 1996 Personal Responsibility Act, included the requirement that single mothers 'work for their welfare' and were given 'no extra payouts for additional children conceived once the mothers were on benefits'.[51] The tabloids approach was marked by strong support for US style welfare reforms because they argue that 'America has found an effective solution',[52] which is:

> Paying benefits only to those who CANNOT work. The able-bodied lose their welfare cheque if they refuse employment. It has transformed lives, rebuilt families, restored the work ethic ... And saved a fortune in taxes.[53]

Overall, the role of poverty and social exclusion in creating an underclass is often dismissed in these tabloid stories. Journalists alternatively would argue that,

> Poverty ceased to exist at some point over the last two decades and instead of finding ever more elaborate statistical methods of feigning a remaining underclass of several hundred thousand, we should take a legitimate, measured pride in the achievement of its abolition. Today's problems are not of poverty, they are of sustaining the once booming economy that defeated it.[54]

Conclusion

As we have seen from this study, Malthusian discursive regimes have remained the most important paradigm in defining the way poverty is reported by the tabloid press in Great Britain. It is a paradigm that seems to evolve and adapt after each economic crisis and subsequent period of austerity but that nevertheless seeks to constantly displace responsibility for the crisis from those in power towards those receiving charity or state benefits. What this research shows is that Malthusianism has mutated in each period into publically 'acceptable' rhetorical forms that are nevertheless able to carry with them the same message: that is, that some people deserve to be rich, some to be poor and that the poor do not deserve to exist.

Indeed, in this study we were able to observe that in times of financial crisis and austerity, Malthusian discursive regimes tend to be used by journalists in the tabloids as the default theoretical explanatory framework for poverty and as a guide to analyse public policy. However, as we also saw, this process has been far from homogenous, particularly after World War II, during the Keynesian 'welfare consensus', in which Malthusian discourses opted for state interventionism to limit the 'expansion' of the poor by means of population control and forced sterilisation.

We also discussed how the 1980s brought about an era in which Malthusian discursive regimes returned to the more laissez-faire worldview. An era in which it was argued that cuts in the welfare budget were necessary to allow the market forces to reduce the numbers of people in poverty. The return of classic liberal economic policy through neo-liberalism also meant a return to a more classical conceptualisation of Malthus and his ideas. The aftermath of the 2007/8 financial crisis with regards to the way the concept of the 'underclass' was employed by journalists in the tabloid press only confirms the tendency of using such rhetorical devices as a decoy to displace responsibility for the crisis in times of austerity. Indeed, our findings indicate that the Malthusian paradigm is present in the British tabloid press and that it deeply reflects the ideology and editorial policy of that segment of the media.

Despite government claims of being in this crisis 'together', the austerity plans have meant instead deep cuts in the welfare budget destined to the poorest and most vulnerable individuals of our society, while the richest continue with their affluent life styles characterised by bank bonuses and real estate bubbles. In light of this, the fourth estate instead of fulfilling its normative claims of speaking truth to power, seem to remain silent in the face of these excesses, celebrating instead lavish behaviour through stories about celebrities (Johansson, 2008) and business people (Boyle & Kelly, 2012) while blaming the most vulnerable for the state we are in.

Disclosure statement

No potential conflict of interest was reported by the authors.

Notes

1. Fraser Nelson, A Triple Blight that Curses us All, *The News of the World*, 26 August 2007.
2. 1st, Benefits of work, *Daily Mail*, 27 May 2008.
3. Iain Duncan Smith, Where gangs are the only family, *Daily Mail*, 24 August 2007.
4. Lorraine Kelly, Knife ads can't cut it, *The Sun*, 31 May 2008.
5. News, Kid crime kings rise, *The Sun*, 10 February 2010.
6. Bob Roberts, We'll give Migrants Amnesty, *The Mirror*, 19 September 2007.
7. Martyn Brown, At last, a return to classroom discipline, *The Express*, 2 September 2011.
8. Amanda Platell, The joker who's brought back spite and envy, *Daily Mail*, 29 November 2008.
9. Kelvin Mackenzie, Ramsay is my telly nightmare, *The Sun*, 22 November 2007.
10. Stephen Glover, The Left claim 'chav' is a term of class hatred. Nonsense. It's today's tragic underclass they should be fighting for, *Daily Mail,* 17 July 2008.
11. Leading Article, Dignity in torment, *The News of the World*, 20 January 2008.
12. Jon Gaunt, Karen's in a class of her own, *The Sun*, 18 April 2008.
13. Richard Littlejohn, Land of the rising scum, *Daily Mail*, 14 November 2008.
14. Jon Gaunt, Karen's in a class of her own, *The Sun*, 18 April 2008.
15. Editorial, Betrayed again, *The Sun*, 5 December 2008.
16. Jon Gaunt, More Shannons in Benefits R Us hell, *The Sun*, 5 December 2008.
17. Kelvin Mackenzie, STOP TEEN YOB ABUSE, *The Sun*, 5 February 2009.
18. Editorial, Holding baby, *The Sun*, 14 February 2009.
19. Jon Gaunt, Chaos?, I can show you chaos, *The Sun*, 22 May 2009.
20. Jon Gaunt, Chuck it in, Mandy, *The Sun*, 13 March 2009.
21. Fergus Shanahan, Slobs AND nobs are cheating taxpayers, *The Sun*, 4 August 2009.
22. Fergus Shanahan, Slobs AND nobs are cheating taxpayers, *The Sun*, 4 August 2009.
23. News Front Page, Labour's lost it, *The Sun*, 30 September 2009.
24. Jon Gaunt, EU boss..I can't Blair it, *The Sun*, 2 October 2009.
25. Lorraine Kelly, They weighed 92st and were held as examples of a feckless underclass who lay in front of the TV stuffing their faces with deep-fried lard, *The Sun*, 6 January 2010.
26. News, Kid crime kings rise, *The Sun*, 10 February 2010.
27. Martell Maxwell, Brandon mum still to blame, *The Sun*, 11 March 2009.
28. Carol Malone, Baby P: They're ALL guilty, *The News of the World*, 16 November 2008.
29. Anna Smith, No glamour in a ned's life, *The News of the World*, 23 January 2011.
30. Fraser Nelson, A Triple Blight that Curses us All, *The News of the World*, 26 August 2007.
31. David Blunkett, Boldness only way to Victory, *The Sun*, 9 January 2008.
32. Editorial, Cut 'em off, *The Sun*, 31 July 2009.
33. News Front Page, Labour's lost it, *The Sun*, 30 September 2009.
34. Jane Moore, Give poor kids their future back, Gordon, *The Sun*, 16 April 2008.
35. Jon Gaunt, Chaos?, I can show you chaos, *The Sun*, 22 May 2009.
36. Julia Hartley-Brewer, Let's be fair on welfare, *Sunday Express*, 14 December 2008.
37. Fergus Shanahan, Slobs AND nobs are cheating taxpayers, *The Sun*, 4 August 2009.
38. Patrick O'Flynn, Why our European Union membership spells doom for welfare reform, *The Express*, 19 June 2010.
39. Patrick O'Flynn, Why our European Union membership spells doom for welfare reform, *The Express*, 19 June 2010.
40. Education Correspondent, White and Male?, Go to the bottom of the class, *Daily Mail*, 8 June 2008.
41. 1st, Is Labour's legacy a welfare underclass, *Daily Mail*, 7 February 2008.

42. Karen Matthews was convicted of 'false imprisonment and perverting the course of justice' after being part of a conspiracy to kidnap her own daughter in February 2008, the case was widely reported in the media.
43. Graeme Wilson, The shambles of our shameless, *The Sun*, 7 October 2010.
44. Leader, Brown's bid for middle class support is doomed, *The Express*, 18 January 2010.
45. Leader, Middle Britain looses again, *The Express*, 14 January 2009.
46. Editorial, Betrayed again, *The Sun*, 5 December 2008.
47. Jon Gaunt, Karen's in a class of her own, *The Sun*, 18 April 2008.
48. Jon Gaunt, Karen's in a class of her own, *The Sun*, 18 April 2008.
49. Fraser Nelson, A Triple Blight that Curses us All, *The News of the World*, 26 August 2007.
50. Jason Beattie, I Predict a Riot; Union leader rages at government assaults on pensions and the NHS, *Daily Mirror*, 10 September 2011.
51. Julia Hartley-Brewer, Spongers are soaking up our hard earned billions, *Sunday Express*, 30 August 2009.
52. Sun Says: Leading Article, Just the job, *The Sun*, 9 November 2007.
53. Sun Says: Leading Article, Just the job, *The Sun*, 9 November 2007.
54. Richard Waghorne, The CPA should crack open the champagne and close its doors, *Daily Mail*, 5 September 2007.

References

Allan, S. (1999). *News culture*. Buckingham: Open University Press.

Avery, J. (1997). *Progress, poverty and population: Re-reading Condorcet, Godwin and Malthus*. London: F. Cass.

Bauman, Z. (1998). *Work, consumerism and the new poor*. Buckingham: Open University Press.

Boltanski, L. (1999). *Distant suffering: Morality, media and politics*. Cambridge: Cambridge University Press.

Boychuk, G. W. (1998). *Patchworks of purpose: The development of provincial social assistance regimes in Canada*. Montreal: McGill-Queen's University Press.

Boyle, R., & Kelly, L. W. (2012). *The television entrepreneurs: Social change and public understanding of business*. Burlington, VT: Ashgate.

Bullock, H. E., Fraser Wyche, K., & Williams, W. R. (2001). Media images of the poor. *Journal of Social Issues*, *57*(2), 229–246. doi:10.1111/0022-4537.00210

Chouliaraki, L. (2013). *The ironic spectator: Solidarity in the age of post-humanitarianism*. Cambridge, MA: Polity.

Cockett, R. (1994). *Thinking the unthinkable: Think-tanks and the economic counter-revolution 1931–1983*. London: HarperCollins.

Cohen, S. (2011). *Folk devils and moral panics the creation of the Mods and Rockers Routledge classics*. Retrieved from https://www.dawsonera.com/guard/protected/dawson.jsp?name=https://lse.ac.uk/idp&dest=http://www.dawsonera.com/depp/reader/protected/external/AbstractView/S9780203828250

Conboy, M. (2002). *The press and popular culture*. London: SAGE.

Conboy, M. (2006). *Tabloid Britain: Constructing a community through language*. London: Routledge.

Connelly, M. J. (2008). *Fatal misconception: The struggle to control world population*. Cambridge, MA: Belknap.

Critcher, C. (2003). *Moral panics and the media*. Buckingham: Open University Press.

Darwin, C. (1958). *The autobiography of Charles Darwin, 1809–1882. With original omissions restored. Edited, with appendix and notes, by … Nora Barlow. [With plates, including portraits.]*. London: Collins.

Daunton, M. J. (1995). *Progress and poverty: An economic and social history of Britain 1700–1850*. Oxford: Oxford University Press.

Deacon, A. (1973). The abuse of social security. *The Political Quarterly*, *44*(3), 345–349. doi:10.1111/j.1467-923X.1973.tb02103.x

Deacon, A. (1978). The scrounging controversy: Public attitudes towards the unemployed in contemporary Britain. *Social Policy & Administration*, *12*(2), 120–135. doi:10.1111/j.1467-9515.1978.tb00127.x

Dijk, T. A. v. (1988). *News as discourse*. Hillsdale, NJ: L. Erlbaum Associates.

Fernández Martínez, D. (2007). From theory to method: A methodological approach within critical discourse analysis. *Critical Discourse Studies*, *4*(2), 125–140. doi:10.1080/17405900701464790

Fowler, R. (1991). *Language in the news: Discourse and ideology in the press*. London: Routledge.

Franklin, B. (1999). *Social policy, the media and misrepresentation*. London: Routledge.

Gans, H. J. (1995). *The war against the poor: The underclass and antipoverty policy*. New York, NY: BasicBooks.

de Goede, M. (1996). Ideology in the US welfare debate: Neo-Liberal representations of poverty. *Discourse & Society*, *7*(3), 317–357. doi:10.1177/0957926596007003003

Golding, P., & Middleton, S. (1982). *Images of welfare: Press and public attitudes to poverty*. Oxford: M. Robertson.

Hackett, R. A. (1984). Decline of a paradigm? Bias and objectivity in news media studies. *Critical Studies in Mass Communication*, *1*(3), 229–259. doi:10.1080/15295038409360036

Harvey, D. (2005). *A brief history of neoliberalism*. New York, NY: Oxford University Press.

Hayward, K., & Yar, M. (2006). The 'chav' phenomenon: Consumption, media and the construction of a new underclass. *Crime, Media, Culture*, *2*(1), 9–28. doi:10.1177/1741659006061708

Hutton, W. (1996). *The state we're in* (Fully rev. ed. ed.). London: Vintage.

I Campos, A. (2014). *El delito de ser pobre : una gestión neoliberal de la marginalidad*. Barcelona: Barcelona: Icaria Editorial.

Johansson, S. (2008). Gossip, sport and pretty girls. *Journalism Practice*, *2*(3), 402–413. doi:10.1080/17512780802281131

Jones, O. (2011). *Chavs: The demonization of the working class*. London: Verso.

Kasun, J. (1988). *The war against population: The economics and ideology of world population control*. San Francisco, CA: Ignatius Press.

Katz, M. B. (1990). *The undeserving poor: From the war on poverty to the war on welfare*. New York, NY: Pantheon Books.

Katz, M. B. (1995). *Improving poor people: The welfare state, the 'underclass,' and urban schools as history*. Princeton, NY: Princeton University Press.

Kendall, D. E. (2005). *Framing class: Media representations of wealth and poverty in America*. Lanham, MD: Rowman & Littlefield.

Klein, N. (2007). *The shock doctrine: The rise of disaster capitalism*. London: Allen Lane.

Leader, B. (2012, August 5). Five years ago, the credit crunch began; today it's worse. How long will it last?, *The Observer*. Retrieved from http://www.theguardian.com/business/2012/aug/05/credit-crunch-august-2007-recession

Lister, R. (2004). *Poverty*. Cambridge, MA.: Polity.

Lugo-Ocando, J. (2015). *Blaming the victim: How global journalism fails those in poverty*. London: Pluto Press.

Lugo-Ocando, J., & Harkins, S. (2015). The poverty of ideas in the newsroom. In *Blaming the victim: How global journalism fails those in poverty* (pp. 36–59). London: Pluto Press.

Malthus, T. R. (1996). *An essay on the principle of population*. London: Routledge.

Marks, R. (2007). *The origins of the modern world: Fate and fortune in the rise of the west* (Rev. and updated ed.). Lanham, MD: Rowman & Littlefield.

McKendrick, J. H., Sinclair, S., Irwin, A., O'Donnell, H., Scott, G., & Dobbie, L. (2008). *Transmitting deprivation: Media, poverty and public opinion in the UK* (pp.1–72). New York: Joseph Rowntree Foundation.

Mills, C. W. (1959). *The sociological imagination*. New York, NY: Oxford University Press.

Nichols, J. (2014). Defend journalism that speaks truth to power: From Ferguson to Washington. *The Nation*. Retrieved from http://www.thenation.com/blog/181309/defend-journalism-speaks-truth-power-ferguson-washington#

Ross, E. B. (1998). *The Malthus factor: Population, poverty and politics in capitalist development*. London: Zed.

Ruse, M. (2009). *Philosophy after Darwin: Classic and contemporary readings*. Princeton, NJ: Princeton University Press.

Serr, K. (2006). *Thinking about poverty*. Annandale, Australia: The Federation Press.

Silva, E. B. (1996). *Good enough mothering; Feminist perspectives on lone motherhood*. London: Routledge.

Spencer, H. (1851). *Social statics: Or the conditions essential to human happiness specified, and the first of them developed*. London: John Chapman.

Steel, J. (2012). *Journalism & free speech*. London: Routledge.

Willson, H. C. (1950). Benthamism, laissez faire, and collectivism. *Journal of the History of Ideas, 11*(3), 357–363. doi:10.2307/2707736

Zizek, S. (2006). *The parallax view*. Cambridge, Mass.; London: MIT.

'I think it's absolutely exorbitant!': how UK television news reported the shareholder vote on executive remuneration at Barclays in 2012

Richard Thomas

Cardiff Business School, Cardiff University, Aberconway Building, Cardiff, UK

ABSTRACT

The most publicised rebellion during the so-called 'Shareholder Spring' of 2012 was at Barclays PLC. Using multi-modal and critical discourse analysis, this paper examines how three UK television channels with different public service obligations covered this story on 27 April 2012. It finds that broadcasters' regulatory obligations do not obviously impact content and that, for example, simple reporting routines contain judgemental phrases. Generally, the multi-dimensional nature of executive pay is simplified and the real balance between private and individual shareholders is obscured. Analysis also reveals that editing and the use of images can subtly construct discourses that may not reflect the reality of the dissent. The paper concludes that established criticisms that business journalism is indolent and that corporate discourses are privileged are not supported, but also that the coverage contributes little to promote wider understanding of executive pay debates.

Introduction

Almost anticipating the controversy surrounding executive remuneration two thousand years later, Plato proposed that the highest-paid Athenians should earn no more than five times more than the lowest (Morrow, 1993). More recently, Drucker suggested the ratio should not exceed 20 (Groom, 2014; Wartzman, 2008), but such advocacy appears idealistic in light of Tesco's Chief Executive earning 500 times more than his shelf-stackers (Judge, 2010), while ratios at Walt Disney apparently exceed 600:1 (Groom, 2014).

Drucker's prognosis that such inequality would generate widespread contempt (Rigby, 2011) proved prophetic in 2012 when 'excessive' pay at several UK corporations became headline news (see English, 2012; Williams, 2012). These rebellions are significant beyond their localised objectives since they implicitly challenge capitalism's basic premise that some people earn more than others (Ott, 2005). Alongside public intolerance of inequality (McCall, 2003), Wilkinson and Pickett (2010) are among those suggesting that widening income disparity is associated with negative health and social outcomes. Executive remuneration, therefore, is a zeitgeist issue, and its prominence within news agendas is potentially enhanced by the prevailing backdrop of austerity and suggestions that the current financial crisis is the result of unfettered profligacy, especially within the financial sector (Lawson, 2009; Shughart, 2009). This paper examines how one remuneration story was reported by three UK television (TV) news bulletins on the same day in April 2012.

TV news bulletins have ritual, iconic and strategic importance (Cushion, 2012; Fiske, 1987). Blending findings that 75% of adults use TV for news (Ofcom, 2014) with suggestions by Fairclough (2003) that 'texts' have causal effects, TV bulletins can be considered a powerful news platform. Callaghan and Schnell (2001, p. 203) summarise their reach by concluding that 'media have the power to actively shape public discourse by selecting from many available frames'. Given the complexity of executive remuneration, audiences may rely on TV news to debunk and contextualise it; its influence is further enhanced by the general decline in newspaper reading, and suggestions that *viewers* are less critical than *readers* (Belk & Kozinets, 2005). Moreover, TV news bulletins contain around a dozen stories versus approximately 300 in a newspaper (Hanley, 2009); since it incorporates the most abridged and refined of news agendas and an inherent time constraint (McCombs & Shaw, 1972), the potential to firstly tell audiences what to think *about* is compelling.

In addition to providing agendas, as 'fluent, intelligible versions of the world' (Montgomery, 2007, p. 20), TV news can also influence what viewers think *about* these issues. 'Framing' describes how news producers arrange information (Tuchman, 1978, p. 193), providing the 'central organizing idea' and story 'essence' (Gamson & Modigliani, 1987, p. 143). Consequently, framing highlights the salience of a particular line of interpretation, or promotes the interests of some groups rather than others (Hannah & Cafferty, 2006; Reese, 2007). According to Entman (1993), framing defines issues, interprets causality, evaluates moral dimensions and prescribes solutions. News reports about executive remuneration can therefore shape opinions (Herbst, 1998) which may themselves then function as 'disciplining devices' for private and public policy-making (Kuhnen & Niessen, 2012, p. 1250). This paper considers the coverage of the shareholder vote regarding remuneration at Barclays PLC as it appeared on BBC, ITV and SKY news bulletins on 27 April 2012. The following appraisal of literature comprises of an examination of the reporting of economic issues generally and a review of general themes associated with executive remuneration practice.

According to normative theories of news production, Economic, Business and Financial journalism – hereafter called 'EBF journalism' (Merrill, 2012) – should be a 'trusted ally' for concerned citizens (Schifferes & Coulter, 2012, p. 2) and 'untangle the complicated' (Seymour, 2009, p. 8). However, it is claimed that practitioners are scarce (Whitney & Wartella, 2000), inadequately trained (Doyle, 2007; Merrill, 2012) and prone to inaccurate reporting (Fost, 2002; Maier, 2002) while the profession generally recruits from a narrow, privileged demographic (Edwards & Cromwell, 2009). Against prescriptions that EBF journalism should hold commerce to account, instead there are accusations that it champions wealth, success and the narrow interests of businesses themselves (Lewis, 2013; McChesney, 2003; Tambini, 2010).

Another debate concerns whether news is 'dumbed down' (see Doyle, 2007; Franklin, 1997). Some argue that simplifying complex issues engages a wider audience (Langer, 1998; Temple, 2006) than simply 'older white males' (Hargreaves & Thomas, 2002, p. 53). However, the BBC, for example, is under increasing commercial pressure (Foster & Meek, 2008) perhaps inevitably resulting in 'simpler' news. Consequently, senior BBC journalists have expressed concern that the channel's news agenda has become increasingly tabloid and celebrity-led (Bingham, 2008; Jury, 2002). Allied with theories of insufficient probing, there are also claims that EBF reporting is overly reliant on sources from influential institutions (Berry, 2013), summarised by Lewis (2013, p. 122) as deferring to the 'same well-heeled sources that created or failed to anticipate the crisis in the first place'. Doyle (2007, p. 441) contends that 'experts' for example, are rarely 'disinterested' and that their insights usually benefit institutional investors. The compelling conclusion is that critics of EBF journalism significantly outnumber its supporters.

Scrutiny of EBF issues increases during time of financial crisis (Anderson, 2004; Kjær & Slaatta, 2007), particularly since in the past several financial scandals have not been anticipated in advance (Doyle, 2007; Tambini, 2010). The leitmotif of 'excess' is prominent within remuneration scholarship (Brown, 1992; Lissy & Morgenstern, 1994), especially as cutbacks are made in the name of 'austerity' (Dittmann, Maug, & Zhang, 2011, p. 1202), at the same time, executives receive increasingly attractive remuneration packages (Gómez-Mejia & Wiseman, 1997). There is also a contentious debate regarding the correlation between remuneration and performance, with some unsurprisingly finding that rewarding apparently substandard performance causes widespread angst (Brown, 1992; Lissy & Morgenstern, 1994; Perkins, 2009). In contrast, other research claims associations between pay levels and growth, share price and profitability (Coughlan & Schmidt, 1985; Deckop, 1988). Executive remuneration packages have also become more complex, and now typically contain a basic salary plus bonuses, stock options and pension elements (Dymond & Murlis, 2008). Consequently, there are suggestions that true remuneration levels are being 'camouflaged' by these complicating dimensions (Bebchuk & Fried, 2004; Kay & Van Putten, 2007), and that remuneration committees are deferential to those whose pay they set (Crystal, 1992; Lambert, Larcker, & Weigelt, 1993).

Within the era of austerity, many 'ordinary' citizens are finding that debt is more difficult to service while borrowing is restricted, welfare payments are cut and non-essential purchases are less affordable. Within the public sector, the enforcement of pay freezes and lower-than-inflation increases has contrasted markedly with reports of MPs claiming expenses for moat cleaning and the maintenance of helipads and swimming pools (Winnett, 2009). Against a similarly grim backdrop within the private sector, stories of corporate apartments finished with '$6,000 shower curtains' and '$15,000 umbrella stands' (English, 2003) have become indexical of the perceived disparity between those controlling and managing large corporations and their rank and file employees. Votes regarding executive remuneration are tangible, public platforms for expressing dissent over such alleged excess; such conflict and the challenging of corporate power offer broadcasters opportunities to provide wider commentaries about austerity and the financial climate.

Notwithstanding the contentious nature of contemporary executive remuneration, there is only a small corpus of research into its media coverage. Core, Guay, and Larcker (2008) consider *newspaper* coverage of executive pay debates and unsurprisingly conclude that high pay results in critical media coverage. Media coverage can also impact executive pay levels (Kuhnen & Niessen, 2012); equally predictably are findings that within US and UK newspapers leaning to the political left, executive pay is framed as a potentially vote-attracting issue (Culpepper, 2012). Tan and Crombie (2011) investigate stakeholder legitimisations regarding the remuneration of the New Zealand Telecom Chief Executive and find that both media and the public consider executive pay as excessive, but cite few examples of discourses used by executives themselves. Hamilton and Zeckhauser (2004) examine coverage of chief executive officers (CEOs) generally between 1970 and 1999 rather than their remuneration per se. They find that when the economy suffered, CEO coverage increased, indicating that 'bad news' attracted EBF journalists. In the same way CEOs are 'saints and then sinners' they suggest, coverage is subject to 'fits and fads' (Hamilton & Zeckhauser, 2004, p. 4) and in general, coverage of CEOs is reactive to the demands of news consumers. Such findings implicitly suggest that the media and their audiences find stories about executive pay especially newsworthy; indeed, a TV news anchor is quoted as suggesting that 'big pay packages for executives, big takeover targets, the huge corporate egos involved – these kinds of stories beat an episode of Dallas any day' (Hamilton & Zeckhauser, 2004, p. 3).

Theoretical approach and sample

This paper adopts epistemological assumptions consistent with critical realism, enhancing explanations of 'how' things happen with dimensions of 'why' (Guba & Lincoln, 2003, p. 211). Wright (2011, p. 160) validates critical realism as 'ethically and politically suited' to media research since it holds newsmakers to account for their output by examining the influencing circumstances and structures. This paper considers, therefore, how such structures and circumstances determine the presentation of the Barclays' shareholder vote.

When examining media output, the theory of *political economy* examines how owner-ship and control influence content (Hartley, 2011). McManus (1991) suggests that political economy exists on macro, meso and micro levels. These respectively relate to the pursuit of corporate profit, the institutional constraints shaping news and the response to demands for certain types of news. The analysis that follows uses this broad taxonomy to evaluate the three news reports in question.

The first of these elements – the pursuit of profit – is an established discourse. Herman and Chomsky (2002) contend that the large corporations owning media outlets have become increasingly concentrated, are solely motivated by financial return and have sym-biotic links with commerce and government. In terms of the type and shape of stories covered, political economy suggests that editors 'follow the money' (Devereux, 1998, p. 102). Consequently, and resonant with EBF journalism research, this analysis examines whether commercial channels offer more listless critiques of the remuneration controversy associated with a bank who may simultaneously provide it with advertising revenue. It also investigates whether the BBC performs according to its public service function and adheres to the Reithian promise to 'inform, educate and entertain' (Cushion, 2012; Debrett, 2010).

Another element of the model proposed by McManus (1991) is the provision of news according to demand. This could be interpreted as adhering to established models of 'news values' or the characteristics within stories and events that editors anticipate their particular audiences will prefer (see Galtung & Ruge, 1965; Harcup & O'Neill, 2001; Harri-son, 2006). There are several elements within executive remuneration stories that news producers may find attractive. First, there is 'negativity' and 'conflict' as stakeholder groups may disagree about pay levels. Furthermore, attention is inevitably focussed on 'elite' personalities and in 2012, such stories also offered 'continuity', in that they were part of the ongoing 'Shareholder Spring'.

Notions of morality may be the most pertinent feature of remuneration stories, especially during post-crisis austerity. Despite claims that people accept inequality in a similar way they accept the weather – factually, rather than morally – since they are apparently powerless to change it (Scott, 1982), Kendall (2012) points out the common-sense notion of morally opposing what may be out of normal reach. The reporting of seemingly limitless remuneration while many slip towards poverty may tap into a readiness to feel outraged within watching audiences; reports can further accentuate emotive responses, for example, by describing a morally charged 'inequality' rather than the less pejorative 'gap' (Ryscavage, 2009, p. 15). Finally, in terms of salaries, ballot results, corporate performance details, other numerical data and 'fact', viewer perceptions that broadcasters are 'spinning' and mediating stories are minimised. This paper asks whether such news values are evident within the presentation of the three reports.

Each report comprises of still photographs, onscreen graphics, video footage and utterances from journalists, politicians, corporate spokespersons and others. The stories analysed were taken from ITV (6.30 pm bulletin), SKY (9 pm bulletin) and the BBC (10 pm bulletin) which are routinely recorded by *Cardiff School of Journalism, Media and Cultural Studies*. The UK's broadcasting system is a 'mixed model' combining public service obligations with commercial elements (Leiss & Botterill, 2005, p. 112) and the channels chosen for analysis reflect the breadth of this model. Ofcom (2014) finds that the BBC, ITV and SKY are the three most widely viewed sources of UK broadcast news, and the *raison d'être* and regulatory burden of each can be contextualised as the institutional constraints noted by McManus (1991). The three channels can be described thus:

BBC – The public service broadcaster is funded by a licence fee, and its output is determined by Royal Charter. Former Chairman Michael Grade asserted that 'the BBC has a duty to set a gold standard in news reporting' in terms of 'accuracy' and 'impartiality' (Machin, 2008, p. 60). However, there are more recent suggestions that it has 'been pushed to the right' (Burrell, 2014).

The other broadcasters considered here have their output determined by Ofcom, a 'light touch' regulatory body (Barnett, 2012).

ITV – This commercial broadcaster comprises of a network of independent regional organisations owned by Carlton-Granada (Cushion, 2012) and is funded by advertising revenue (Johnson & Turnock, 2005). Among UK commercial broadcasters, ITV carries the heaviest public service regulatory burden (Cushion, Lewis, & Ramsay, 2012).

SKY – This satellite commercial broadcaster is owned by News Corporation (Schlesinger, 2006) and is funded by subscriptions and advertising. Despite being obliged to provide impartial journalism, it is not actually obliged to provide news or current affairs at all; consequently, of the three channels, it has the lightest regulatory obligations (Cushion et al., 2012). Indeed, Cushion (2010) suggests that SKY News is a rather unexpected enterprise, given the rest of Rupert Murdoch's broadcasting portfolio, also noting suspicions from others that it may be strategically attempting to upgrade SKY's wider brand image.

Research method

Firstly, 'text' is used here in its widest definition to include TV news reports. Widdowson (2000, p. 22) asserts that consumers of texts understand them in 'normal pragmatic ways, inferring meanings'. Consequently, and consistent with critical realism (Farrelly, 2010; Iosifide, 2011), social actor speech within these reports was analysed using Critical Discourse Analysis (CDA). Viewing language as 'everywhere' and 'always political' (Gee, 1999, p. 1), CDA aims to reveal 'forensic goals, hidden meanings and value structures' (Coupland & Jaworski, 2006, p. 33). It connects texts to social structures, which in this case could include broadcasting corporations, political parties and shareholder alliances. CDA examines how language is ideologically commandeered (Machin & Mayr, 2012) and pertinently for studying contentious remuneration debates, Montgomery (2007, p. 20) implicitly ratifies CDA by suggesting that 'reflective commentary' of broadcast news considers 'bias, (mis)representation, inaccuracy, distortion, ideology, "dumbing-down" and selective construction'.

Montgomery (2007) also asserts that broadcasting employs different operational practices from those used in print; news is consumed in real time, and in an order determined by the TV news editor. Analysing TV news therefore requires techniques that are specifically sensitive to it and accordingly, CDA increasingly incorporates examining modes of visual communication as well as verbal ones. Analysis of words is enhanced by considering 'images, layouts, gestures, and sounds' to provide 'enriching and insightful analysis' (Lazar, 2007, p. 144). Pertinent for news analysis, multi-modal approaches propose that like words, images also carry ideological loadings (Kress & Van Leeuwen, 1996; Machin, 2007).

The analytical techniques associated with CDA have been applied to news broadcasts internationally, for example, to examine coverage of Hurricane Katrina (Johnson, Sonnett, Dolan, Reppen, & Johnson, 2010), the reporting of severe acute respiratory syndrome in Belgium (Joye, 2010) and conflict in the former Yugoslavia (Pankov, Mihelj, & Bajt, 2011). This research takes a similar approach to Ekstrom (2001), in that it quantifies some rudimentary variables to supplement CDA; the small quantitative element includes timing report lengths and the lengths of the journalistic contributions within them.

This paper addresses the following questions:

> What discourses and news frames characterise the news reports covering the Barclays shareholder vote on executive remuneration on 27th April 2012 as shown BBC, ITV and SKY? Which types of social actors are interviewed and quoted within the reports?

and

> How do different levels of regulatory obligation shape how the three broadcasters present the story?

Ahead of a discussion about the wider implications of the findings, each report is described and presented in a two-columned table reflecting the simultaneous nature of verbal and visual dimensions (see Tables 1–3). The descriptions include report lengths measured from the beginning of the first word relating to the item (excluding any appearances in headlines at the start of the bulletins) and the length of journalistic contributions, which are defined as the verbal commentaries made by anchors or reporters, rather than those offered by other social actors or groups.

Table 1. The BBC report

Visual	Verbal
Backdrop of Barclays logo and photograph of CEO Bob Diamond	Anchor Fiona Bruce introduces the story
Graphic explaining details of Diamond's proposed pay	Business Editor Robert Peston describes shareholder unhappiness
Vox populis with shareholders outside the meeting, speaking to unseen interviewer	Shareholders give their views – they are critical of the pay by a factor of 3:1
Peston speaks to camera outside shareholder meeting	Peston explains the imbalance between Barclays' share dividends and their total payroll costs
Tim Bush (Pensions and Investment Research Group) speaks to unseen interviewer	Comments on remuneration levels
Sarah Wilson (Manifest) speaks to unseen interviewer	Comments on remuneration levels
Secretary of State for Business, Innovation and Skills Vince Cable speaks to unseen interviewer	Comments about how rewards should be appropriate
Barclays CEO Bob Diamond drinks wine at a social event	Peston concludes the report

Notes: Length of report: 3 minutes: 14 seconds. Length of journalistic contribution: 1 minute: 58 seconds (60.8% of total report).

Findings

Lexical choices (i.e. words specifically selected ahead of appropriate alternatives) reveal overriding discourses (Machin & Mayr, 2012) and convey value judgements and meanings (Richardson, 2007). Consequently, in the BBC report (See Table 1), Fiona introduces the story with evaluative selection, describing the 'powerful message' about 'big' bonuses and Bob Diamond's 'huge' pay. Furthermore, the term 'revolt' to describe shareholder dissent evokes a larger-scale conflict despite the vote against being only 'nearly 27%'.

Social actor 'agency' describes those with 'power' (Machin, 2007, p. 123). Noting the 'powerful message', their 'stand' and 'protest', Bruce gives agency to shareholders rather than to Barclays who are positioned on the receiving end of the voter dissent. Throughout the report, despite one ambiguous reference to 'big shareholders', neither Bruce nor Peston differentiates between private and institutional shareholders, and via the technique of *collectivization* (van Leeuwen, 1996), frequent references to 'many' represents investors as a homogenous group. Describing investors as cognate implies shared traits and mentalities (Reisigl & Wodak, 2001), and here it is generally unclear whether the protest includes institutional, private shareholders or both.

However, it is inferred from the appearance, clothing, proximity and a lack of evidence to the contrary that the contributing shareholders within the vox populis are private individuals (Figure 1). Three of these shareholders express discontent about Diamond's remuneration in terms of their dividend payments. One in particular makes strong lexical choices of 'exorbitant' pay and 'paltry' dividends and notably, a 27% shareholder 'revolt' is not reflected onscreen; critical shareholders outnumber supportive ones by 3:1.

By suggesting that Barclays have 'short-changed' shareholders, Robert Peston establishes a moral backdrop invoking the bank's rightful duties and responsibilities (see Harré & Van Langenhove, 1999). He accentuates the negativity and embellishes the conflict by asserting that shareholder disquiet has 'gone global', although his corroborative evidence involves only two other countries.

Whoever the 'big shareholders' are, they apparently have no voice in the report and their agency is removed. Tim Bush of *Pensions and Investment Research Consultants* (PIRC) establishes the familiar structural opposition between reward and performance

*"Too much bonuses, not
enough going back to
the shareholders..."*

*"I think it's absolutely
exorbitant what Bob
Diamond is getting –
for the amount of
dividend we get it's
absolutely paltry..."*

*"If he can have that much
in salary, why can't they
give – afford to give the
shareholders more than
3p a share in dividends..."*

Figure 1. Shareholders are critical of the pay award. BBC 10pm bulletin, 27 April 2012 http://bobnational.net/record/98446

(Figure 2) and his statement is notable for its high modality – the measure of the 'degree of commitment to the factuality of statements' (Saeed, 1997, p. 125).

Bush's lexical choices of 'significant', 'whatsoever', performance going 'backwards' and rewarding 'failure' make for a damning critique. The absence of any modal qualifiers like 'possibly' and 'probably' defining the strength of a claim (Flick, 1998; Quinton & Smallbone, 2006) enhances it further. Sarah Wilson from *Manifest* uses the metaphor of change at the 'top table', invoking associations with fine dining. Bob Diamond is later seen drinking wine, reinforcing notions of indulgence (Figure 3). Barclays themselves are indirectly quoted, and their Chairman offers a concessionary apology, for not listening to shareholder views well enough, rather than for the levels of pay involved. Arguably, this expression of regret, such as it is, is nullified by an uncompromising and highly modal assertion that removing bonuses 'is not an option'.

*"There's a significant
reward here for effectively
no performance whatsoever
– this is a company whose
performance has gone
backwards. This is a reward
for failure."*

Figure 2. The comments by Tim Bush. BBC 10pm bulletin, 27 April 2012 http://bobnational.net/record/98446

"His current pay won't be affected by the shareholder vote, although Barclays says it is paying attention to what shareholders want and hopes they too will have something to toast –bigger dividends – in years to come."

Figure 3. The concluding image. BBC 10pm bulletin, 27 April 2012 http://bobnational.net/record/98446

In April 2012, the minister overseeing any legislative process concerning shareholder power was Vince Cable. His contribution to this report reflects the political element within debates about executive remuneration, and whether governments should intervene in such matters within neoliberal economic systems. Referring to shareholders, he suggests that ' ... they, like me want to see good business and successful business properly rewarded ... ' This associates him with common-sense notions about fair reward, resonant with the concept of *conforming/decoupling*, where legitimisation is achieved by associating oneself with what appear to be acceptable values (Meyer & Rowan, 1977). By suggesting that 'where pay is excessive and unreasonable, shareholders have got to take responsibility and act ... ' Cable places agency with investors and perhaps mitigates government obligations, consistent with a free-market ethos. Moreover, his comments could be interpreted as a further call to action aimed towards investors.

This is the lead story within the BBC bulletin. As the corporation does not rely on advertising revenue, positioning shareholder disquiet and controversial remuneration as apparently the day's top story supports theories that the BBC may be comfortable criticising commercial organisations. Furthermore, it develops a political dimension to the story absent from the other reports considered here, underpinning notions that it offers an 'establishment view' (Hargreaves, 2003, p. 27). In sum, notwithstanding the BBC's imperative for high standards of objectivity, the report describes Barclays' intransigence regarding bonus payments, its unwillingness to compromise, and concludes with Bob Diamond drinking wine. The conclusion is that the general theme of conflict is preferred to any explanation about the cause, effect and wider implications of executive remuneration or indeed any sort of justification for them.

In the SKY report (see Table 2), Mark Longhurst opens by reporting that 'more than a quarter of Barclays' shareholders voted against the bank's controversial pay deals'. With the vote set as the dominant clause, Longhurst establishes 'protest' as the story's central frame. 'Rhetoric' is the process of persuasion (Burke, 1969) and within the concept, Atkinson (1984) posits that developing a 'contrast' is a familiar device; by describing the vote as 'a quarter against' rather than 'three quarters for', Longhurst institutes an early discourse of conflict, perpetuated by suggestions that high remuneration prevails despite poor corporate results.

Table 2. The SKY report

Visual	Verbal
Plain backdrop	Anchor Mark Longhurst introduces the story
Shareholder protests outside the AGM and a brief exchange between disagreeing shareholders	Reporter Tadhg Enright describes the disagreements
Cllr. Peter Brayshaw (Local Authority Pension Fund) speaks to unseen interviewer	Comments about the wider implications of executive remuneration
Louise Rouse (Fair Pensions Campaigner speaks to unseen interviewer	Comments about the wider implications of protest
Bob Diamond making a short statement to a Commons Select Committee	Suggests that 'banker remorse' should end
Graphic outlining proposed pay, and a statement by Barclays Chairman Marcus Aguis	Enright outlines details of remuneration package
Tadhg Enright speaks to camera outside the meeting	Explains balance between dividends and payroll
Simon Walker (Institute of Directors) speaks to unseen interviewer	Calls for balance to be restored
Shareholders leave meeting	Enright concludes the report

Notes: Length of report: 3 minutes: 8 seconds. Length of journalistic contribution: 1 minute: 53 seconds (60.1% of total report).

Reporter Tadhg Enright continues the conflict binary between executives and shareholders by describing the increasing gap between salaries and dividends. Van Leeuwen and Wodak (1999) outline the linguistic strategy of *rationalisation* as legitimising a position by associating it with values widely understood as valid; here, Enright contextualises the vote by suggesting that the issue is relevant to the retirement pensions received by the population at large. This is the only report that contextualises this issue quite so broadly.

Moreover, SKY's coverage is also notable, in that it more clearly delineates corporate shareholders from private ones, emphasised by contributions from Louise Rouse and Cllr. Peter Brayshaw. Rouse represents *ShareAction,* which further research reveals to be a charity promoting responsible investment by pension funds and fund managers. In citing 'ordinary' people and jobs, Brayshaw invokes a moral justification (Van Leeuwen & Wodak, 1999) by referring to the specific – and reasonably assumed to be popular – notion that public service pensions must be honoured (Figure 4).

Enright enhances this point by suggesting that institutional investors 'are pension funds that many, if not most of us, depend on to fund our retirements'; in so doing, he connects the story to a much wider audience than simply the business community. He also describes the vote as 'democracy at work', although institutional investors 'tend not to speak out'.

"Dinner ladies, refuse collectors, people on relatively low pay – we have to pay their pensions – we want to pay their pensions – we need a good return on our investment to do that..."

Figure 4. An explanation of the wider relevance of the vote SKY 9pm bulletin, 27 April 2012 no BOB resource available

The verbal exchange between two unidentified men outside the meeting highlights a lack of shareholder consensus; one protestor invokes a rational argument indicating the potential consequences of continued protest, but the exchange is generally rather esoteric and ambiguous. This advances the theme of conflict beyond the Barclays/Shareholder binary; disagreement is now shown to exist within the shareholder community itself. Simon Walker from the *Institute of Directors* then describes Bob Diamond as a 'superstar'; this is exemplar of the discursive device of 'identity ascription' which maps traits and attitudes to social actors (see Antaki, 1998; Whittle & Mueller, 2011). The choice to include descriptions of a highly paid 'superstar' is in notable contrast to those with lower-ranking jobs whose pensions may be threatened.

This distinction is strengthened further when Diamond asserts that the 'period of remorse and apology for banks ... needs to be over'. However, this is an isolated prescription, with no accompanying reasoning and may be considered contentious and inflammatory; using a quote from 2011 and therefore out of context adds to the case that a discourse of 'conflict' is being determinedly constructed. Furthermore, Barclays Chairman Marcus Aguis then demonstrates low modality by preceding the concession of some wrongdoing with the approximator 'evidently' (Figure 5), suggesting something less than his full agreement that wrong has actually been done. Thereafter, he apologises for poor communication rather than for high pay levels, and promises no more than better 'engagement' with shareholders in the future, exemplar of evading the central point of high pay with 'euphemism, question-begging and sheer cloudy vagueness' (Orwell, 1971).

One manifestation of SKY's lesser regulatory encumbrance could be a more low-brow approach to news (Hargreaves & Thomas, 2002) and a preference for dramatising and featuring stories more often found in tabloid newspapers (Cushion & Lewis, 2009). Here, for example, SKY builds the conflict binary and focuses specific and unflattering attention on two senior Barclays executives, presenting them as phlegmatic, belligerent and only grudgingly apologetic. Nevertheless, SKY's approach is inconsistent with what may be reasonably expected from a lightly regulated commercial channel. Unlike the other channels, SKY expresses executive remuneration within a wider context and also makes attempts to explain the real shareholder power dynamic and the low potential impact of the dissenting vote.

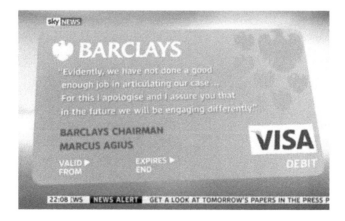

Figure 5. The Chairman's 'apology' SKY 9pm bulletin, 27 April 2012 no BOB resource available

Table 3. The ITV report

Visual	Verbal
Plain backdrop	Anchor Alastair Stewart introduces the story
Unknown man – later identified to be David Stredder (UK Individual Shareholders Society) – prepares to leave home	Business Editor Laura Kuenssberg describes the shareholder stand
Stredder speaks to unseen interviewer at an unidentified railway station	Comments about the incongruence of executive pay within the general economy
Graphic explaining the composition of the proposed pay and magnitude of the vote against it	Kuenssberg provides commentary
Stredder enters the meeting with protesters in the background	Kuenssberg explains that overseas voters dominated the vote
Main door is bolted	Kuenssberg explains that cameras were barred from entering
Kuenssberg speaks to camera outside meeting	Kuenssberg explains that cameras were barred from the meeting and describes the general mood inside
Frank Clark (Barclays Shareholder) speaks to unseen interviewer	Defends high pay
Lucy Marcus (Corporate Consultant) speaks to unseen interviewer	Advocates more transparent remuneration
Long shot of meeting and Stredder's return home	Kuenssberg providing summarising voiceover

Notes: Length of report: 2 minutes: 38 seconds. Length of journalistic contribution: 1 minute: 58 seconds (74.7% of total report).

For ITV (see Table 3), Anchor Alastair Stewart opens with the striking lexical choices of 'remarkable' barracking, shareholder 'fury' and 'bumper' pay. Many may concur that Diamond's pay is high by most ordinary measures, but arguably, ITV purposefully and consciously appraises this salary as high even within the context of the prevailing executive pay culture. Once again, lexical choices initiate discourses of conflict and protest; furthermore, the use of 'remarkable' aligns the story with the traditional news value of 'unexpectedness' (Galtung & Ruge, 1965; Harcup & O'Neill, 2001).

In common with the BBC report, ITV Business Editor Laura Kuenssberg does not offer any real insight into the difference between private and institutional shareholders or the numerical split, but describes a homogenous 'thousands of others' who 'are off to stand up to a rich and powerful institution'. By establishing one man – David Stredder – as representative of the revolt, Kuenssberg establishes a conflict where one side is identified with and clearly valorised (Montgomery, 2007); perhaps the wider audience may naturally identify with David Stredder as a contemporary 'David' attempting to slay 'Goliath' (Figure 6).

"Not just the usual morning routine, but the day that David Stredder and thousands of other shareholders set off to stand up to a rich and powerful institution."

Figure 6. David Stredder begins his journey. ITV 6.30pm bulletin, 27 April 2012 http://bobnational.net/record/98093

Kuenssberg uses further evaluative lexical choices describing 'booing' and 'laughter' at the shareholder vote, rather than more neutral descriptions such as 'Barclays' explanation did not satisfy the shareholders', or something similar. Kuenssberg also describes being prevented from entering the meeting and highlights the obstruction (alongside images of doors being bolted) by stating that 'protestors were kept out and we couldn't take our cameras in' (Figure 7). Seemingly, opposition and protest are accompanied by secrecy and obstruction.

Contrasting with thematic framings of news which give general evidence within wider contexts (Darwish, 2010) evident within the other reports, Kuenssberg employs an episodic construction featuring David Stredder's journey to the Barclays meeting as the central element. He is seen leaving home, arriving in London, entering the meeting and finally beginning his return journey some time later. This narrative spans the entire report and is indicative of the general shareholder quest. In contrast with the other reports, however, Kuenessberg explains the multi-dimensional composition of the executive pay package by explaining that although the pay was 'set at six point three million' if you 'count long term incentives' then the total 'is more than seventeen'.

As with the BBC report, airtime is given to a shareholder who apparently supports the pay award. Frank Clark – ambiguously identified as a 'Barclays Shareholder' but presumably speaking only for himself – uses a basic economic rationalisation whereby 'if we pay him twenty million pounds and he brings in a hundred million pounds, we're making eighty million pounds profit'. ITV choose a sound bite from Clark which, as in case of the SKY report, ascribes 'superstar' status to an unnamed Barclays executive. This character is apparently personally and singularly responsible for profitable results, the details of which are not referred to elsewhere in this or any of the other reports. Clark's coda of ' … what they moaning about?' emphasises disunity within the shareholder community. The vaguely labelled 'Corporate Consultant' Lucy Marcus describes a time of extraordinary change, which without further elaboration, sits incongruously alongside the reality of a non-binding dissenting vote amounting to just 27% against.

Only ITV does not specifically mention Bob Diamond, and they position the story seventh in their running order. Both may be unsurprising, given that ITV is funded by advertising revenue, provided by corporations like Barclays and others like them. By these measures, ITV's coverage seems pro-business, in that they are not explicitly critical

"There was some heckling, some booing and even laughter at the bank's explanation after shareholder after shareholder complained about pay … protestors were kept out and we couldn't take our cameras in…"

Figure 7. ITV is locked out of the shareholder meeting. ITV 6.30pm bulletin, 27 April 2012 http://bobnational.net/record/98093

of specific personalities and do not prioritise the story within their running order. None-theless, their tone and framing are *explicitly* critical; for example, Kuenssberg's descriptions of being prevented entry to the annual general meeting (AGM) and the general share-holder derision are elements absent from the other reports. In this respect, ITV contravenes common-sense notions that they might take a more benign stance regarding corporate controversies.

With an episodic framing focusing on David Stredder's journey, however, ITV signifi-cantly simplifies executive remuneration for public consumption. Riker (1993) and Ness (2008) assert that episodic framings are more likely to generate viewer empathy and inter-est, perhaps amplified here by a 'David versus Goliath' narrative reflecting the 'underdog' taking on a powerful global banking institution. Within this sample at least, such construc-tions undermine notions that only corporate elites feature within EBF journalism (Davis, 2000). However, episodic framings also reduce complex issues 'to the level of anecdotal evidence' (Iyengar, 1991, pp. 136–137) where context is removed and coverage reduced to a 'fleeting parade of events' (Dimitrova & Strömbäck, 2012, p. 493), meaning under-standings are 'disorganized and isolated' (de Vreese, 2003, p. 38). In sum, instead of offer-ing wider analysis, ITV represents the general issue of executive pay with one shareholder's literal and metaphorical journey and their barred entry to an unruly AGM. It is a good example perhaps, of 'image crowding out rational analysis' (Bird, 2000, p. 221).

Discussion

Despite 'consensual' views that journalists seek the truth (Machin, 2008, p. 62), media scho-larship proposes that news is not objective reality, but a construction of it (Potter, 2010). Consequently, representations of the shareholder vote comprise of the visual and verbal elements determined by news editors. Explicitly or implicitly, consciously or unconsciously, *some* elements of reality are included while others are excluded or marginalised (Mon-tgomery, 2007). Consequently, social actors are seemingly powerless over the ways they are edited and contextualised; therefore, conclusions here can only be drawn about edi-torial choices and the ways channels decided to present the Barclays vote.

As a precursor to the discussion of findings, a BBC News report on 15 May 2009 is exem-plar of how TV news might shape understandings of executive pay. Surrounded by bottles of champagne, Robert Peston describes a 'big buck bonus culture' within the banking sector, connoting excess and affluence, and confirming the importance of visual elements within news reports. Such imagery is 'highly salient for viewers' (Gilens, 1996, p. 528) to the extent that it can even 'take precedence over the story itself' (Robinson, Else, Sherlock, & Zass-Ogilvie, 2009, p. 15). This paper has sought to advance such ideas, and coverage of the Barclays remuneration vote across three broadcasters also enables some direct com-parison. To address the first two research questions, however, there are also common themes that may have wider relevance.

First, the reports are all of similar length and characterised by the discourse of conflict. This story might not actually have been considered newsworthy to begin with – after all, 73% of shareholders did not vote against the pay award. Instead, the facts – that pay is widely perceived as high and some shareholders disputed it – are actively constructed using the emotive language of 'revolt'. Out-of-context apologies and belligerent state-ments about bonuses alongside images of wine drinking and socialising enhance likely outrage from the watching audience. Furthermore, and resonating with themes within EBF reporting and remuneration research, experts often have unclear affiliations, there is a well-defined theme of 'excess' and seemingly the links between pay and performance are tenuous. By marginalising or ignoring the complicating dimensions of executive remuneration, there is a general simplification consistent with theories that some stories will attract news editors more than others. Narratives about conflict, and even 'conflict within conflict' are highlighted, while justifying high remuneration, its cause and effect, and explanations of the wider logics of capitalism are generally ignored. None of the reports makes even the briefest of attempts to defend such high remuneration levels.

In the BBC and ITV reports, but to a lesser degree SKY, attention is concentrated on private shareholders who are seen as implicitly holding sufficient power to affect change, although coverage of private shareholders is disproportionate with the real investor power dynamic. The reality is that 'other businesses' own corporations like Barclays (Watson, 2008, p. 186) and that institutional investors are more influential than private ones (Goergen & Renneboog, 2001); the Office for National Statistics (2012) provides emphatic confirmation by showing that in 2012, individuals owned only 11.5% of available UK shares. Only SKY make it clear that institutional shareholders hold the balance of power, and that even if those voting against remuneration policy had won by even a significant majority, it would not have been binding. ITV's implicit narrative of private shareholding therefore obscures the realities of corporate ownership; 'David', or for that matter even many 'Davids' acting together will never slay 'Goliath'. Meanwhile, the absence of large shareholders within the reports may be explained by their generally passive stance regarding such issues (Goergen & Renneboog, 2001; Sheehan, 2011).

In addition to the ambiguous power dynamic, there are claims that the 'Shareholder Spring' itself may simply be a media construction. Hyde (2012), for example, questions the associating of shareholder rebellion with the 'Arab Spring'; she challenges how 'brutal regimes' can be compared to the 'courage' needed to attend an AGM 'at the Canary Wharf Hilton' to complain about unsatisfactory dividends. Robert Peston concurs the 'Shareholder Spring' was a 'myth' (see Hosking, 2012; Moore, 2013); just weeks after the report in this sample was broadcast, he notes that dissenting shareholder votes in 2012 were significantly less than the levels recorded, for example, in 2002 and 2003 (Peston, 2012). Indeed, while a 27% vote against the Barclays remuneration policy in 2012 merited a lead position and a report lasting over three minutes within the BBC report, in 2014, the Barclays vote against was 34% (Pratley, 2014; Spanier, 2014); yet, it did not appear at all in the corresponding BBC bulletin. Shareholder disagreement is part of daily corporate life, but without sharp focus on a central protagonist (Diamond) and other simultaneous protests (the wider 'Shareholder Spring'), the 2014 vote seemingly lacked sufficient momentum to propel it onto TV news agendas.

Evaluative lexical choices evident within the reports exemplify the paradox in contemporary TV news reporting as defined by Pounds (2012). First, TV news is legally bound to standards of impartiality more demanding than those applied to the written press (Montgomery, 2007). However, the strong visual dimension offers more opportunities to evoke emotion within presentations and the responses to them. While research suggests that printed media shows no such 'emotion' (Martin & White, 2005) and despite normative suggestions that news anchors should operate within restricted emotional ranges without revealing their social positioning (Montgomery, 2007), Pounds (2012) suggests that emotion is pervasive in TV news via verbal (lexical choice and voice intonation) and non-verbal means (facial expression, gestures and body language). Despite concerns that 'emotionalizing' news could indicate falling journalistic standards (Pantti, 2010), the three news anchors in this sample make evaluative choices. The judgemental language they use indicates that increasingly, editors and journalists are the chief sense-makers about executive remuneration, privileging some discourses and suppressing others (see Kjaer & Slaatta, 2007). This is especially true in the case of ITV, where commentary and interpretation account for almost 75% of the report time. While these scripts and choices *possibly* signal institutional and personal agendas, it can be concluded more certainly that none of the featured 'experts' could be reasonably described as neutral or impartial. Tim Bush, Sarah Walker and Lucy Marcus represent PIRC, *Manifest* and *Marcus Venture Consulting*, respectively; all are organisations closely allied to institutional shareholders. Simon Walker represents the *Institute of Directors* – their mission is to develop the interests of its members – by definition these are the recipients of high-end salaries.

However, established theories that EBF journalism is insufficiently critical of business are not supported by this small qualitatively analysed sample. Indeed, arguably, there are elements of schadenfreude regarding the difficulties experienced by Barclays, and the use of adjectives such as 'bumper' and 'huge' challenge accusations that EBF journalism is 'teeming with reverence for the accumulation of wealth' (Solomon, 2001). Within this research sample, therefore, the 'age of austerity' may be at least partly responsible for a considerable shift away from the supposed traditional norms of EBF journalism. Furthermore, and indicative of executive remuneration's position within contemporary political agendas (Kuhnen & Niessen, 2012), it is conceivable that the reporting of the wider 'Shareholder Spring' played some part in the development of the *Enterprise and Regulatory Reform Bill* which received Royal Assent in April 2013. This bill provides binding votes for shareholders regarding executive remuneration, meaning that instead of being symbolic but ultimately powerless, shareholder rebellions over pay now actually determine policy.

However, in terms of the wider ideals of accuracy and diversity within journalism, the conclusions are less positive. In answer to the first research question, the reports are characterised by simplified reports of congruent length, narratives of protest and conflict, a narrow range of social actor contributions and assertive, evaluative reporting which does not generally finesse the concept of shareholding. In sum, and returning to the model proposed by McManus (1991), the pursuit of corporate profit (courting potential advertisers) and the institutional constraints (regulatory burdens) that shape news are not obviously evident within these reports. However, there *is* evidence that certain news values influence story presentation into forms and frames that viewers may find more appealing.

ITV is arguably the most implicitly critical of Barclays, especially given their descriptions of secrecy and raucous criticism during the shareholder meeting. They alone attempt to unpick Diamond's multi-layered and possibly 'camouflaged' remuneration package, but their shorter, episodic presentation reduces the issue to the simplest form within the three reports. SKY provides what must be considered as the most comprehensive coverage, and makes attempts to contextualise and explain the wider implications of shareholder dissent. By referring to public sector pensions, they also potentially broaden the audience beyond the narrow demographic suggested by some EBF journalism research. Whether, as has been suggested, this is part of a highbrow upgrade of their brand or not, it seems that in this instance, SKY operates over and above the requirements of a low regulatory burden and provides the most informative and recondite expression of the vote.

Omitting social actor groups like remuneration committees, trade unions, institutional shareholders, academic commentators and truly independent experts, and misrepresenting shareholder power may have wider implications. Consistent with findings by Tan and Crombie (2011), there are no *direct* contributions from any highly paid executives, although they, like other social groups, may have refused to appear. However, it seems unlikely that trade unions, for example, would have turned down this opportunity, so it could be reasonably concluded that they were not asked to appear; if they were, they certainly did not appear in the final edited packages. Notwithstanding the time constraints within TV reporting, in the case of the BBC, articulating executive remuneration in such narrow terms arguably breaches their impartiality model, especially notable when public service broadcasters are apparently considered to be the most trustworthy news suppliers (see Cushion, 2012). Redefined as a 'wagon wheel' incorporating a wider spectrum of opinion than the traditional left-wing/right-wing 'see-saw' binary (Bridcut, 2007, p. 7), the concept of 'impartiality' is key to conclusions regarding the final research question. In the instance of the Barclays vote, therefore, contributions from interested groups like trade unions and remuneration committees may have more closely achieved 'wagon wheel impartiality'.

SKY's generally more informative report may support notions that despite continual financial losses, the channel is attempting to become 'something more respectable than a purveyor of football, films and American dramas' (Blighty, 2011). Data produced by Broadcasters' Audience Research Board (2014) reveal that at somewhere less than 750,000 viewers, SKY News bulletins lag some way behind the BBC 10 pm bulletin (regularly over 4 million) and the ITV 6.30 pm bulletin (regularly over 2.5 million). Notwithstanding audience size, it is still influential; in 2005, even the then head of BBC TV news told colleagues that SKY News 'remains the first port of call for key opinion formers' (Robinson, 2005). SKY's audience may therefore be smaller, but seemingly includes policy-makers and commercial elites. However, despite its apparent eminence and possible strategic position as the legitimising 'jewel in the crown', Rupert Murdoch was prepared to sacrifice SKY News as part of the attempt to buy all the shares in BSkyB before the phone hacking scandal at the *News of the World* scuppered the deal (Cushion et al., 2012).

Conclusion

Despite SKY's prominence here, this three-way analysis supports notions that despite varying regulatory burdens, TV news is to a large degree homogenous in terms of agenda and presentation (Barnett, 2012). Despite aspirations to provide 'wagon wheel' impartiality, the BBC presented the Barclays story in narrow terms and so it is difficult to resist the conclusion by Berry (2013, p. 268) that 'if it is to fulfil its mandate to provide a broad spectrum of opinion, there is a need to open up the parameters of economic debate in its most influential news programmes'. If the UK's public service broadcaster does not provide such a range of opinion and the widest of possible pictures, commercial channels with less regulatory obligations can hardly be relied upon to do so, despite SKY 'punching above its weight' within this small sample. This research suggests that journalism is still capable of holding business to account, but while as a collective, the three channels provide a reasonable analysis, no single report has the whole story of the Barclays vote. If Ofcom regulations were less, and broadcasters were given a completely free rein in terms of their editorial view (Barnett, 2012), then the result may have been three reports, that when viewed in parallel, offer a wider analysis with contributions from executives, remuneration committees, politicians, trade unions and all types of shareholder.

The reports and others like them may have encouraged executives to become more reflective about criticism of their pay. Moreover, they may have also played a part in reforming the remuneration practices of publically listed companies. However, in terms of accuracy and a more cerebral approach, it is hard to conclude anything other than that TV news has not advanced executive remuneration debates much beyond the 20-year-old assessment that the issue has reached 'Marie Antoinette proportions' and that people are 'disgusted' (Lublin, 1996). The executive remuneration narrative at Barclays is further complicated by increases in its bonus payments despite falling profits (Groom, 2014) and the shedding of thousands of its UK jobs (BBC, 2014). In this most recent context, therefore, the general compulsion to simplify is even less useful in helping viewers to make sense of these wider debates.

CDA has revealed the thrust of these broadcast reports, and references to political economy and varying regulatory obligations have enabled some conclusions about the possible ideological motivations of SKY, BBC and ITV. Given that much of UK programming concerning business and commerce such as *The Apprentice*, *Undercover Boss* and *Dragon's Den* is primarily produced to entertain, it falls to factual genres like news to inform wider understandings of commercial issues such as remuneration practice. During times of austerity, much of the population experiences some degree of economic discomfort; it seems reasonable that it should be widely represented and that diverse stakeholder and social groups should be provided with a voice. These findings suggest that without erudite, probing journalism, wider news audiences may not be given access to justifications for, and less emotional criticisms of executive pay, wide-ranging social actor opinion, the con-textualising of the issue within the wider economic system, or insights into the realities of private and institutional stockholding. For different reasons and to different degrees, it seems that these three broadcasters have missed the opportunity to nuance concepts of austerity, shareholder agency and inequality, and so have some distance to travel in order to move beyond simple notions of 'fat cats' and protest.

Acknowledgement

The author wishes to thank Dr Stephen Cushion for his invaluable comments during the draft stage of this paper.

Disclosure statement

No potential conflict of interest was reported by the author.

References

Anderson, B. (2004). *News flash: Journalism, infotainment, and the bottom-line business of broadcast news*. San Francisco, CA: Jossey-Bass.

Antaki, C. (1998). Identity ascriptions in their time and place: 'Fagin' and 'the terminally dim'. In C. Antaki & S. Widdicombe (Eds.), *Identities in talk* (pp. 71–86). London: Sage.

Atkinson, M. (1984). *Our master's voices*. London: Methuen.

Barnett, S. (2012). The *rise and fall of television journalism*: Just *wires and lights in a box*? London: Bloomsbury Press.

BBC. (2014, May 8). Barclays to cut 19,000 jobs over three years. *BBC news website*. Retrieved April 17, 2014, from http://www.bbc.co.uk/news/business-27321589

Bebchuk, L. & Fried, J. (2004). Pay without *performance: The unfulfilled promise of executive compensation*. Cambridge: Harvard University Press.

Belk, R., & Kozinets, R. (2005). Videography in marketing and consumer research. *Qualitative Market Research: An International Journal, 8*(2), 128–141.

Berry, M. (2013). The today programme and the banking crisis. *Journalism, 14*(2), 253–270.

Bingham, J. (2008). 'Dumbed down' BBC no longer knows what it is for, say former staff. The Telegraph. Media and Telecoms.

Bird, S. (2000). Audience demands in a murderous marketplace. In J. Tulloch & C. Sparks (Eds.), *Tabloid tales* (pp. 213–228). New York, NY: Rowman and Littlefield.

Blighty. (2011, May 3). The sky and the limit. The Economist. Retrieved May 20, 2012, from http://www.economist.com/blogs/blighty/2011/03/news_corporation_and_bskyb

Bridcut, J. (2007). From seesaw to wagon wheel: Safeguarding impartiality in the 21st Century. BBC Trust. Retrieved May 2, 2014, from http://www.bbc.co.uk/bbctrust/assets/files/pdf/review_report_research/impartiality_21century/report.pdf

Broadcasters' Audience Research Board. (2014). Top 30s. Retrieved on May 15, 2014, from http://www.barb.co.uk/viewing/weekly-top-30?_s=4

Brown, D. (1992). Can we put the brakes on CEO pay? *Management Review, 81*(5), 10–15.

Burke, K. (1969). *A grammar of motives*. Berkeley, CA: University of California Press.

Burrell, I. (2014, February 14). BBC accused of political bias – on the right, not the left. The Independent. Retrieved May 7, 2014, from http://www.independent.co.uk/news/uk/politics/bbc-accused-ofpolitical-bias–on-the-right-not-the-left-9129639.html

Callaghan, K. & Schnell, F. (2001). Assessing the democratic debate: How the news media frame elite policy discourse. *Political Communication, 18*, 183–213.

Core, J., Guay, W., & Larcker, D. (2008). The power of the pen and executive compensation. *Journal of Financial Economics, 88*, 1–25.

Coughlan, A., & Schmidt, R. (1985). Executive compensation, management turnover and firm performance: An empirical investigation. *Journal of Accounting and Economics, 7*, 43–66.

Coupland, N., & Jaworski, A. (2006). *The discourse reader*. London: Routledge.

Crystal, G. (1992). *In search of excess*. New York, NY: Norton and Co.

Culpepper, P. (2012). *The politics of executive pay in the United Kingdom and the United States*. European University Institute. Retrieved May 4, 2014, from http://federation.ens.fr/ydepot/semin/texte1213/CUL2013POL.pdf

Cushion, S. (2010). Rolling service, market logic: The race to be Britain's most watched news channel. In S. Cushion & J. Lewis (Eds.), The *rise of 24-hour news television: Global perspectives* (pp. 113–132). New York, NY: Peter Lang.

Cushion, S. (2012). *Television journalism*. London: Sage.

Cushion, S., & Lewis, J. (2009). Towards a 'Foxification' of 24-hour news channels in Britain? An analysis of market-driven and publicly-funded news coverage. *Journalism, 10*, 131–153.

Cushion, S., Lewis, J., & Ramsay, G. (2012). The impact of interventionist regulation in reshaping news agendas: A comparative analysis of public and commercially funded television journalism. *Journalism, 13*, 831–849.

Darwish, A. (2010). *A journalist's guide to live direct and unbiased news translation*. Melbourne: Writescope.

Davis, A. (2000). Public relations, business news and the reproduction of corporate elite power. *Journalism, 1*, 282–304.

Debrett, M. (2010). *Reinventing public service television for the digital future*. Chicago, IL: Intellect.

Deckop, J. (1988). Determinants of chief executive officer compensation. *Industrial and Labor Relations Review, 41*(2), 215–226.

Devereux, E. (1998). *Devils and angels: Television, ideology and the coverage of poverty*. Luton: John Libbey Media.

Dimitrova, D., & Strömbäck, J. (2012). Election news in Sweden and the United States: A comparative study of sources and media frames. *Journalism, 13*(5), 604–619.

Dittmann, I., Maug, E., & Zhang, D. (2011). Restricting CEO pay. *Journal of Corporate Finance, 17*, 1200–1220.

Doyle, G. (2007). Financial news journalism: A post-Enron analysis of approaches towards economic and financial news production in the UK. *Journalism, 7*(4), 433–452.

Dymond, J., & Murlis, H. (2008). Executive rewards 'don't you just give them loads of money? In S. Corby, G. Burrell, S. Palmer, M. Marchington, E. Lindop, & P. Thompson (Eds.), Rethinking *reward* (pp. 157–180). Basingstoke: Palgrave Macmillan.

Edwards, D., & Cromwell, D. (2009). *Newspeak in the 21st century*. London: Pluto Press.

English, S. (2003, November 26). The shower curtain that cost $6,000. The Telegraph. Retrieved September 20, 2014, from http://www.telegraph.co.uk/finance/2870083/The-shower-curtain-that-cost-6000.html

English, S. (2012, May 9). Shareholder revolt grows as Aviva's boss Andrew Moss falls on his sword. The Independent. Retrieved March 10, 2014, from http://www.independent.co.uk/news/business/news/shareholder-revolt-grows-as-avivas-boss-andrew-moss-falls-on-his-sword-7723321.html

Entman, R. (1993). Framing: Towards clarification of fractured paradigm. *Journal of Communication, 43*, 51–58.

Ekström, M. (2001). Politicians interviewed on television news. *Discourse and Society, 12*(5), 563–584.

Fairclough, N. (2003). Analysing *discourse: Textual analysis for social research*. London: Routledge.

Farrelly, M. (2010). Critical discourse analysis in political studies: An illustrative analysis of the 'empowerment' agenda. *Politics, 30*(2), 98–104.

Fiske, J. (1987). Television culture. London: Methuen.

Flick, U. (1998). An *introduction to qualitative research*. London: Sage.

Fost, D. (2002, March 3). Stung by Enron, business journalists increase their vigilance. San Francisco Chronicle, G1.

Foster, R., & Meek, K. (2008). Public *service broadcasting* in the United Kingdom: A *longer term view*. London: Social Market Foundation.

Franklin, B. (1997). Newszak and *news media*. London: Arnold.

Galtung, J., & Ruge, M. (1965). The structure of foreign news. The presentation of the Congo, Cuba and Cyprus crises in four Norwegian newspapers. *Journal of Peace Research, 2*, 64–90.

Gamson, W., & Modigliani, A. (1987). The changing culture of affirmative action. In R. Braungart (Ed.), *Research in political sociology* (Vol. *3*, pp. 137–77). Greenwich, CT: JAI Press.

Gee, J. (1999). *An introduction to discourse analysis theory and method* (2nd ed.). New York, NY: Routledge.

Gilens, M. (1996). Race and poverty in America: Public misperceptions and the American news media. *Public Opinion Quarterly, 60*(4), 515–535.

Goergen, M., & Renneboog, L. (2001). Strong managers and passive institutional investors in the U.K.: Stylized facts. In F. Barca & M. Becht (Eds.), The *control of corporate* Europe (pp. 258–284). Oxford: Oxford University Press.

Gómez-Mejia, L., & Wiseman, R. (1997). Reframing executive compensation: An assessment and outlook. *Journal of Management, 23*(3), 291–374.

Groom, B. (2014, March 10). If only Plato was running Barclays. *Financial Times*. Retrieved May 2, 2014, from http://www.ft.com/cms/s/0/c0ecff02-a84a-11e3-a946-00144feab7de.html#axzz30m5Qem9l

Guba, E., & Lincoln, Y. (2003). Competing paradigms and perspectives. In N. Denzin & Y. Lincoln (Eds.), *The landscape of qualitative research: Theories and issues* (2nd ed.) (pp. 105–117). Thousand Oaks, CA: Sage.

Hamilton, J., & Zeckhauser, R. (2004). *Media coverage of CEOs: Who? what? where? when? why?* Harvard University. Retrieved May 2, 2014, from http://www.anderson.ucla.edu/faculty_pages/romain.wacziarg/mediapapers/HamiltonZeckhauser.pdf

Hannah, G., & Cafferty, T. (2006). Attribute and responsibility framing effects in television news coverage of poverty. *Journal of Applied Social Psychology, 36*(12), 2993–3014.

Hanley, T. (2009). *Engaging public support for eradicating UK poverty*. York: Joseph Rowntree Foundation.

Harcup, T., & O'Neill, D. (2001). What is news? Galtung and ruge revisited. *Journalism Studies, 2*(2), 261–280.

Hargreaves, I. (2003). *Truth or dare?* Oxford: Oxford University Press.

Hargreaves, I., & Thomas, J. (2002). New news, old news. Ofcom. Retrieved May 4, from http://www.ofcom.org.uk/static/archive/bsc/pdfs/research/news.pdf

Harré, R., & Van Langenhove, L. (1999). The dynamics of social episodes. In R. Harre & L. Van Langenhove (Eds.), *Positioning theory* (pp. 1–13). Oxford: Blackwell.

Harrison, J. (2006). *News*. London: Routledge.

Hartley, J. (2011). *Communication, cultural and media studies: The key concepts*. London: Routledge.

Herbst, S. (1998). *Reading public opinion: How political actors view the democratic process*. Chicago, IL: University of Chicago Press.

Herman, E., & Chomsky, N. (2002). *Manufacturing consent: The political economy of the mass media*. New York, NY: Pantheon Books.

Hosking, P. (2012, November 19). Call that an uprising? Investor rebellions over pay were 'something of an illusion. The Times. Banking and Finance.

Hyde, M. (2012, May 12). Comment: This is no shareholder spring, just a new type of self-interest. *The Guardian*, p. 42.

Iosifide, T. (2011). *Qualitative methods in migration studies: A critical realist perspective*. Farnham: Ashgate.

Iyengar, S. (1991). *Is anyone responsible? How television frames political issues*. Chicago, IL: University of Chicago Press.

Johnson, C., & Turnock, R. (2005). Introduction: Approaching the histories of ITV. In C. Johnson & R. Turnock (Eds.), *ITV cultures: Independent television over fifty years* (pp. 1–12). Maidenhead: Open University Press.

Johnson, K., Sonnett, J., Dolan, M., Reppen, R., & Johnson, L. (2010). Interjournalistic discourse about African Americans in television news coverage of Hurricane Katrina. *Discourse & Communication, 4* (3), 243–261.

Joye, S. (2010). News discourses on distant suffering: A critical discourse analysis of the 2003 SARS outbreak. *Discourse & Society, 21*(5), 586–601.

Judge, P. (2010, November 14). How we lost grip of top pay. *The Sunday Times*, p. 2.

Jury, L. (2002, March 29). John Simpson joins attack on BBC's dumbed-down 'Six O'Clock News'. *The Independent*, p. 9.

Kay, I., & Van Putten, S. (2007). *Myths and realities of executive pay*. New York, NY: Cambridge University Press.

Kendall, D. (2012). *Framing class: Media representations of wealth and poverty in America* (2nd ed.). Lanham, MD: Rowman and Littlefield.

Kjaer, P., & Slaatta, T. (2007). *Mediating business: The expansion of business journalism*. Copenhagen: Copenhagen Business School Press.

Kress, G., & Van Leeuwen, T. (1996). *Reading images: The grammar of visual design*. London: Routledge.

Kuhnen, C., & Niessen, A. (2012). Public opinion and executive compensation. *Management Science*, *58*(7), 1249–1272.

Lambert, R., Larcker, D., & Weigelt, K. (1993). The structure of organizational incentives. *Administrative Science Quarterly*, *38*, 438–461.

Langer, J. (1998). *Tabloid television: Popular journalism and the 'other news'*. London: Routledge.

Lawson, R. (2009, February 1). Keeping directors in check. *The Guardian*. Retrieved May 7, from http://www.theguardian.com/commentisfree/2009/feb/01/company-directors-shareholders.

Lazar, M. (2007). Feminist critical discourse analysis: Articulating a feminist discourse praxis. *Critical Discourse Studies*, *4*(2), 141–164.

van Leeuwen, T. (1996). The representation of social actors in discourse. In C. Caldas-Coulthard & M. Coulthard (Eds.), *Texts and practices: Readings in critical discourse analysis* (pp. 32–70). London: Routledge.

Leiss, W., & Botterill, J. (2005). *Social communication in advertising: Consumption in the mediated marketplace*. New York: Routledge.

Lewis, J. (2013). *Beyond consumer capitalism: Media and the limits to imagination*. Cambridge: Polity.

Lissy, W., & Morgenstern, M. (1994). Currents in compensation and benefits. *Compensation and Benefits Review*, *26*, 8–15.

Lublin, J. (1996, April 11). America's New Continental Divide! The executives vs. the rest. *Wall Street Journal*, p. 1.

Machin, D. (2007). *Introduction to multimodal analysis*. London: Hodder Arnold.

Machin, D. (2008). News discourse I: Understanding the social goings-on behind news texts. In A. Mayr (Ed.), *Language and power: An introduction to institutional discourse*. (pp. 60–89). London: Continuum.

Machin, D., & Mayr, A. (2012). *How to do critical discourse analysis: A multimodal introduction*. Los Angeles, CA: Sage.

Maier, S. (2002). Numbers in the news: A mathematics audit of a daily newspaper. *Journalism Studies*, *3*(3), 507–519.

Martin, J., & White, P. (2005). *The language of evaluation. Appraisal in English*. Basingstoke: Palgrave.

McCall, L. (2003). *Do they know and do they care? Americans' awareness of rising inequality*. Working paper. New Brunswick, NJ: Rutgers University.

McChesney, R. (2003). The problem of journalism: A political economic contribution to an explanation of the crisis in contemporary US journalism. *Journalism Studies*, *4*(3), 299–329.

McCombs, M., & Shaw, D. (1972). The agenda-setting function of mass media. *Public Opinion Quarterly*, *36*(2), 176–187.

McManus, J. (1991). *Market driven journalism: Let the citizens beware?* London: Sage.

Merrill, G. (2012). The revolution must wait: Economic, business and financial journalisms beyond the 2008 crisis. *Ethical Space: The International Journal of Communication Ethics*, *9*(1), 41–51.

Meyer, J., & Rowan, B. (1977). Institutionalized organizations: Formal structure as myth and ceremony. *American Journal of Sociology*, *83*, 340–363.

Montgomery, M. (2007). *The discourse of broadcast news: A linguistic approach*. London: Routledge.

Moore, J. (2013). Figures reveal shareholder spring' a myth. *i-Independent*, p. 40.

Morrow, G. (1993). *Plato's Cretan city*. Princeton, NJ: Princeton University Press.

Ness, C. (2008). *Female terrorism and militancy: Agency, utility, and organization*. Abingdon: Routledge.

Ofcom. (2014). *News consumption in the UK*. London: Ofcom.

Office for National Statistics. (2012). *Ownership of UK quoted shares 2012*. London: Dandy.

Orwell, G. (1971). *Collected essays*. (Vol. 4). New York, NY: Harvest Books.

Ott, J. (2005). Level and inequality of happiness in nations: Does greater happiness of a greater number imply greater inequality in happiness? *Journal of Happiness*, *6*(4), 397–420.

Pankov, M., Mihelj, S., & Bajt, V. (2011). Nationalism, gender and the multivocality of war discourse in television news. *Media Culture & Society*, *33*(7), 1043–1059.

Pantti, M. (2010). The value of emotion: An examination of television journalists' notion on emotionality. *European Journal of Communication*, *25*(2), 168–181.

Perkins, S. (2009). Executive reward. In G. White & J. Druker (Eds.), *Reward management: A critical text* (pp. 148–169). London: Routledge.

Peston, R. (2012, June 12). The myth of a shareholder spring. *BBC News*. Retrieved May 10, 2014, from http://www.bbc.co.uk/news/business-18407587

Potter, W. (2010). *Media literacy* (5th ed.). Thousand Oaks, CA: Sage.

Pounds, G. (2012). Multimodal expression of authorial affect in a British television news programme. *Discourse, Context and Media, 1*(2–3), 68–81.

Pratley, N. (2014, April 26). If the bonus cap doesn't fit, why is the treasury putting it on RBS? *The Guardian*, p. 37.

Quinton, S., & Smallbone, T. (2006). *Postgraduate research in business: A critical guide*. London: Sage.

Reese, S. (2007). The framing project: A bridging model for media research revisited. *Journal of Communication, 57*(1), 148–154.

Reisigl, M., & Wodak, R. (2001). *Discourse and discrimination*. London: Routledge.

Richardson, J. (2007). *Analysing newspapers: An approach from critical discourse analysis*. Basingstoke: Palgrave.

Rigby, R. (2011). *28 business thinkers who changed the world*. London : Kogan Page.

Riker, W. (1993). *Agenda formation*. Ann Arbor: University of Michigan.

Robinson, F., Else, R., Sherlock, M., & Zass-Ogilvie, I. (2009). *Poverty in the media: Being seen and getting heard*. York: Joseph Rowntree Foundation.

Robinson, J. (2005, November 20). BBC news admits 'opinion-formers' prefer Sky. *The Guardian*. Retrieved May 17, 2014, from http://www.theguardian.com/media/2005/nov/20/tvnews.bbc

Ryscavage, P. (2009). *Rethinking the income gap: The second middle class revolution*. New Brunswick, NJ: Transaction.

Saeed, J. (1997). *Semantics*. Oxford: Blackwell.

Schifferes, S., & Coulter, S. (2012). Downloading disaster: BBC news online coverage of the global financial crisis. *Journalism, 14*(2), 228–252.

Schlesinger, P. (2006). Is there a crisis in British journalism? *Media Culture and Society, 28*(2), 299–307.

Scott, J. (1982). *The upper classes: Property and privilege in Britain*. London: Macmillan.

Seymour, D. (2009). *Reporting poverty in the UK: A practical guide for journalists*. York: Joseph Rowntree Foundation.

Sheehan, K. (2011). Great expectations: Institutional investors, executive remuneration, and 'say on pay'. In J. Hawley, S. Kamath, & A. Williams (Eds.), *Corporate governance failures: The role of institutional investors in the global financial crisis* (pp. 115–43). Philadelphia: University of Pennsylvania Press.

Shughart, W. (2009). Foreword. In C. Rowley & N. Smith (Eds.), *Economic contractions in the United States: A failure of government* (pp. xv–xviii). Fairfax, VA: The Locke Institute.

Solomon, N. (2001, November 8). Bloomberg's Victory and the Triumph of Business News. *FAIR*. Retrieved May 10, 2014, from http://fair.org/media-beat-column/bloombergs-victory-and-the-triumph-of-business-news/

Spanier, G. (2014). Pearson shareholders raise pressure on pay. *The Evening Standard*, p. 55.

Tambini, D. (2010). What are financial journalists for? *Journalism Studies, 11*(2), 158–174.

Tan, V., & Crombie, N. (2011). *The legitimacy of CEO pay: The discourse of telecom, the media and the public*. Working Paper. Retrieved May 9, 2014, from http://ir.canterbury.ac.nz/bitstream/10092/6219/1/12636336_TelecomCeoPay-WorkingPaper.pdf

Temple, M. (2006). Dumbing down is good for you. *British Politics, 1*(2), 257–273.

Tuchman, G. (1978). *Making news: A study in the construction of reality*. New York, NY: Free Press.

Van Leeuwen, T., & Wodak, R. (1999). Legitimizing immigration control: A discourse-historical analysis. *Discourse Studies, 1*(1), 83–118.

de Vreese, C. (2003). *Framing Europe. Television news and European integration*. Amsterdam: Aksant Academic Publishers.

Wartzman, R. (2008, September 12). Put a cap on CEO pay. *Bloomberg Businessweek*. Retrieved May 7, 2014, from http://www.businessweek.com/stories/2008-09-12/put-a-cap-on-ceo-paybusinessweek-business-news-stock-market-and-financial-advice

Watson, T. (2008). *Sociology, work and industry* (5th ed.). London: Routledge.

Whitney, C., & Wartella, E. (2000). On U.S. journalism education. *Journalism: Theory, Practice, Criticism, 1*(1), 52–55.

Whittle, A., & Mueller, F. (2011). The language of interests: The contribution of discursive psychology. *Human Relations*, *64*(3), 415–435.

Widdowson, H. (2000). On the limitations of linguistics applied. *Applied Linguistics*, *21*(1), 3–25.

Wilkinson, R., & Pickett, K. (2010). *The spirit level: Why equality is better for everyone*. London: Penguin.

Williams, S. (2012, July 20). Share holder rebels: The unlikely activists. *The Telegraph*. Retrieved May 10, 2014, from http://www.telegraph.co.uk/journalists/sally-williams/9395405/Shareholder-rebels-The-unlikely-activists.html

Winnett, R. (2009, May 11). MPs' expenses: paying bills for Tory grandees. *The Telegraph*. Retrieved May 10, 2014, from http://www.telegraph.co.uk/news/newstopics/mps-expenses/5310200/MPs-expenses-Paying-bills-for-Tory-grandees.html

Wright, K. (2011). Reality without scare quotes. *Journalism Studies*, *12*(2), 156–171.

ORGANIZING THE (SOCIOMATERIAL) ECONOMY
Ritual, agency, and economic models

Amanda Szabo

ABSTRACT

Employing sociomateriality, communicative constitution of organization (CCO), critical discourse analysis (CDA), performativity, and ritual, this article offers a discursive explanation of the economy: that discourse organizes the economy. This process-oriented and relational explanation proposes discourse as an entry point for understanding and perhaps foreclosing financial crisis and austerity. An instance of ritual use in a US city's council meetings about municipalizing a power utility (turning the privately owned energy utility into a city-owned energy utility) is analyzed with CDA, revealing how ritual positioned the city council and the economic model in relation to grant economic models agency in shaping decision-making and producing economic effects. A blending of CCO literatures with literature on ritual is recommended, illustrating the striking similarity between the CCO concept of authoritative text and ritual, and suggesting that perhaps rituals are authoritative texts.

CDA should shift from critique of structures to critique of strategies – of attempts, in the context of the failure of existing structures, to transform them in particular directions. (Fairclough, 2010, p. 14)

A full consideration of financial crisis and the responding impulse of austerity must grapple with how economic existence is being organized, of what economic reality is taken to be, and how an economy of coordinated activity and coordinated human and nonhuman subjects and actors is arising. To view economy as an accumulation of abstract things like Gross Domestic Product is to reduce the ongoing formative processes that are always making it and us together into a snapshot, and to reduce the myriad possibilities for intervention in making economic realities differently. If discourse is productive of reality as critical discourse analysts (Blommaert, 2005; Fairclough, 2010; Fairclough & Wodak, 1997) hold, discourse is also productive of reality that is economic. Viewing the economy as discursive positions financial crisis as an interruption in the discursive processes that have been stabilizing it, and austerity as a discursive construction seeking to perform stable economic alignments, albeit an asymmetrical discursive construction. Seeing the process of economic organizing as central to any concerns about austerity and financial crisis, this article focuses most on the process of organizing the economic – how discourse is stabilizing and performing economic texts (in this case, economic models) into existence.

Given this premise, this article focuses on one example of how economic models are given agency and authority through ritual and text during a long-term decision-making process of whether a US city should municipalize their power utility (bring it into city ownership rather than private ownership). I found that rituals capacitate economic models as authoritative actants capable of analyzing and calculating risk, predicting, approving, recommending, planning, and setting parameters. This article also suggests a discursive explanation for the organizing of the economy, and uses various conceptual approaches toward this end.[1] First in this article, I figure the economy as sociomaterial – as intricate alignments that entangle and produce people and things so that the division between the social and material is impossible, each being inherent and essential in the other. Second, I motion toward the role of discourse in the economy by engaging critical discourse analysis' (CDA) and others' understanding of discourse, symbolic and linguistic interaction, as productive of a politicized reality with performativity that explain how theories and economic models become accurate when appropriated discursively. Third, I engage the Montreal School of communicative constitution of organization (CCO), through concepts of authoritative texts, co-orientation, and ventriloquism, to contribute an understanding of how the material and texts are purposed through communication to produce stabilizing and organizing effects on the economic. Fourth, a description of ritual foregrounds how communication comes to coordinate, entangle, and be entangled in relations of authority and collectivity. Faced with prominent similarities, I propose that rituals are (figurative) authoritative texts and that acknowledging this sameness could expand both CCO and discourse scholars' ability to explain discursive organizing. After the conceptual foundation is laid, I contextualize, present, and analyze data of the documents and discourse involved in the city council decision process on municipalizing the electric utility. As this process divulged explicit and public engagement with economic forecasts and models, it revealed the common and complex ways that economic reality is produced through interactions between discourse and text. I conclude with a discussion that foregrounds the contributions of this approach: If discourse enables and stabilizes relations between infrastructures, money, resources, technology, cities, consumers, labor, authority, politics, and desire, then perhaps discourses are the origin of economies, and perhaps attention to discourse provides productive opportunities to intervene in financial crises and austerity measures.

Sociomaterial, Authoritative Texts, Ritual, and Discursive Economies

Sociomaterial

Imagining 'the economy' may evoke images of numerical figures, banks, physical, and digital stock markets, the illusive concept of credit and debt, consumer goods, and money. What often elides consideration is the role of humans and relations in constituting an economy. Sociomateriality, which I propose economies are, begs a divergence from separating the human from the material, instead holding that human and nonhuman actants (actors and actants) align temporarily and produce certain effects which make things happen (Orlikowski & Scott, 2008). The relation is foregrounded, and the character-istics produced result from the interpenetration of one actant/actor on the other. For instance, a person could be seen as a particular effect resulting from the interpenetration of biology, bodily form, food, tools, clothes, and voice, with human and material agency that presses upon and makes these things through an ongoing process of mutual consti-tution (Orlikowski, 2007). The economy as sociomaterial foregrounds the particular way the material assurance of money or product interpenetrates with systems of trust and human networks to make trade possible (Buenza, Hardie, & MacKenzie, 2006), and a socio-material understanding of austerity might highlight the alignment and interpenetration of the political forces, strategic communications, and states of affairs (Kittel & Obinger, 2003; Pierson, 1998).

Discursive Economies

The methods of these particular alignments seem illusive – why do certain actants align with certain actors, and how do they express their agency upon one another? Barad (2003) suggests that it is discourse that performs relationships and entities, which are always already material, into being. Her use of discourse, though, deviates from communi-cation to draw instead on Foucault's concept: Discourse is *'specific material reconfigurings of the world through which local determinations of boundaries, properties, and meanings are differentially enacted'* (Barad, 2003, p. 819, emphasis in original). Barad's use is similar to Laclau and Mouffe's (1985) (Foucauldian) conception of discourse as the 'structured totality resulting from the articulatory practice' (p. 105), articulations being the groupings that result from suturing certain variables to certain other variables in one specific way. These articulations limit the myriad possible relationships these variables could have, and in this way, make one way of relating hegemonic. Among these definitions, economies could be discourses considered robustly as political, collective, and societal effects. Considering economies as discursive in this (Foucauldian) way highlights the political processes of their production and interpretation, and their relational (as well as sociomaterial) nature.

While a Foucauldian discursive understanding of the economy yields a productively politicized view of economic organization, a look at how discourse as symbolic and linguistic interaction produces the economy, which will be the focus of this article, hones in on how everyday interactions and communicative exchanges organize sociomaterial into the economy. CDA scholars (Blommaert, 2005; Fairclough, 2010; Fairclough & Wodak, 1997) see discourse as semiotic interaction and as being socially constitutive, just as it is also made by the social, recognizing also that it fuses relations with material (Fairclough, 2010). du Gay and Pryke (2002) adopt this view and infuse it with a recognition of dis-course as the signifying tool which allows the material to be constructed into an object that can be used toward economic ends. Discourses' ability to produce something econ-omic, then, lies in its ability to motivate the social into using the material in coordinated ways.

Further, investigating performativity reveals how discourse can enact economic theories and models into being. Callon (1998, 2006) and Ferraro, Pfeffer, and Sutton (2005) suggest that economists' theories and economic models propose specific relation-ships among variables, and the proposition of these relations, as they gain traction and recognition in broader society, actually produce the foundation for those associations in social life; the propositions are performed into being real. Callon (1998, 2006) calls these proposed relationships *agencements*, or assemblages. These propositions gain societal tractions when they influence institutional design which in turn influences behavior, when they assume social norms, and shape language (Ferraro et al., 2005), and these propositions maintain their influence because of their application in management practices, the privileged status of economics as an academic discipline, and in the power economists have to advise policy (Ferraro et al., 2005).[2]

What is less recognized, but very essential to the performativity concept is that it takes symbolic and linguistic interaction with these theories and models for them to be performed. Performativity, when considered in the case of financial crisis, reveals this important communicative caveat. Colander et al. (2009) blamed the 2008 financial crisis on economists' neglect of how people really act, omission of the vulnerability and limitations of their models, and unheeding of the hegemony of their theories in enacting economic arrangements. Given those failures of the economists, the models obfuscated the real conditions and needs in the market (which, viewed through different lenses, may have been very evident) and thus the models failed to perform a reality that preserved economic integrity. In wanting to prevent future financial crises from blindsiding the public and economists again, Colander et al. (2009) beg for clearer comprehension of how interactions between actors organize larger systems like the economy. In short, collective communicative construction of the models that could accurately represent relations in society was the missing piece. CCO scholarship offers this missing piece through its understanding of the unique relation between discourses and texts.

Communicative Constitution of Organization

CDA scholars (Blommaert, 2005; Fairclough, 2010; Fairclough & Wodak, 1997) often see communication as productive of the social and the social as productive of communication, but CCO scholars focus most on the former:[3] they 'start *from* communication in order *to* explain organization and organizing, and not the other way around' (Cooren, 2012, p. 4). The Montreal school of CCO used in this article claims that texts, especially authoritative texts, and the nonhuman come to have agency (Cooren, 2004) through co-orientation (Kuhn, 2008), which coordinates action.

Some CCO scholars conceptualize discourse (conversation) in dialectical relation to texts through co-orientation: conversations shape texts, which go onto shape conversations, which go onto shape texts, and so on. This relating perpetuates authoritative texts (Koschmann, Kuhn, & Pfarrer, 2012) and is an essential organizing practice (Kuhn, 2008): Just as a phrase elicits coordinated action from its hearers, these texts come to include, coordinate, and control actors into being organized – or co-oriented – toward shared tasks (Koschmann et al., 2012). Significantly, co-orientation offers fixity: conversations become stabilized into texts (as when someone types up meeting notes that become a less-changeable record), and thereby become resistant to change, preserving arrangements that can be called upon in the future (Cooren, 2004). These texts become authoritative texts when they are abstracted from the conversation, but still induce a dominant reading that ensures various actors will converge around that dominant reading of it, producing the effect of organization (Koschmann, 2012).

Authoritative texts are 'an abstract textual representation of the collective that portrays its structure and direction, shows how activities are coordinated, and indicates relations of authority' (Koschmann, 2012, p. 68). They *do something to* actors, and could be either figurative or concrete (Kuhn, 2008). A concrete text is often written down, like employee handbooks, memos, and laws. Conversely, figurative texts are 'abstract representations of practice sites, communities, and firms' (Kuhn, 2008, p. 1234), such as understood codes of professionalism in an office (Koschmann et al., 2012). When authoritative texts are invoked relations of authority and relations among actors and actants are also invoked (Kuhn). When invoked, authoritative texts make the organization present: *they organize.*

In order to be an authoritative text, a text must: (1) be 'bound up with practice and the production of value' (Kuhn, 2008, p. 1238) so that it ensures its structures and use continues, (2) marshal consent, and (3) attract capital (Kuhn). A text is 'bound up in practice and the production of value', when it has more effects than just utilitarian effects. For example, when someone references the employee handbook, that reference serves not just as a citation of a policy (purely utilitarian effect), but an acknowledgement of one's dedication to the company or an indication of their 'rightness' in asserting that certain norms should be followed. To marshal consent, a text must get actors to use it in a certain way (Kuhn), like when people agree to be moved by a phrase in a particular way (Koschmann et al., 2012), such as upon the utterance of a phrase 'it's a small world' colleagues would immediately clean up their papers to not interfere with others' space. Texts can attract economic (money), social (connections), cultural (knowledge or social value), or symbolic (status) capital (Kuhn). Capital 'makes the games of society – not least, the economic game – something other than simple games of chance offering at every moment the possibility of a miracle' (Bourdieu, 1986, p. 241). In this way, the ability to attract capital is the ability to particularize which of various social or *economic* games actors play. To the degree that texts gain capital and consent, they organize relations.

Cooren's (2010) concept of ventriloquism offers a unique explanation of organizations as texts relating through collectives, and collectives relating through texts. When collectives invoke a text, they give it a voice, a body, a form. In turn, texts invoke collectives in the reading and authoring of them, so that when read, texts instantiate a collective. Like a ventriloquist to its dummy (and the dummy to its ventriloquist), each is required in order for either to speak and exist: the ventriloquist could not speak or be a ventriloquist without the dummy, and the dummy could not speak or be a ventriloquist dummy without the ventriloquist. Cooren believes that systems are organized by collectives consistently and frequently purposing a text in a particular way and stabilized because interaction with the fixity of text ensures that the collective can be made present again and again across space and time.

In all, CCO explains organization as a process of groups relating to texts, a process that alters and enables each. Because it is through communication that groups relate with texts (and vice versa), regularly inducing this communication is essential for perpetuating an organization, and organizational stability (read also: economic stability). Scholarship on ritual reiterates how communication organizes collectives, and accounts for the regular triggering (stabilizing) of this communication.

Rituals and Organizing

This section reveals the way rituals derive authority and organize a collective, similarly to authoritative texts. Goffman (1967) states rituals are the key to the organization of society as they impart human nature onto humans and thereby purpose them into usable interactants in society. While there are many different definitions of ritual (Islam & Zyphur, 2009; Senft & Basso, 2009), I draw on the definitions from Philipsen (1992): ritual is 'a structured sequence of actions the correct performance of which pays homage to a sacred object' and Knuf (1993) who further operationalized ritual to require 'invariant behaviors' and that 'Referential meanings of the words and symbols employed become subordinate to the meaning of the ritual as a whole' (p. 88). Through this combination, three qualities are required for a ritual to be present: (1) invariant behaviors, or, the same sequential speaking behaviors being performed at multiple times and by multiple speakers, (2) these behaviors, words used, and symbols employed must be subordinate to the significance of the whole practice, and (3) there must be a focus on a sacred object (Philipsen, 1993). In rituals, what is done and said is much less important than the fact that it is all being done. Knuf (1993) explains:

> Because the behavior is invariant, so that there is no correct alternative in the situation, it loses its informative value … so that the referential meanings of the words and symbols employed become subordinate to the meanings of the ritual as a whole. (p. 88)

Because there is no literal meaning of rituals, other meanings are instantiated, like the paying of homage to a sacred object (Philipsen, 1993), which could be peace (Katriel, 1985) or understanding (Nuciforo, 2013).

In considering how rituals organize collectives, their agency becomes significant. Observing daily rituals at an AIDS relief organization, Koschmann and McDonald (2015) found rituals do have agency – to impose, remind, and signal. They were able to 'make present the full force of the organization – its values, norms, and relations of power' (p. 34), and thus were crucial to the organization performing its daily work in as an organization. While rituals do '"move" people' (Knuf, 1993, p. 93), this movement (of themselves and of others) is beyond the intention of the human performers. In fact, rituals operate on latent cultural levels where norms and rules also operate, so that an individual will not be fully conscious of performing or intending to perform them (Islam & Zyphur, 2009). Because rituals have agency and this agency is not the product of human intention, rituals' agency is not reducible to human action. In fact, if an act comes fully from an actor, it is not a ritual (Bloch, 2006). Therefore, rituals are somewhat societally induced.

How and why are rituals able to move people? In part they derive this capacity from deference or 'the authority of others to guarantee the value of what is said or done' (Bloch, 2006, p. 497). Rituals, in exacting deference from their performers, instantiate relations of power and authority, which is especially useful during moments of transition or situations that require capacities beyond an individual's ability (Bloch, 2006). During these periods, people often seek to depend on a stable set of relations and look to authorities to defer to. These periods are when rituals' ability to organize becomes valuable. Islam and Zyphur (2009) claim that through the performance of rituals individuals forgo their social differences and exercise their shared membership, becoming more collective. For example, Aden et al. (2009) found that ritual performances of watch party rituals for Nebraska State fans 'spin a web of communal connection' (p. 26), creating a community of Cornhuskers across dispersed locations. Philipsen (1987) explains this cohesive capacity of rituals through their ability to marshal consent; 'especially nonrational consensus. Their form provides for the celebration of what is shared by participating in known sequences of coordinated action, which, by definition, require – and once enacted, implicate – the exploitation of shared rules' (p. 251). Ritual's 'essential function is the maximization of certainty' (Knuf, 1993, p. 88), and a ritual view of communication sustains a society across time (Carey, 1989). Rituals serve as valuable actants when they marshal consent for authority, coordinate action, and forge relations, thereby manifesting order during uncertain periods (Knuf, 1993).

So, rituals organize relations (Aden et al., 2009; Islam & Zyphur, 2009) that can weather changing times, express authority and elicit the deference and consent to authority by human actors (Bloch, 2006; Philipsen, 1987). Because of these features, they are more meaningful as a whole, than in parts (Philipsen, 1993). These qualities are very similar to the qualities of authoritative texts (marshalling consent, attracting capital, and producing value that enables the continuation of structures). Table 1 summarizes the shared qualities between rituals (Philipsen, 1993) and (figurative) authoritative texts (Kuhn, 2008) so exactly that I find rituals to be authoritative texts.

The table reveals that the minimum requirements for communication to be a ritual also meet the minimum requirements for authoritative texts, allowing an analysis of rituals as authoritative texts. This recognition could blend ritual understanding of how communication organizes and authorizes with CCO understandings of the same to yield more nuanced understanding of this important phenomenon, particularly the understanding of how rituals are regularly induced could benefit CCO conceptions, perhaps even its slippery conceptions of power.

Setting and Data

The data for this study are drawn from two of many city council meetings held in a Colorado, USA city which took place during a nine-year-long decision-making process on the

Table 1. Literature on rituals as authoritative texts.

Requirements for authoritative texts	How rituals fulfill the requirements for authoritative texts
To be 'bound up with practice', toward the production of value so they ensure the organization and the text continues (Kuhn, 2008)	As rituals are performed with invariant behavior (Knuf, 1993), they are also 'bound up with practice'. If the whole is greater than the sum of its parts, than its performance produces value. And, rituals organize human actors (Goffman, 1967; Koschmann & McDonald, 2015) into coordinated relations (Aden et al., 2009; Islam & Zyphur, 2009)
To marshal consent (Kuhn, 2008)	As ritual performers submit to carry out invariant behaviors that propel the ordering of the collective, the consent of those performing the ritual is marshalled (Philipsen, 1987)
To attract social, economic, cultural, and/or symbolic capital (Kuhn, 2008)	Though not all forms of capital have to be attracted, in this ritual, they are: social capital is attracted as multiple people adhere to the same communication, cultural capital is attracted through ritual by getting people to observe the cultural norms rituals entail, symbolic capital is attracted by observing cultural norms and having one's status in the community affirmed through that performance (Goffman, 1967), and economic capital is raised in this particular ritual by marshalling the resources of the city toward the municipalization project

topic of whether to municipalize their energy utility or not: they could either renew their contract with the private energy provider (the current contract was ending soon), change the contract with the private provider, or acquire the electric utility and allow the city to run it (called municipalization).[4] Municipalizing the utility would allow the city, and the environmentally conscious residents they represent, more control over the types and costs of energy resources used, enabling more environmental and cheaper alternatives. While the environmental significance of these meetings is apparent, these meetings also provided a novel economic moment in which the city publicly made explicit and available its economic assumptions and goals, which are so often embedded, hidden, and taken for granted.

My contact with these data began the summer of 2013 while I was assisting another researcher with a project using these municipalization data, mostly by making transcripts of these meetings. We requested DVDs of the video-recordings of all the city council meetings on municipalization, which are open to the public and recorded for public viewing on the local government television channel. As I transcribed two particular meetings, the conversations stood out to me: a roundtable on 9 October 2012 presented some of the final details of the metrics to the council so that they could understand it before the other meeting I analyzed – the 15 November 2012 meeting wherein the council approved (authorized) the metrics to be used in their decision analysis and to inform their decision-making.[5] During these meetings, eight city council members, the mayor, financial advisory staff, and various other city staff explored municipalization in front of any citizens who wanted to see it.

Upon first listening to the two meetings, I was struck that the council was authorizing models to make thousands of their decisions, or at least to define and structure their decisions in specific ways that make a big difference on what they choose. Intrigued by this authorization process and the role of these models in decision-making, I delved deeper conceptually trying to understand how they were able to invest their authority and how they were able to treat these models like an actant in their decision-making. In other words, I heeded Fairclough's (1993) attention to 'discourse analysis which aims to systematically explore often opaque relationships of causality and determination between (a) discursive practices, events and texts, and (b) wider social and cultural structures, relations and processes through discourse' (p. 135). Because rituals enact a deference to and instantiation of external authority and can organize human and nonhuman resources during periods of uncertainty and change (Bloch, 2006), I thought rituals may explain the phenomenon I heard, so I analyzed these meetings for rituals. I looked for invariant behavior, the correct performance of which is more valuable than the sum of each step, and when, if ever, homage was paid to a sacred object (Philipsen, 1993).

The Economic Model as Actant

In order to meet the environmental goals the city hoped for, the city is mandated by a charter to prove that the first day the utility opens it will be able to supply energy at the same rate or cheaper than the private provider and at the same reliability or greater reliability than them. To prove the possibility of meeting these requirements, the city must use energy and economic models that can forecast the future capacities of a not-yet-existent utility. Over the course of municipalization discussions, three different

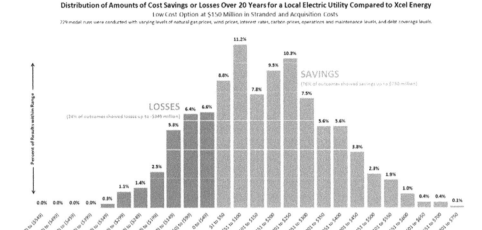

Figure 1. Histogram projecting probabilities of cost savings with municipal utility over 20 years. © [City]. Reproduced by permission of the Energy Strategy and Electric Utility Development.

models were made to predict how a variety of different situations would affect energy resource use and costs over a 20-year period: one model considered the energy load (amount of energy the city will need in the future); a second model considered different energy resources (wind, natural gas, coal, solar, etc.) to come up with optimum combinations of cost-effective, reliable, and environmentally friendly energy; and finally the third model which is the focus of this paper is the financial model. This spreadsheet-based financial model takes the data from the energy resource model and combines other costs (bond and initial loan costs, stranded costs they could be mandated to inherit from the private provider's debt, energy transmission costs, taxes, operations and maintenance, funding for infrastructural improvement and energy-efficiency programs, and acquisition costs) to model the costs of energy per unit based on a variety of financial situations as well as whether the city could afford to municipalize. All of these data are compared to the financial, reliability, and energy source models of staying with the private energy provider (City, n.d., *Modeling City's Energy Future*) (Figure 1).

The models' agency lies partly in how the charter positions them – as furnished with the ability to foreclose municipalization if they cannot show a probability of meeting reliability and cost standards. The agenda for the city council study session on 8 August 2012 states (italics added):

> The metrics were developed using the charter's guiding language, with a team of city staff and members of the public. These metrics *will set the parameters* the strategies must achieve for future go/no go decisions.

Here, the metrics do something – set parameters. The 23 July 2013 study session, which presented updated data from the model to the council as one of the last presentations of these data before the city actually decides to acquire the utility, illustrates this agency powerfully:

None of the new modeling and subsequent results changes the key conclusion that a local electric utility is possible under the charter metrics. They do, however, underscore the importance of having clear plans to manage stranded and acquisition cost rulings and other potential risks if and before they occur …

DEBT SERVICE COVERAGE

Metric status: Achieved …

INCREASED RENEWABLES, DECREASED EMISSIONS

Metric status: Achieved …

COMPARABLE RELIABILITY

Metric status: Achieved …

In this excerpt, the ability of the models to 'achieve' the charter requirements ultimately approves municipalization as an option. The models are also able to 'underscore' and thus recommend (for instance, the mitigation of stranded and acquisition cost rulings). Further, in mentioning that they do not, this document reveals that the models and their results had the ability to change a 'key conclusion that a local electric utility is possible'.

So, one agency the models have is to approve or not approve municipalization. While the council ultimately decides, if the models say the city cannot meet the requirements, the decision is invalid.

Beyond enabling or disabling municipalization, the models also advise on and predict municipalization through probabilistic decision analysis. Decision analysis identified six of the greatest uncertainties municipalization faces and developed a range of outcomes with each of those – a high, low, and medium outcome, and then ran these 729 variations through the model. This processes yielded probabilistic trends about whether the city will be better off municipalizing or not. One of the metrics produced is below (City, n.d., *What is 'Decision Analysis'?*):

The city explains their use of this decision-analysis tool (City, n.d., Good Decision-Making):

Decision analysis is the practice of addressing decision-making in a formal manner. Risk is the likelihood of a negative outcome, and it can be analyzed probabilistically by looking at the severity of adverse consequences and the likelihood of each consequence. Risk analysis helps identify the factors that could jeopardize the success of a project. It also helps develop procedures to reduce the likelihood of these factors occurring or institute countermeasures for those factors that cannot be mitigated

Decision analysis identifies risk, develops ways to reduce the risk, and functions as a tool to ground community discussions in 'facts'. The acting of this analysis as an actant on human planning is quite evident: it is able to analyze probabilistically and calculate risks that human actors are not able to do, and it is able to advise human actors on a 'factual level' as well as 'develop procedures' and 'institute countermeasures'; the latter being two things normally only attributed to human or institutional actions.

In all, economic models as engaged in this municipalization process are able to analyze and calculate risk, to predict, to approve, to recommend, to plan, and to set parameters. But it is co-orientation through (ritual) discourse that enables these agencies, making the next section about the economic model ritual very important.

The Economic Model Ritual

I found three instances of ritual over about an hour's time in the first meeting. In the second meeting, which lasted 2 hours and 53 minutes, 12 instances of ritual were found, for a total of 15 ritual instances across the 2 meetings. In analyzing ritual, it is important that there are at least three to prove there are 'invariant behaviors' (Knuf, 1993). These 15 instances more than represent that minimum. The import of the ritual can be analyzed by delving into one example, revealing through one excerpt, presented momentarily, the role that ritual plays in sociomaterial alignment, nonhuman agency, and co-orientation.

The patterned stages of the economic model ritual begin with (1) a council person (CP) mentioning some public concern. This could be a concern about which she or he thinks the public might care, a concern that the public has either in union mentioned or an individual has mentioned, or a concern that she or he has on behalf of the public's interest. Often, this concern is stated directly by the CP, but occasionally it is implied (such as 'what would happen if this goes to litigation?'). Then (2) the next stage addresses the economic models or the economic advisors as a venue for addressing the issue. Either the CP herself or himself or another CP, staff, or the financial advisor (FA) suggests that they check the model or consult a financial expert to address the concern. Next, (3) most often the FA but occasionally another CP will respond saying that they either did or can include said concern in the model. Often this will be a statement to the effect of 'Yes, we can/have included this in the modeling'. (4) In the last stage, which is sometimes absent, the original CP (and sometimes another CP) either celebrates the ability of the model or the FA (something like 'Yes, thank you, that's what we should do') or moves to make sure that the findings of the model are addressed in later decision-making ('please be sure to report back next council session', or 'Can you send out those figures when you get them?'). Overall, the stages are as follows:

(1) Some public concern is mentioned.
(2) Consulting the model/FAs is suggested.
(3) The power of the model/advisor is upheld to be capable and entrusted with the concern.
(4) (The capability of the model/advisor is affirmed, and sometimes future decision processes are set up.)

In the interests of illustration, I share one example of the economic model ritual, taken from the 15 November 2012 meeting. Below a CP explores economic model's ability to accurately represent the costs of municipalized energy to the community. The stages are indicated to the right.

CP: Council person
FA: Financial advisor on staff
OFA: Other financial advisory staff person

This excerpt reveals how the CP assures that the model is capable of handling the specific analysis of their community, and that this is a priority in the construction of the model. In the first economic model ritual step, CP, in lines 1–5, mentions the public concern about access to 'certain data' (line 2), which seems to relate to 'actual rate data' (line 8). This concern, at least for CP, relates in some way to the public having 'confidence that we have a handle on' (line 11) how this process might affect the public and

⌐―1st Stage―⌐	1	CP: Um one of the things that's been challenging is if you don't- we don't have access
	2	to certain data, um that would be very helpful, and I'm assuming that we still won't
	3	have access to that come the- come March. Um so that is a source of concern for a lot
	4	of folks, you've seen it in the questions on the emails, and certainly things that have
	5	been presented to each of us. Um is there- is there a way to introduce any more
	6	certainty, uh you said we're gonna know more, yes, we will know more about a lot of
	7	other things, but we're not necessarily gonna know more about the actual costs, the
	8	actual rate data, that we don't now have from Xcel by- by customer class, which is
	9	what I'm trying to ask about in a convoluted way here. Um so I'm trying to get at
2nd Stage	10	whether we will have any better way of assessing that, are we able to give our
	11	community any more confidence that we have a handle on the comparisons that are
	12	most relevant to them?
	13	FA: Well- and we are hoping- we're- we're doing um a lot of work to try to get to that
	14	level. We will not be at the level of being able to design 28 different rate schedules.
	15	But we are um you know right now, we are- we're very confident in the residential,
	16	commercial, industrial grouping and the average cost, um what we're trying to do is
	17	get some information where we can- we can delve a little bit deeper. I don't know- I
	18	can't sit here today and say if we'll have anything better than that, but we are getting
	19	some data um that's helping us understand where the cost drivers are, and
3rd Stage―(2nd Stage)	20	potentially what customers are contributing those cost drivers, and with that
	21	information, we can do a little bit more analysis, and Jonathan I don't know if you
	22	wanna add anything to that.
	23	OFA: Yeah, just- just briefly, um part of our process right now of course is refining all
	24	of our load information, so instead of just looking uh using one year's worth of data,
	25	using a proxy of Fort Collins, we're using updated information to really build out a
	26	low profile that is 20 years out, that's much more sophisticated and much more uh
	27	focused on Boulder's load, part of that will be to work uh with some energy
	28	customers, large customers, maybe mid-sized customers, residential customers, and
	29	get some of the data from them that then our hopes are we can then reverse
	30	engineer some of the rate design, um you may have seen in some recent articles that
	31	the information is somehow public at the PUC [Public Utilities Commision], it's not.
	32	There is information about rate classes, the three big rate classes. Residential,
	33	commercial, and industrial. As Heather mentioned, there are 28 rate schedules
	34	including street lighting. The way the rates are designed is not public information.
	35	That is not available at the PUC, and so we can work to reverse engineer it in a way
	36	that gives us some more confidence, and that is part of the process that we hope to
	37	accomplish in the next couple of months as part of the low profiling and- and rate
	38	process
	39	CP: Yeah, and that would- this is one the same thing, so I'm gonna jump in here. And
	40	that would speak to one of the other things I was curious about, which is the use of
4th Stage	41	the average, which appeared to be raising concern for some of our largest electricity
	42	users, and a response that you provided uh in regards to a question about that,
	43	saying that you would be willing to work with the larger customers to try to get at
		the data through them. And I'm hoping that that is the case, that we will be doing
		that so that some of the folks that are very nervous about the average being the um
		data point we're using in our- in our analysis is not necessarily relevant for them.
	42	that are very nervous about the average being the um data point we're using in our-
	43	in our analysis is not necessarily relevant for them.

their individual rates. To get that confidence for the public, CP asks if there is a 'better way of assessing' (line 10) what the rates might be, fulfilling the second step of the economic model ritual by asking the FAs (probably implying an assumption that they would consult the economic model). FA hesitates to directly say that they will have that data (line 13, lines 16–17), but affirms the council that the staff are already trying to find that data (lines 12–13, lines 15–16, lines 17–19), and mentions that these data will be put into 'analysis' (line 20) to give a more detailed response (lines 18–20) that may instill more confidence, executing the third economic model ritual step. FA then asks OFA (line 20), another financial staff person, for insights into meeting the concerns of the public. This move to ask another advisor could be a re-expression of the second ritual step, and shows a self-referencing of FAs. OFA addresses the specifics of what they are doing (lines 21–27) apparently to assure the council that they are working toward offering answers that may ease the public's concern, and that these results are promising (lines 32–35). OFA mentions specifically that their processes are designed to 'give us some more confidence' (line 33), and lists a time period in which it should be accomplished (lines 33–35), which again completes the third economic model ritual step. CP acknowledges ('yeah', line 36) what OFA has just said, completing part of the fourth economic model ritual step. CP then raises another different but related concern about the use of average rates (lines 37–38), which may not accurately reflect all of the energy users. CP addresses and celebrates the offer of OFA to work directly with these users to ensure that they get the relevant information about how they will be affected, specifically trying to get OFA to follow through with this plan (lines 39–43). Imploring OFA to follow through on the idea completes the second part of the fourth ritual step, ending the economic model ritual.

Analysis: The Economic Model Ritual and Authoritative Text

This ritual does not stand out as odd, but its ubiquity reveals the common ways that economic models are brought into relation with collectives to organize a Community/Economy assemblage, which is the ritual's sacred object. To show this process, I argue that the excerpt above meets the requirements for ritual (it has invariant behaviors, the whole of it is more than the sum of its parts, and it pays homage to a sacred object – Knuf, 1993), thus it also meets the requirements of an authoritative text and in meeting these requirements, the economic model ritual organizes the economy. First, the excerpt is an instance of the economic model ritual. The same stages were performed sequentially 15 times across two meetings (though I only included one instance for the sake of space), fulfilling the performance of invariant behaviors. More to the meat of this article, the ritual is more than the sum of its parts in that it animates the model as an actant, so that the sacred object of Community/Economy could be produced.

Taken separately, each stage seems like a simple question and answer that seeks nothing more than arriving at information about the capacity of a technical device, which is part of the value of this exchange but not all of the value. Taken together and taken in context, this ritual exchange vets the model as a competent and capable actant in which to invest community concerns, and to allow shaping the future of the community. This vetting can be seen in the emphasis on the model being 'relevant' (lines 11 and 43) to the community. To make these data points more relevant would instill more 'confidence' in the public (lines 11, 14, and 33). Without this relevance or confidence, it would be unlikely for an economic model to be perceived as an actant worthy of investing the council's authority in. With confidence in the model, the council can accept a close relationship and can authorize the models to inform their decision-making on behalf of the community, establishing strong sociomaterial relations capable of planning for the complex and uncertain future of their community.

The most successful outcome of the sociomaterial relationship that the ritual establishes would be the production of a successful sociomaterial product: a robust Community/Economy, the economic model ritual's sacred object. A community 'consists of a group of people who are bound together in some relation of shared sentiment and mutual responsibility' (Philipsen, 1992, p. 14). Specifically, a shared sentiment of collectively observing rituals can form a community (Philipsen, 1992, 1993), so it makes sense that the sacred object of many rituals might be 'community'. A sacred object is normally located by an attention to how interactants fashion symbolic linkages, and through these linkages, uphold precious (social, political, and moral) values (Philipsen, 1992, 1993). For the city council meeting data, community as a focus is overtly present through it being stated 43 times in the 15 November 2012 meeting. This attention to community is used to form a link between the community and the models. The diffusing of community concerns, the establishment of relevance of the model to the community, and instilling confidence in the modeling process (what the FAs tried to do lines 14–27) serve to lubricate the community's acceptance of and the council's authorization of these models as actants in the community. Once accepted as actants, the models can be co-oriented around to project the community across space and time, perpetuating its (economic) existence. The models, when ritually engaged, are thus able to organize and stabilize the Community/Economy, making Community/Economy the sacred object and inclusion the value that is preserved in the paying of homage.

The Economic Model Ritual as Authoritative Text

This paper argues that a ritual already is an authoritative text. As the rituals follow invariant performance of the same stages, the economic model ritual is 'bound up with practice', and *produces value* in ensuring that the Community/Economy and this ritual is sustained (Kuhn, 2008), while also marshalling council people's consent to defer to the model's authority. The economic model ritual also attracts social capital by getting council members to purpose the model as actant, cultural capital when the model is authorized as a knowledge actant to calculate and recommend, symbolic capital in awarding authority to the model in the decision-making process and to the council people for participating in the socially sanctioned practice of ritual (Goffman, 1967). Economic capital is attracted by the economic model ritual as well: On January, 2014, the council sent an official letter of intent to acquire to the private energy provider, which would not have happened had the models not approved municipalization per the charter requirements.

Recognizing the economic model ritual as authoritative text contextualizes this discursive practice as ventriloquism and co-orientation. As the economic model ritual is performed, the community pregnant with the model and the model pregnant with the community is made present, or ventriloquized. Because texts offer fixity, the community is capable of co-orienting with the text, and being ventriloquized and organized in various moments and places.

Discussion

This paper proposes that the achievement of a new municipal utility was a ritual achievement. In moments of concern or uncertainty about the future of a municipal utility, the model was called upon to provide the answers the community needed to move forward (either with or without municipalizing). Through the economic model ritual, the community became coordinated (organized) in regard to a municipal utility (their future energy needs were represented and they were able to forecast their future involvement in a municipalized utility).

Toward organizing an economy, the economic model ritual co-oriented people with text to produce sociomaterial alignments. A charter was created through political processes that authorized a municipal energy utility only if the municipal utility could be shown to produce the same level of reliability and cost to consumer that the private energy utility does. This charter, when adopted and integrated into the practices of the city council, authorized and legitimated the use of economic models in particular ways. The models (including the economic model) were created through calculative devices interacting with human efforts, and then presented to the council (by a human, voice, and presentation devices). The council interacted (through the economic model ritual) with human and nonhuman representations of the economic models as they sought to understand and edit the models to include their concerns and understanding of the issues. The model was changed to reflect council concerns and yield the answers the council desired. These answers the model yielded were integrated into a final decision. In the case of municipalizing the energy utility, the council (in part ventriloquizing and ventriloquized by the economic models) approved and directed their staff to write the January 2014 letter that was sent to the private electricity provider indicating that the city would acquire the utility for municipal use.

Throughout this process, the influence of texts – to analyze and calculate risk, to predict, to approve, to recommend, to plan, and to set parameters – is evident. Texts assembled the (present and future) community into certain relations that were subjected to interactions with a municipalized future, and this ability for texts to predict and organize the community facilitated a municipalized future. Additionally, texts are able to be called upon in multiple times and multiple places, allowing the instantiation of the municipalized community to occur across space and time, and thereby cohere, endure, and spread.

I imagine this ritual, sociomaterial, and textual process is very similar to many policy decisions, especially decisions on economic matters – there is a legal constraint on how the decisions should be made (like the council's charter) and the decision-making body adopts these constraints while struggling with texts (like economic models) that help them foresee, estimate, and predict what will be the best decision for the people they represent. Through this process of interacting with various texts and calculative actants, decision-makers adhere to norms like the economic model ritual so that they purpose the texts 'appropriately' and consistently from person to person and saturate these texts or the interpretation of these texts with their ideological positions, concerns, or desires. These interpretations and modifications to the text change how others in the future address and interact with them, and what kind of community is invoked when the texts are brought up.

This description reveals the incredible amount of influence and authority that texts and the discursive purposing of texts have in ordering economic realities. Not only do texts often assume arrangements, when they invoke the texts, communities and users of the texts ventriloquize them and embody the arrangements texts assume. But as the economic model ritual reveals, texts are also vulnerable to how they are appropriated and to being edited. In the case of financial crisis, the economic models and theories were not sufficiently edited to reflect the existing sociomaterial relations, making the predictions the theories and the models had ineffective and destructive (Colander et al., 2009). Viewed from this lens, more use of the economic model ritual would have included and entangled the financial models with community concerns and could prevent the inaccurate economic predictions and irrelevant economic recommendations.

Considering austerity provides even more moral implications for this article's analysis. Though the impact of this economic model ritual – whether it did accurately represent the economic effects of municipalization on the community – are yet to be seen (at this point of writing, the municipal utility has yet to be implemented), based on the conceptualization of a discursive economy I propose, the perpetuation of a Community/Economy requires the value of community inclusion in relating with economic texts (theories, models, etc). The texts themselves are fluid, their ability to produce economic effects depend on how they are engaged. Economic theories and models only work to the extent that a full Community/Economy co-orients with the economic texts, so that the texts become pregnant with Community/Economy, and birth the Community/Economy as the texts are engaged. Structures that seek to represent ideologies rather than the local community relations (structures like the International Monetary Fund or experts who have little local knowledge) must be legitimated by the local community lest their influence only distance the economic texts from relation with and coordination of the community. The tighter the connection and the more inclusive the text and the co-orienting to the texts, the more accurate the texts are in representing and ventriloquizing a robust community, and the more stable that Community/Economy could become.

Conclusion

This article has brought together various concepts (sociomateriality; CCO concepts of authoritative texts, co-orientation, and ventriloquism; CDA, performativity; and ritual) to service a discursive explanation of the economy: That discourse, especially when structured, routinized, and widely adopted like rituals are, invokes various economic texts to organize sociomaterial arrangements while also allowing the sociomaterial to organize the texts. A full description of this occurrence is not presented in this article but remnants of talk (the economic ritual used in city council meetings) and of texts (various city documents that authorized the economic models) are presented to point toward the complex and perpetual process of economic co-orientation. This admittedly limited description suggests that humans are entangled in arrangements that are in part outside of their control because they lie also in texts and material relations, but in part humans animate and construct these texts which animate the sociomaterial through communication. In this view, economic organizing lies in communication processes that link people and texts, rather than just in texts or in people, therefore, communication should be central to a solution to and understanding the problem of financial crisis and austerity. The authoring of economic texts (policies, models, and documents) must attend carefully to how, what, and who the texts invoke if the texts are to be accurate, legitimate, and are to gain traction in aligning sociomaterial. The power of ritual and other consistent communication patterns – wherein the power of economic ordering might lie – could be leveraged for economic stability if inclusive and representative relations are established (as it appears this city council attempted) or toward economic coercion if inclusive relations are neglected (say, for short-sighted political gains). In the latter case resisting relations, disturbing ritual performances, or neglecting models and other performative texts while offering alternate relations, rituals, and texts could prove effective economic resistance strategies.

Further empirical investigations into the discursive organization of the economy are needed. I have suggested many conceptual tools toward this end and provided ritual in one city council as an instance, but more instances of discourse as it orders or fails to order economies are necessary as well as longer term and broader scoped analyses of how discourse has or has not played out in the ordering of the economic world.

Acknowledgements

Author acknowledges the gracious support of David Boromisza-Habashi, Matt Koschmann, Tim Kuhn, Matthew Kopec, Nicholas Burk, Leah Sprain, and Larry Frey for their commentary during the development of this manuscript and the two anonymous reviewers for their suggestions, all of which enhanced this article.

Disclosure statement

No potential conflict of interest was reported by the author.

Notes

1. Rather than using these concepts as full frameworks, which would elicit theoretical and conceptual contradictions, I am using them as heuristics to shed light on different aspects of a complex phenomenon that is not yet well understood.
2. The Black-Sholes option pricing theory illustrates the theory of performativity excellently. When the theory was first introduced, its predictions of exchanges at the Chicago Board Options Exchange were not very accurate. As (cultural, ideological, and practical) adoption increased (in part due to an availability of technology that allowed the theory to be consulted in real time in the trading pit), the Black-Sholes theory normalized options trading and compelled pricers to price according to the model. Thus, the options pricing theory became much more accurate in its predictions (MacKenzie & Millo, 2003). MacKenzie and Millo (2003) attribute this 'self-fulfilling' ability to social forces like the respect traders exhibited for certain norms, reputation, and interpersonal networks that enabled the collective adoption of the theory, which in turn made it predictive.
3. While economies are not traditionally considered an 'organization,' CCO explores not just organizations, but also the process of organizing (Cooren, Kuhn, Cornelissen, & Clark, 2011).
4. If energy municipalization was adopted (which it was), the city would buy the utility and its distribution system from the private energy provider, set up a separate city department to operate the utility, and the energy utility would become a public utility, serving all the clients, residents, and users that the private provider did, but users would pay the city, and decisions about the operation of the utility would be opened to political and democratic processes.
5. IRB Protocol #: 13-0070. The city's name will be redacted, and substituted for 'city'.

Update

An update for the book edition: In the summer of 2016, the city is still pursuing legal and regulatory steps for energy municipalization—hopeful that a city-run energy utility will be in its future, but has not yet municipalized as anticipated when the article for the special issue was finalized.

References

Aden, R. C., Borchers, T. A., Grim Buxbaum, A., Cronn-Mills, K., Davis, S., Dollar, N. J., … Amato Ruggerio, A. (2009). Communities of cornhuskers: The generation of place through sports fans' rituals. *Qualitative Research Reports in Communication*, *10*(1), 26–37. doi:10.1080/17459430902839017

Barad, K. (2003). Posthumanist performativity: Toward an understanding of how matter comes to matter. *Signs: Journal of Women in Culture and Society*, *28*(3), 801–831.

Bloch, M. (2006). Deference. In M. Stausberg, J. A. M. Snoek, & J. Kreinath (Eds.), *Theorizing rituals: Issues, topics, approaches, concepts* (pp. 495–506). Leiden, NL: Brill.

Blommaert, J. (2005). *Discourse: A critical introduction*. Cambridge: Cambridge University Press.

Bourdieu, P. (1986). The forms of capital. In J. Richardson (Ed.), *Handbook of theory and research for the sociology of education* (pp. 241–258). New York, NY: Greenwood.

Buenza, D., Hardie, I., & MacKenzie, D. (2006). A price is a social thing: Towards a material sociology of arbitrage. *Organization Studies*, *27*(5), 721–745. doi:10.1177/0170840606065923

Callon, M. (1998). *The laws of the markets*. Oxford, MA: Blackwell.

Callon, M. (2006). *What does it mean to say economics is performative?* Working paper. Paris: Ecole des Mines.

Carey, J. (1989). *Communication as culture: Essays on media and society*. Winchester, MA: Unwin Hyman.

City. (n.d.). *Modeling city's energy future*. Unpublished presentation. Retrieved from http://prezi.com/ecxfrtirjhbc/view/#18_11382753

City. (n.d.). *What is 'decision analysis'?* Unpublished presentation. Retrieved from https://www-static.bouldercolorado.gov/docs/WhatisDecisionAnalysis-1-201305151611.pdf

City. (n.d.). *Good decision-making: Recognizing and evaluating risks and opportunities*. Retrieved from https://bouldercolorado.gov/energy-future/energy-future-decision-making

Colander, D., Goldberg, M., Haas, A., Juselius, K., Kirman, A., Lux, T., & Sloth, B. (2009). The financial crisis and the systemic failure of the economics profession. *Critical Review: A Journal of Politics and Society*, *21*(2–3), 249–267. doi:10.1080/08913810902934109

Cooren, F. (2004). Textual agency: How texts do things in organizational settings. *Organization*, *11*(3), 373–393.

Cooren, F. (2010). *Action and agency in dialogue: Passion, incarnation and ventriloquism* (Vol. 6). Philadelphia, PA: John Benjamins Publishing.

Cooren, F. (2012). Communication theory at the center: Ventriloquism and the communicative constitution of reality. *Journal of Communication*, *62*(1), 1–20.

Cooren, F., Kuhn, T., Cornelissen, J. P., & Clark, T. (2011). Communication, organizing and organization: An overview and introduction to the special issue. *Organization Studies*, *32*(9), 1149–1170.

du Gay, P., & Pryke, M. (2002). Cultural economy: An introduction. In P. du Gay & M. Pryke (Eds.), *Cultural economy* (pp. 1–20). Thousand Oaks, CA: Sage.

Fairclough, N. (1993). Critical discourse analysis and the marketization of public discourse: The universities. *Discourse & Society*, *4*(2), 133–168. doi:10.1177/0957926593004002002

Fairclough, N. (2010). *Critical discourse analysis: The critical study of language* (2nd ed.). New York, NY: Routledge.

Fairclough, N., & Wodak, R. (1997). Critical discourse analysis. In T. A. van Dijk (Ed.), *Discourse as social interaction* (pp. 258–284). *Discourse studies: A multidisciplinary introduction* (Vol. 2). London: Sage.

Ferraro, F., Pfeffer, J., & Sutton, R. I. (2005). Economics language and assumptions: How theories can become self-fulfilling. *Academy of Management Review*, *30*(1), 8–24. doi:10.5465/AMR.2005.15281412

Goffman, E. (1967). *Interaction ritual: Essays on face-to-face behavior*. New York, NY: Pantheon.

Islam, G., & Zyphur, M. J. (2009). Rituals in organizations: A review and expansion of current theory. *Group & Organization Management*, *34*(1), 114–139.

Katriel, T. (1985). Brogez: Ritual and strategy in Israeli children's conflicts. *Language in Society*, *14*, 467–490.

Kittel, B., & Obinger, H. (2003). Political parties, institutions, and the dynamics of social expenditure in times of austerity. *Journal of European Public Policy*, *10*(1), 20–45. doi:10.1080/1350176032000046912

Knuf, J. (1993). 'Ritual' in organizational culture theory: Some theoretical reflections and a plea for greater terminological rigor. In S. Deetz (Ed.), *Communication Yearbook*, *16*, 60–104.

Koschmann, M. A. (2012). The communicative constitution of collective identity in interorganizational collaboration. *Management Communication Quarterly*, *27*(1), 61–89. doi:10.1177/089331891244314

Koschmann, M. A., Kuhn, T. R., & Pfarrer, M. D. (2012). A communicative framework of value in cross-sector partnerships. *Academy of Management Review*, *37*(3), 332–354. doi:10.5465/amr.2010.0314

Koschmann, M. A., & McDonald, J. (2015). Organizational rituals, communication, and the question of agency. *Management Communication Quarterly*, *29*(2), 229–256.

Kuhn, T. (2008). A communicative theory of the firm: Developing an alternative perspective on intra-organizational power and stakeholder relationships. *Organization Studies*, *29*(8–9), 1227–1254. doi:10.1177/0170840608094778

Laclau, E., & Mouffe, C. (1985). *Hegemony and socialist strategy: Towards a radical democratic politics*. London: Verso.

MacKenzie, D., & Millo, Y. (2003). Constructing a market, performing theory: The historical sociology of a financial derivatives exchange. *American Journal of Sociology*, *109*(1), 107–145. doi:10.1086/374404

Nuciforo, E. V. (2013). Russian toasting and drinking as communication ritual. *Russian Journal of Communication*, *5*(2), 161–175.

Orlikowski, W. J. (2007). Sociomaterial practices: Exploring technology at work. *Organization Studies*, *28*(9), 1435–1448.

Orlikowski, W. J., & Scott, S. V. (2008). Sociomateriality: Challenging the separation of technology, work and organization. *The Academy of Management Annals*, *2*(1), 433–474.

Philipsen, G. (1987). The prospect for cultural communication. In L. Kincaid (Ed.), *Communication theory: Eastern and western perspectives* (pp. 245–254). New York, NY: Academic Press.

Philipsen, G. (1992). *Speaking culturally: Explorations in social communication*. Albany, NY: SUNY Press.

Philipsen, G. (1993). Ritual as a heuristic device in studies of organizational discourse. In S. Deetz (Ed.), *Communication Yearbook*, *16*, 104–112.

Pierson, P. (1998). Irresistible forces, immovable objects: Post-industrial welfare states confront permanent austerity. *Journal of European Public Policy*, *5*(4), 539–560. doi:10.1080/13501769880000011

Senft, G., & Basso, E. B. (Eds.). (2009). *Ritual communication*. Oxford: Berg.

Index